Short Stories by Latin American Women:
The Magic and the Real

Compiled and Edited
by
Celia Correas de Zapata

Arte Público Press
Houston
Texas
1990

Publication of *Short Stories by Latin American Women: The Magic and the Real* is made possible through support from the National Endowment for the Arts, a federal agency, and the Texas Commission for the Arts. Special thanks to Wayne Beck for assembling biographical data on the authors.

Cover art: En la Luz de la Luna, by Nivia González. Copyright @ 1988 Nivia González. Reproduced with permission of DagenBela Graphics, Inc., San Antonio, Texas.

Arte Público Press
University of Houston
Houston, Texas 77204-2090

Short Stories by Latin American Women: The Magic and the Real [edited by] Celia Correas de Zapata.
   p. cm.
   ISBN 1-55885-002-3
   1. Latin American fiction–Women authors. 2. Short stories, Latin American. 3. Latin American fiction–20th century. I. Correas de Zapata, Celia.
PQ7085.S48 1989   89-36298
863–dc20   CIP

Table of Contents

Foreword

The short story form is similar to poetry. An emotion wells up; nurtured by the author, it emerges one day amid pain and rejoicing to seek its fortune in a wider world of readers.

A good short story begins with the overpowering need to communicate a single idea or feeling. You have let it go all at once without hesitating, trusting to your intuition and your luck. It's like shooting an arrow. There is no second chance, it's a make-or-break proposition. The very first sentence sets the tone for the entire story, the rhythm, the tension, the point of it all. Without a good start, you might as well throw it away and not waste any more time on it—or, perhaps, file it away under "work in progress" until you can reconsider it afresh, maybe in two or three years. Novels can be written intermittently and rehashed endlessly because the complexity of their structure allows numerous errors and false starts to slip by undetected, but the short story has to be handled very carefully so as to achieve the firmness and transparency of a watercolor. Time and space are in short supply, nothing extraneous can be tolerated. The setting, characters and action must be precisely delineated; the development and culmination of the story can leave no loose ends.

At times what is most important is what is left unsaid. Indeed, the author is most vulnerable in the short story because it is not just a literary form but also a baring of the soul.

That is why this anthology is so valuable; it lays open the emotions of writers who, in turn, speak for others still shrouded in silence. For women in Latin America, setting down a short story is like screaming out loud; it breaks the rules, violates the code of silence into which we were born. Through these stories, each author selected by Dr. Zapata shouts out defiantly and reveals our experience to the world.

Until very recently, Latin American literature was—with very few exceptions—a man's game. The world was run by men and written about by men who, consequently, wrote us, our role and our place in their world. The result was a crude patriarchal myth reinforced by separation, mutual ignorance and machismo. Only recently have women stormed the literary bastions *en masse* and seized the right to write themselves, to define themselves. Characterizations of women in contemporary Latin American literature have grown more varied; we have broken out of the stereotypical scheme of madonnas, child-women and whores to portray real human beings, rebellious, anxious, concerned,

5

advancing together—women that love, fear and hate. Writer's passions and anguish emerge from the darkness to which they were banished, redefining femininity in a welter of voices striving to create in letters women we can all recognize. Within the framework of traditional literary forms, they write about women as they are, as they always have been—as men, blinded by their own myths, have been unable to see us. In so doing, they reveal new dimensions in our lives, bringing new dignity to all of us.

Women's writing in Latin America is characterized by a subversive kind of happiness. You have to read between the lines, passing beyond the rage, the weariness and frustration. It comes from a newfound power of expression and the sheer joy of exercising it to denounce ancient injustices and to clamor for changes. When a woman writes, she calls on us to show more love and respect for each other: why don't we just band together and set this upside-down world back on its feet?

Isabel Allende

Introduction

There never really was a *women's literature*, strictly speaking, in Latin America. Once can say, however, that women scattered across the continent entered the world of letters almost simultaneously during the romantic period. There were, of course, exceptional cases of women that wrote from the time of the Conquest: the Indian princess Anacaona wrote song lyrics, *areitos*, in the isle of Santo Domingo according to the chronicler Fernández de Oviedo (1515). The beauty and attainments of Sor Juana Inés de la Cruz dazzled Viceroy Mancera's court in seventeenth-century Mexico. Now, towards the end of the twentieth century, the courage and accomplishments of this forerunner have finally attracted critical attention and reevaluation of her works (cf. Octavio Paz's *Sor Juana Inés de la Cruz, Or the Pitfalls of Faith*). Colonialism, slavery, tyranny and exile inform the work of the nineteenth-century women writers starting with the drama of Gertrudis Gómez de Avellaneda (the Cuban-Spanish author of *Sab* and *Guatimozín*). The novels of Juana Manso and Juana Manuela Gorriti witness to the tyranny of Rosas in the Rio de la Plata region. Two Peruvians, Mercedes Cabello de Carbonera and Clorinda Matto de Turner became masters of realism and were rewarded by the hostility of their church and society.

After the publication of Rubén Dario's *Azul* in 1888, modernism made itself felt in poetry, prose, drama and the novel; simultaneously, a greater number of Latin American women started writing. According to Manuel Ugarte,

> ... it will be seen that Delmira Agustini's work was necessary for the later development of writers across the continent like Gabriela Mistral, Alfonsina Storni and the Venezuelan Teresa de la Parra, whose *Memorias de la Mamá Blanca* are really prose poems.
>
> (*Spanish-American writers of 1900*)

This group of writers publishing in the twenties is responsible for a fundamental change of tactics in the struggle against a traditionally male-dominated society. They went from "being objects of desire to being agents of desire" in the words of Uruguayan critic Helén Ferro, who also noted that their literary manifesto is a complete break with

7

all that went before. Teresa de la Parra satirized marriages of convenience in her novel *Ifigenia, diario de una señorita que escribió porque se aburría* (1925). Surrealism puts in an appearance in María Luisa Bombal's *La última niebla* in 1935. The novel's juxtaposition of realism and fantasy is a founding contribution to the school of magical realism which reached its zenith with the publication of Gabriel García Márquez's *One Hundred Years of Solitude* in 1967. According to Enrique Anderson Imbert one must distinguish carefully between literature of the fantastic and magical realism. The German critic Franz Roh coined the phrase "magical realism" in 1925 to describe a trend in modern art. Roh found–according to Anderson Imbert–that there was a kind of Hegelian dialectic in painting: "thesis: impressionism; antithesis: expressionism; synthesis: magical realism."[1] Applying these ideas to literature, the Argentine critic sees a parallel scheme of thesis (reality, realism), antithesis (the supernatural, literature of the fantastic) and their synthesis, the literature of magical realism.

From the great variety of critical definitions available, we have chosen to adopt Anderson Imbert's three basic ones:

– reality (realism)
– the supernatural (literature of the fantastic)
– the strange (magical realism)

To fully understand magical realism, however, one must also take into account its lyrical character. Graciela Sola notes that, unlike realism, it seeks to endow its subject with a heightened sense of reality much like a poem:

> Call it surrealism, *magical realism* or whatever you like, it is evident that this poetry escapes the categories of conventional criticism in spite of the common features it shares with all real art.[2] (author's emphasis)

In this anthology we propose to show the lyrical basis of the realistic, surrealistic and supernatural elements in the stories of 32 authors. Without glossing over the uniqueness of each one, it should be pointed out that the anthology is characterized by a fundamental unity of style underlying the diverse themes. In contrast to the lonely efforts of sor

---

[1] Celia Correas de Zapata, *Ensayos hispanoamericanos* (Buenos Aires: Ediciones Corregidor, 1978): 239.

[2] Zapata, *op.cit.* p. 241.

Juana Inés de la Cruz in the seventeenth century, modern women writers enjoy a shared esthetics and poetic sensitivity that pervades the anthology.

Each one emerges from a cultural matrix that conditions her work. Their lands and their history appear in stories by Argentines, Mexicans and Puerto Ricans. Humor and sarcasm appear in both the observation of individual psychology and tales of the absurd. Love is tinged with surrealism even within realistic (even pessimistic) settings. The language of the literature of the fantastic most approximates standard Spanish usage in the realistic mode even when sprinkled with regionalism.

In 1980, Lygia Johnson and I brought out a Spanish-language anthology of Latin American women's writing entitled *Detrás de la reja* (*Behind the Grilled Windows*). The publisher, Monte Avila of Caracas, requested that we group the stories around a set of unifying themes: women as adolescent, unmarried, wife, widow and also spinster. The heroines of *Detrás de la reja* are prisoners of fear, religion, lust, nature, tyrannical mothers and deceitful relatives; they are also victims of obsessions, unseen (and therefore ineluctable) circumstances, hate, curiosity, customs and old age. In this anthology, however, our characters are not stereotypes; they are flesh-and-blood individuals endowed with free will. They can either take reality or leave it, escaping to an alternate reality giving greater scope to their fantasies.

The gulf between the two anthologies is not only thematic but also esthetic. We have tried to show in this selection that the exclusively "epic" stage of women's literature referred to by Virginia Woolf and Victoria Ocampo has been replaced by a new sensibility.

I should add, though, that we have here not a separate movement but a definite raising of consciousness as regards the situation of women writers and their greater public acceptance.

When I first started researching the topic of Latin American women writers in 1973, I was surprised by their omission from literary criticism and histories written by men. The better ones tipped their hat in passing to this poet or that and were obliged to mention Sor Juana Inés de la Cruz, a freak or prodigy of nature never to be encountered again. At our insistence, however, critics began revising their histories and anthologies and so women gained a foothold in the literary enterprise. Even now, however, women's works draw less attention than men's when all is said and done. In all fairness, though, the critics have not had a very large corpus of women's work to deal with: women writers entered drama, the novel and the essay relatively recently. This last form is the newest for women: the essay is a philosophical unertaking in that it requires a freedom and a tradition of independent thinking that have been denied to women for centuries. We still need specialized anthologies like the present one to put their work before the public; academic notice, while valuable, is not enough. The opportunity to address a wider reading public throughout the Western Hemisphere is critical to obtaining this recognition.

One of the basic purposes of this anthology is to make available to universities and to the public at large the works of authors of merit and to dispel the image of the shawled, silent Latin American woman. Although it does correspond to reality in the more backward areas of the continent, those silent women are increasingly the beneficiaries of the struggles of those who *do* speak up. I concluded the Prologue to the 1980 anthology with a quote by Amary de Reincourt who noted that "Men *make* history; the daughters of Pandora *are* history." Nowadays, however, I no longer hold to that definition; both men and women *make* history and *are* history itself. Together, we write in an effort to better the world in which we live.

Celia Correas de Zapata

An Act of Vengeance

Isabel Allende

On that glorious noonday when Dulce Rosa Orellano was crowned with the jasmines of Carnival Queen, the mothers of the other candidates murmured that it was unfair for her to win just because she was the only daughter of the most powerful man in the entire province, Senator Anselmo Orellano. They admitted that the girl was charming and that she played the piano and danced like no other, but there were other competitors for the prize who were far more beautiful. They saw her standing on the platform in her organdy dress and with her crown of flowers, and as she waved at the crowd they cursed her through their clenched teeth. For that reason, some of them were overjoyed some months later when misfortune entered the Orellano's house sowing such a crop of death that thirty years were required to reap it.

On the night of the queen's election, a dance was held in the Santa Teresa Town Hall, and young men from the remotest villages came to meet Dulce Rosa. She was so happy and danced with such grace that many failed to perceive that she was not the most beautiful, and when they returned to where they had come from they all declared that they had never before seen a face like hers. Thus she acquired an unmerited reputation for beauty and later testimony was never able to prove to the contrary. The exaggerated descriptions of her translucent skin and her diaphanous eyes were passed from mouth to mouth, and each individual added something to them from his own imagination. Poets from distant cities composed sonnets to a hypothetical maiden whose name was Dulce Rosa.

Rumors of the beauty who was flourishing in Senator Orellanos' house also reached the ears of Tadeo Céspedes, who never dreamed he would be able to meet her, since during all his twenty-five years he had neither had time to learn poetry nor to look at women. He was concerned only with the Civil War. Ever since he had begun to shave he had had a weapon in his hands, and he had lived for a long time amidst the sound of exploding gunpowder. He had forgotten his mother's kisses and even the songs of mass. He did not always have reason to go into battle, because during several periods of truce there were no adversaries within reach of his guerrilla band. But even in times of forced peace he lived like a corsair. He was a man habituated to violence. He crossed the country in every direction, fighting visible enemies when he found them, and battling shadows when he was forced to invent them. He would have continued in the same way if his party had not won the presidential election. Overnight he went from a clandestine existence to wielding power, and all pretext for continuing the rebellion had ended for him.

Tadeo Céspedes's final mission was the punitive expedition against Santa Teresa. With a hundred and twenty men he entered the town under cover of darkness to teach everyone a lesson and eliminate the leaders of the opposition. They shot out the windows in the public buildings, destroyed the church door, and rode their horses right up to the main altar, crushing Father Clemente when he tried to block their way. They burned the trees that the Ladies' Club had planted in the square; amidst all the clamor of battle, they continued at a gallop toward Senator Orellano's house which rose up proudly on top of the hill.

After having locked his daughter in the room at the farthest corner of the patio and turned the dogs loose, the Senator waited for Tadeo Céspedes at the head of a dozen loyal servants. At that moment he regretted, as he had so many other times in his life, not having had male descendants who could help him to take up arms and defend the honor of his house. He felt very old, but he did not have time to think about it, because he had spied on the hillside the terrible flash of a hundred and twenty torches that terrorized the night as they advanced. He distributed the last of the ammunition in silence. Everything had been said, and each of them knew that before morning he would be required to die like a man at his battle station.

"The last man alive will take the key to the room where my daughter is hidden and carry out his duty," said the Senator as he heard the first shots.

All the men had been present when Dulce Rosa was born and had held her on their knees when she was barely able to walk; they had told her ghost stories on winter afternoons; they had listened to her play the piano and they had applauded in tears on the day of her coronation as Carnival Queen. Her father could die in peace, because the girl would never fall alive into the hands of Tadeo Céspedes. The one thing that never crossed Senator Orellano's mind was that, in spite of his recklessness in battle, he would be the last to die. He saw his friends fall one by one and finally realized that it was useless to continue resisting. He had a bullet in his stomach and his vision was blurred. He was barely able to distinguish the shadows that were climbing the high walls surrounding his property, but he still had the presence of mind to drag himself to the third patio. The dogs recognized his scent despite the sweat, blood, and sadness that covered him and moved aside to let him pass. He inserted the key in the lock and through the mist that covered his eyes saw Dulce Rosa waiting for him. The girl was wearing the same organdy dress that she had worn for the Carnival and had adorned her hair with the flowers from the crown.

"It's time, my child," he said, cocking his revolver as a puddle of blood spread about his feet.

"Don't kill me, father," she replied in a firm voice. "Let me live so that I can avenge us both."

Senator Anselmo Orellano looked into his daughter's fifteen-year-old face and imagined what Tadeo Céspedes would do to her, but he saw great strength in Dulce Rosa's transparent eyes, and he knew that she would survive to punish his executioner. The girl sat down on the bed and he took his place at her side, pointing his revolver at the door.

When the uproar from the dying dogs had faded, the bar across the door was shattered, the bolt flew off, and the first group of men burst into the room. The Senator managed to fire six shots before losing consciousness. Tadeo Céspedes thought he was dreaming when he saw an angel crowned in jasmines holding a dying old man in her arms. But he did not possess sufficient pity to look for a second time, since he was drunk with violence and enervated by hours of combat.

"The woman is mine," he said, before any of his men could put his hands on her.

A leaden Friday dawned, tinged with the glare from the fire. The silence was thick upon the hill. The final moans had faded when Dulce Rosa was able to stand and walk to the fountain in the garden. The previous day it had been surrounded by magnolias, and now it was nothing but a tumultuous pool amidst the debris. After having removed the few strips of organdy that were all that remained of her dress, she stood nude before what had been the fountain. She submerged herself in the cold water. The sun rose behind the birches, and the girl watched the water turn red as she washed away the blood that flowed from between her legs along with that of her father which had dried in her hair. Once she was clean, calm, and without tears, she returned to the ruined house to look for something to cover herself. Picking up a linen sheet, she went outside to bring back the Senator's remains. They had tied him behind a horse and dragged him up and down the hillside until little remained but a pitiable mound of rags. But guided by love, the daughter was able to recognize him without hesitation. She wrapped him in the sheet and sat down by his side to watch the dawn grow into day. That is how her neighbors from Santa Teresa found her when they finally dared to climb up to the Orellano villa. They helped Dulce Rosa to bury her dead and to extinguish the vestiges of the fire. They begged her to go and live with her godmother in another town where no one knew her story, but she refused. Then they formed crews to rebuild the house and gave her six ferocious dogs to protect her.

From the moment they had carried her father away, still alive, and Tadeo Céspedes had closed the door behind them and unbuckled his leather belt, Dulce Rosa lived for revenge. In the thirty years that followed, that thought kept her awake at night and filled her days, but it did not completely obliterate her laughter nor dry up her good disposition. Her reputation for beauty increased as troubadors went everywhere proclaiming her imaginary enchantments until she became a living legend. She arose every morning at four o'clock to oversee the farm and household chores, roam her property on horseback, buy and sell, haggling like a Syrian, breed livestock, and cultivate the magnolias and jasmines in her garden. In the afternoon she would remove her trousers, her boots, and her weapons, and put on the lovely dresses which had come from the capital in aromatic trunks. At nightfall visitors would begin to arrive and would find her playing the piano while the servants prepared trays of sweets and glasses of orgeat. Many people asked themselves how it was possible that the girl had not ended up in a straitjacket in a sanitarium or as a novitiate with the Carmelite nuns. Nevertheless, since there were frequent parties at the Orellano villa, with the passage of time people stopped talking about the tragedy and erased the murdered Senator from their memories. Some gentlemen who possessed both fame and fortune managed to overcome the repugnance they felt because of the rape and, attracted by Dulce Rosa's beauty and sensitivity, proposed marriage. She rejected them all, for her only mission on Earth was vengeance.

Tadeo Céspedes was also unable to get that night out of his mind. The hangover from all the killing and the euphoria from the rape left him as he was on his way to the capital a few hours later to report the results of his punitive expedition. It was then that he remembered the child in a party dress and crowned with jasmines, who endured him in silence in that dark room where the air was impregnated with the odor of gunpowder. He saw her once again in the final scene, lying on the floor, barely covered by her reddened rags, sunk in the compassionate embrace of unconsciousness, and he continued to see her that way every night of his life just as he fell asleep. Peace, the exercise of government, and the use of power turned him into a settled, hard-working man. With the passage of time, memories of the Civil War faded away and the people began to call him Don Tadeo. He bought a ranch on the other side of the mountains, devoted himself to administering justice, and ended up as mayor. If it had not been for Dulce Rosa Orellano's tireless phantom, perhaps he might have attained a certain degree of happiness. But in all the women who crossed his path, he saw the face of the Carnival Queen. And even worse, the songs by popular poets, often containing verses that mentioned her name, would not permit him to expel her from his heart. The young woman's image grew within him, occupying him completely, until one day he could stand it no longer. He was at the head of a long banquet table celebrating his fifty-fifth birthday, surrounded by friends and colleagues, when he thought he saw in the tablecloth a child lying naked among jasmine blossoms, and understood that the nightmare would not leave him in peace even after his death. He struck the table with his fist, causing the dishes to shake, and asked for his hat and cane.

"Where are you going, Don Tadeo?" asked the Prefect.

"To repair some ancient damage," he said as he left without taking leave of anyone.

It was not necessary for him to search for her, because he always knew that she would be found in the same house where her misfortune had occurred, and it was in that direction that he pointed his car. By then good highways had been built and distances seemed shorter. The scenery had changed during the decades that had passed, but as he rounded the last curve by the hill, the villa appeared just as he remembered it before his troops had taken it in the attack. There were the solid walls made of river rock that he had destroyed with dynamite charges, there the ancient wooden coffers he had set afire, there the trees where he had hung the bodies of the Senator's men, there the patio where he had slaughtered the dogs. He stopped his vehicle a hundred meters from the door and dared not continue because he felt his heart exploding inside his chest. He was going to turn around and go back to where he came from, when a figure surrounded by the halo of her skirt appeared in the yard. He closed his eyes, hoping with all his might that she would not recognize him. In the soft twilight, he perceived that Dulce Rosa Orellano was advancing toward him, floating along the garden paths. He noted her hair, her candid face, the harmony of her gestures, the swirl of her dress, and he thought he was suspended in a dream that had lasted for thirty years.

"You've finally come, Tadeo Céspedes," she said as she looked at him, not allowing herself to be deceived by his mayor's suit or his gentlemanly gray hair, because he still had the same pirate's hands.

"You've pursued me endlessly. In my whole life I've never been able to love anyone but you," he murmured, his voice choked with shame.

Dulce Rosa gave a satisfied sigh. At last her time had come. But she looked into his eyes and failed to discover a single trace of the executioner, only fresh tears. She searched her heart for the hatred she had cultivated throughout those thirty years, but she was incapable of finding it. She evoked the instant that she had asked her father to make his sacrifice and let her live so that she could carry out her duty; she relived the embrace of the man whom she had cursed so many times, and remembered the early morning when she had wrapped some tragic remains in a linen sheet. She went over her perfect plan of vengeance, but did not feel the expected happiness; instead she felt its opposite, a profound melancholy. Tadeo Céspedes delicately took her hand and kissed the palm, wetting it with his tears. Then she understood with horror that by thinking about him every moment, and savoring his punishment in advance, her feelings had become reversed and she had fallen in love with him.

During the following days both of them opened the floodgates of repressed love and, for the first time since their cruel fate was decided, opened themselves to receive the other's proximity. They strolled through the gardens talking about themselves and omitting nothing, even that fatal night which had twisted the direction of their lives. As evening fell, she played the piano and he smoked, listening to her until he felt his bones go soft and the happiness envelop him like a blanket and obliterate the nightmares of the past. After dinner he went to

Santa Teresa where no one still remembered the ancient tale of horror. He took a room in the best hotel and from there organized his wedding. He wanted a party with fanfare, extravagance, and noise, one in which the entire town would participate. He discovered love at an age when other men have already lost their illusions, and that returned to him his youthful vigor. He wanted to surround Dulce Rosa with affection and beauty, to give her everything that money could buy, to see if he could compensate in his later years for the evil he had done as a young man. At times panic possessed him. He searched her face for the smallest sign of rancor, but he saw only the light of shared love and that gave him back his confidence. Thus a month of happiness passed.

Two days before the wedding, when they were already setting up the tables for the party in the garden, slaughtering the birds and pigs for the feast, and cutting the flowers to decorate the house, Dulce Rosa Orellano tried on her wedding dress. She saw herself reflected in the mirror, just as she had on the day of her coronation as Carnival Queen, and realized that she could no longer continue to deceive her own heart. She knew that she could not carry out the vengeance she had planned because she loved the killer, but she was also unable to quiet the Senator's ghost. She dismissed the seamstress, took the scissors, and went to the room on the third patio which had remained unoccupied during all that time.

Tadeo Céspedes searched for her everywhere, calling out to her desperately. The barking of the dogs led him to the other side of the house. With the help of the gardeners he broke down the barred door and entered the room where thirty years before he had seen an angel crowned with jasmines. He found Dulce Rosa Orellano just as he had seen her in his dreams every night of his existence, lying motionless in the same bloody organdy dress. He realized that in order to pay for his guilt he would have to live until he was ninety with the memory of the only woman his soul could ever love.

Translated by E. D. Carter, Jr.

Sophie and the Angel

Dora Alonso

Sophie was way past eighty and wrapped herself up in dark clothes. Her blouse was decorated with an old gold and enamel brooch shaped like a fig leaf.

She was not shy, just very discreet. Flattened and diminished by age, she seemed like a bit of crumpled paper blown about by the wind: gliding, stopping at times, starting up and bouncing along, steadied by the parasol she used as a cane. Just listening you could tell when she was passing by, given away by the tapping of the tip of the parasol. You came to associate two sharp, small eyes and a pair of bushy eyebrows with it. Her hair was always neatly done: two small combs holding the white mane in check.

In spite of her appearance, the old lady had a busy spiritual life and didn't seem to be bored in her hillside home. She occupied all the recesses and shelves, as comfy in each room as a crab in its shell. She easily negotiated the big, rambling house in the dark and would stroll in the patio under the same leafy tamarind tree that had witnessed her forbears' coming and going in their carriages.

The house on the hillside had been in the family forever. Some great-grandmother, dispatched in a fit of rage by her jealous husband next to the ancient tree, seemed to hold her descendants in thrall within the walls of the ruined manor. Sophie was the last in the line. Her small, lonely figure was practically invisible to her neighbors, although they often noticed the tapping of her parasol. She chirped or mumbled her greetings, and ended up fading into the street and its surroundings.

During the past few years things had changed; life and novelty swirled around the forgotten reef she had become, although she refused to take notice. Ensconced among the begonias and old furniture, she defied and loathed change.

Sophie was left completely alone when Agueda, her old servant and only companion, suddenly departed. Agueda had died, feather duster in hand, before a painting of the Sacred Heart; even if the strange events to come weren't her fault, she was eventually blamed for them.

Agueda, unlike the other woman, was constituted of one part laundry soap and one part reality, the human reality of motherhood several times over. She counterbalanced Sophie, ready to pull her back to the real world when Sophie got overly absorbed in her church visits and commerce with celestial figures. Even though Agueda assiduously dusted the altars and saints, she was part of the new life around them, learning about volunteer work and all the new ideas in the air. She suddenly died, however, leaving Sophie abandoned to her incessant devotions, more isolated than she had ever been before. The flowers on her tomb were still moist when Sophie had her first hallucination.

It was seven-thirty and Sophie was starting to nod off in her sitting-groom rocking-chair in the chiaroscuro of the evening. Then the cat came walking up to her on its hind legs, head bowed, distinctly announcing, "Warm up some coffee, you have a visitor." The angel made his entrance before she had time to react. She didn't realize he was an angel at first; even if she had seen him gliding along near the ridged roof in full tunic tied at the waist with a red cord, she would have seen him carrying an electric guitar instead of a lyre. He was a seraphic figure looking about twenty years old with shoulder-length hair and beautiful smiling eyes. His sandals glowed softly golden and the cat rubbed up against them immediately as soon as he sat down. Sophie fell to her knees and couldn't get up. The radiant spirit moved his hand as if to pick up something in the air and an unknown force picked her up and set her down in her chair where she sat in ecstasy. When she came to, the sun was tinged with blue as it filtered through the frosted glass of the sitting room windows. Sophie shuddered as she recalled what had happened. Anxiously she called the cat, but as she cautiously examined the small black animal, he looked so inoffensive and unremarkable that she calmed down and wrote it all off as a dream. That night in her room she arranged some flowers on the altar and lighted a small lamp under the image of the Virgin. Kneeling where Agueda had collapsed amid clouds of dust, she kissed one of the family relics and prayed for a long time. Once her prayers were done, she got ready for bed. Wearing a chaste nightgown she climbed onto the bed as if it were a burial mound. The room was stuffy. Street noises seemed to filter in from another world: a child screaming, a bus, neighborhood committee announcements over a loudspeaker.

The punctual nine o'clock cannon reverberated through the house like a warning as Sophie mumbled her last prayers for the evening. At the muffled explosion the cat jumped off the kneeler cushion where he usually slept curled up and, walking on his hind legs, went to the bedroom door and opened it. The delicious aroma of guava flooded the room and Sophie noticed that her fingers were covered with rings. She trembled like a sheet of paper inside her large gown as something leapt inside her chest. The angel smiled at her by her bedside. He played his guitar for a long while, lulling Sophie to sleep. After the second time, the messenger of light did not startle her anymore and his visits became regular.

On the fifteenth one he brought her a young unicorn. Sophie was delighted, and within a week the small beast had learned to follow her around and eat from her hand. After the unicorn came a clepsydra which helped amuse her as she awaited his next appearance.

She had no doubts about the celestial credentials of her visitor, although at one time she considered going to confession for guidance and advice. She desisted, however, fearing criticism of the unusual relationship that now occupied her, so things just stayed the way they were.

Their familiarity grew all the time, until it took an unexpected turn, revealing something hitherto well concealed in the lengthy canasta games and conversation. They sat very close to each other on the couch in the half light of the spacious living room as they shared the delicious old fashioned sweets and fresh lemonade that Sophie had made herself, singing as she prepared them.

Long forgotten whims of the distant young lady she had been had suddenly come into bloom. Like a mischievous child she would occasionally muss her friend's feathers with a small wrinkled and veined hand and, just to please her, the spirit of light would demonstrate takeoffs, hover and fly around. Her smiling eyes would follow him to where he would land back in the patio, alighting under the tamarind where the remains of her great-grandmother sweetened its sour fruits.

In the intimacy of those hours under the foliage they exchanged confidences. She told him of her childhood, her languid youth, her religious aspirations and about the late Agueda. He talked about his position in the last of the Nine Choirs, frequent missions on behalf of Divine Providence, and sacred mysteries. And, perceiving his attentive listener's uneasiness about his true identity, he cunningly reassured her about the rightness of it all, how they were no longer bound by outmoded prudery and old fashioned hypocrisy. Sophie would just sigh, trusting him and going along with everything.

She often thought that she was living a delightful dream. Saturdays had been set aside for dancing and the music from the radio wrapped them up in its sensual cadences ... If for some reason her seraphic fiancé failed to appear, Sophie, impatient, could not hide her jealousy. Little quarrels would burst out, warming the encounters and farewells. One evening there was a kiss. How she wept, clutching her pillow! The very idea of falling into mortal sin drove her to despair and she beat her breast in vain, as the pounding merely echoed the same rhythm as that of her lover's music. Upset, exasperated, she mistreated the cat, doubled her prayers, and refused to feed the unicorn. "This has to stop," she would repeat, fearfully, "once and for all." Several days later, after much sorrow and deliberation, she informed the angel of her decision. She had not reckoned, however, that her spirited suitor would be incapable of waiting for her or giving her up. Stubborn and incensed by her drastic breaking-off, he thoroughly shocked her with his cunningly insolent and lascivious behavior. In between riffs on his guitar he would suddenly lift the skirts of the abashed lady who would run off, unable to escape his importunings.

The house no longer smelled of guava when he came but of an unknown and disturbing fragrance that weakened Sophie's knees, embarrassing her. All the tricks in the book were being used against her and when she realized that she could not hold out much longer, she decided to take matters to the top (though not before a judicious quantity of contrite tears).

The frightened virgin scribbled long, revealing letters in a trembling hand, describing her trials and the traps and designs against her chastity—how the bed would get undone as soon as she had made it, how her panties would not lie straight in the dresser and how he would show up in her bathtub with nothing except his crossed wings.

The astonished nuncio secretly forwarded the report to the parish priest with instructions to clear things up as tactfully and discreetly as possible. She was to be made to understand how sinful and unhealthy her illusions had become. Sophie listened to the fatherly admonishment with bowed head. Firm but gentle reasoning convinced her of her mistake, and she was invited to make a sincere confession of it. Obedient and very much comforted, Sophie spoke candidly for a long while. She gratefully accepted the conclusions of her religious advisor who blamed not her but the isolation in which she was living and her wandering imagination given full play by her idleness. Sophie told of her imagined encounters, quarrels and reconciliations with the celestial spirit. She was not interrupted except for a brief comment on the participation of a cat—and a black cat at that—in the episode. Sophie was absolved in exchange for a definite promise to get rid of the cat, and to come right back at the first sign of further irregularities.

The old lady was filled with joy; with devout pride she showed the priest her bedroom, the well-cared for altar, holy images, kneeler ... The parish priest nodded, satisfied that he had handled things in the best possible way.

There was, unfortunately, a long white feather of unquestionably angelic origin poking out luridly—and inexcusably—from beneath the sheets of her bed.

Translated by Beatriz Teleki

Asthmatic

Helena Araujo

You say you want to know how it all started? Well, there was a ruckus at Valle University and the students at National U. wanted to stage a demonstration. Apparently in Cali they were asking for more power for the Student Council, and when they got turned down, they decided to take over the president's office. But damn! those sons of bitches had it together. Not only did they take over the office, they went through the files and found papers from the Ford and Rockefeller Foundations, and an IDB contract to boot. From then on there was no stopping them: fliers, marches, meetings, they did it all. Finally, one afternoon they wound up in a fracas outside the Government Administration building, and then there were troops swarming the University before you could blink an eye. Between the barricades and the rock-throwing, they kicked the shit out of I don't know how many guys. Pretty soon the National U. staged a demonstration in Bogotá, but the pigs turned out right away and hauled in a bunch of people. It was two days after that—two?—that's right, two days later, the private universities and some high schools joined the movement. They were going to organize a huge march downtown, starting from the university campus.

Some of us read about it in the newspaper the night before at Daniel's place, so instead of talking about Lenin or Ho Chi Minh, we got into discussing the movement. Man! We yacked for hours and never agreed on a single thing. One was all for the comrades, another for the China-lovers, and one guy wanted to get the rest of the senior class into it. That seemed a little risky, though. Up to then we'd been underground, so to speak, nobody knew about the meetings. Why blow our cover, just like that? Agreed, and it was Herrera who came up with marching incognito. For a change, García liked the idea and even thought it would define us as supporters of a classless society. But Daniel and Hurtado boycotted it. They thought we couldn't just improvise our first action from one minute to the next. After all, what were we? A party? A dissident faction? When you got right down to it, what was our political platform? Silence. There we all were, yawning and trying to pretend we weren't sleepy, and finally it occurred to Láinez that we should write a statement of solidarity with the students in Cali. But García insisted on getting backing from some organization: there weren't enough of us. Forget that! Daniel started waving his fists around like maracas, cutting in on people right and left. If we hadn't joined a movement, why not come right out and speak for ourselves?

Just before daylight, dog-tired after all that wrangling, we decided to snack on some bread and salami. Then we opened a bottle of booze. So when Daniel jumped up, slapped his forehead, yelled yeeehah! Got it! and said something about a kidnapping, we were all half tight. Kidnapping! Holy shit! Every jaw in the room dropped. We sat around like a freeze-frame in that mess we'd made—cushions everywhere, cigarette butts, dirty dishes. I can still see Daniel kneeling in the middle with us all around him, Hurtado like a Buddha in a trance and Herrera squatting on his heels, emptying his glass. The light was filtering in from Jiménez Street through the raindrops on the windows; we'd turned out the light-bulb covered with a basket we used for a lamp. For safety, supposedly. Yes, we were sitting around in the dark except for a blink of neon now and then. García was smoking, with those quick, muscular movements of his; Láinez sat up, Herrera came over to see if Daniel was serious. Hurtado was sitting with his arms around his knees. Naturally, García spoke up first. He vetoed the proposal in his best sportscaster voice, waved his hairy hands around, called it petit bourgeois exhibitionism. Then Herrera, all caution, called it sensationalism. But Hurtado and Láinez didn't seem convinced. When Daniel ignored the rest of us and started to chortle about how great it would be, just like in the movies, Hurtado and Láinez laughed along with him.

"Imagine the look on Monseigneur's face if he finds out!" Láinez half-hiccuped.

Then I chimed in, "He'd shit in his pants, he'd be so pissed!"

Well, then Herrera went all pop-eyed, held his finger in front of his mouth and shushed us. We had to be serious, he said. Naturally, Hurtado didn't miss the chance to give us a lecture on urban guerrilla warfare. He and Herrera had been assigned a Tupamaro text to analyze and he decided to recite it for us. We thought he'd never shut up, we were dying to get some sleep. García was listening straight-faced, almost solemn, but the rest of us were yawning. Daniel opened another bottle. It was his idea, after all, he was entitled. I can still see him standing there, swigging booze. He couldn't have come from anywhere but Cartagena. He was part Black (and damn proud of it) and the rest of us looked puny next to him. My skin seemed pastier and my posture looked worse. Herrera looked like an albino frog, to the point that his throat seemed to puff out when he talked. García was short too, with thin lips; he blinked a lot. Hurtado was fat and clumsy. He looked like a sad old senator with that long hair of his. Láinez we called The Little Flea because he was so pale and had no beard at all, and because he was always blushing. Even back then he was drawing good caricatures, and the year after that he enrolled in Fine Arts. Of the five, only Herrera had a scholarship. He used to get sarcastic about being just a plebeian. García's family had money, but he wouldn't allow us to mention pedigree around him. The rest of us were upcoming oligarchs with famous grandfathers or great-grandfathers. Whereas we were feeling like upper-class scaredy-cats that night (we didn't let on, naturally), Daniel (the only one over eighteen, with his own apartment) went right on partying, handing the bottle around, talking a blue streak and laughing his head off about how well it would all turn out, just like in the movies.

I don't remember who decided the first thing we had to do was make hoods. Láinez knew more about sewing than anybody else, so he got some scissors and started hunting for cloth. Since there wasn't any handy, he grabbed a sheet off the bed. He cut out some squares. Then he folded them to make points and cut two holes in each one. He and I scrounged around for a while and finally found a spool of thread and another pair of scissors the cleaning lady had left lying around. Somehow we got a couple of needles threaded and worked on the booze and the hoods, pricking our fingers and cussing, while the rest of the guys figured out how to get some weapons. I remember they ran through the entire armory, from toy pistols to kitchen knives. Hurtado and Herrera were acting all grown up and trying to put a damper on the party. Finally they suggested the CO_2 pistol Herrera's dad kept to use against muggers. We went along with the idea and promised to pick it up on our way to school, since Herrera's house was on the way. The pistol, of course, was to threaten the pig with while we disarmed him. Because we were going to disarm him, right? That would be García's job, right? García here, García there, García everywhere, and now the big jerk wanted to pull out! Scratching his head like he had dandruff and running off at the mouth about bourgeois sensationalism. And that would screw us over, because we needed him. He was taking karate lessons and had already come out of a couple of fights with flying colors. So we had to sit back and let him rave and not push him, he'd come around eventually, and then Hurtado, well, Hurtado was simply brilliant. He took García aside and gave him this incredible pep talk about what our action would mean: In return for letting the pig go, we'd demand freedom for all the students they'd jailed, no more, no less, how does that grab you? That was it. García had no choice; he caved in. I remember that Láinez got so excited over everybody agreeing he started turning cartwheels on the bed. It took us a while to pound it out of him with cushions and get a little order going again. The important thing was to plan, organize, get the timing down; the thing had to go off like clockwork. Well, García said, throwing his chest out, disarming the pig would be no big deal, but where would we hide him afterward?

I think by that time we'd emptied the second bottle, otherwise I don't know how we would ever have thought of the gatehouse. That was Daniel's idea, too. "Got it! Hell, yes!" He wiggled his fingers through the holes in his hood and guffawed. "The gate house, where else!" He showed all those perfect white teeth in a big grin, rolled up the hood and threw it to Láinez in a football pass. Láinez dropped it, naturally. At that point García left us all thunderstruck by finally agreeing, in his sportscaster voice, of course. The idea seemed okay to him because the gate house was only feet from where the pig stood guard, right? Right, right. It was Herrera who broke in then to say they'd give us the afternoon off from school, like they always did when there was a demonstration. Hurtado mentioned that the gatekeeper might be standing next to the entrance where the frieze was, the one with the keys we always called "the keys to the kingdom." The gatehouse was right there. It would be easy to dump the gatekeeper. He was some kind of ex-sacristan or something, one of the principal's flunkies. Láinez was yelling "Dump the gatekeeper! Dump the gatekeeper!" when he started gagging. We barely had time to shove him into the bathroom before he heaved. That was when García decided to make some black coffee. We'd try to lay out a detailed plan of action once we sobered up.

Hurtado and Herrera took charge of the timing. According to them, the whole operation would take seven or eight minutes if we worked fast. Things would happen more or less like this: At noon Daniel and I would stay in the library finishing an assignment after everybody else left. The other guys would hide in the bathroom until the priest who taught Scholastic Studies called roll and went into the refectory for lunch. Then Daniel would go down and ask the gatekeeper to go to the store for a soda. As soon as he left, Daniel would go into the courtyard and whistle. That was our signal. We'd get downstairs and into the gate-house, pronto. Then came García's starring role. With or without the hood? We spent the rest of the time we had arguing over that stupid little detail. Daniel insisted the most, because with the hood it would be like in the movies. Láinez, too, since he'd designed the hoods (baggy, wrinkled, shapeless, but what the hell). Although, come to think of it, at that hour Fifteenth Street, where the entrance to the high school was, would be deserted. It was narrow and the courtyard wall ran all along one side, no problem. The big thing, of course, was efficiency. Set-tling the last details and swallowing some breakfast took up the time between then and the first class. More coffee, more, and then one for the road from the bottle as we left the apartment. Seeing that the bot-tle was empty, we decided to buy another one for Daniel to hide in his bookbag, in case we got cold feet.

In the end we bought not one but three bottles (the smallest size) of Black Seal and split them so we could all take a belt now and then. We needed fuel after the all-nighter. I can only speak for myself, but I know that when I crossed the courtyard at school, there were cockroaches running around in my belly, I needed to take a leak, and my hands were clammy. The other guys didn't seem to be in any better shape. Daniel sat next to me in class looking hollow-eyed and green. We lost track of Herrera and Hurtado because we were in A section and they were in B. As for Láinez, he called attention to himself during History by looking dumber than usual, giggling for no particular reason and picking one ear non-stop. García, on the other hand, was cool as cool can be. His hair was every which way, though, and he had some impressive bags under his eyes. He'd said he would disarm the policeman with a knee jab, or a lock or a twist, so he'd be able to drag him into the gatehouse. Yeah, but what if he yelled? What if he kicked and struggled? Forget it! It would be over so fast he wouldn't have time. At least, that was what García said, and we had to believe him. During the eleven o'clock break we checked to see if the pig had arrived. Sure enough, there he was: khaki shirt, white helmet, bayonet, all in place.

At noon we carried out the first stage of the plan and, incredible as it may seem, it went like clockwork. We had no problem staying in the library. The priest sailed through roll call without a hitch and went away with everybody else for lunch. When the time came, Daniel went downstairs. A minute later we heard him whistle from the courtyard, and tore downstairs and into the gatehouse. This was a dinky little room with one crummy window, a high ceiling and a bare lightbulb hanging down from a braided wire. There was a table and one chair, and a telephone. The afternoon was overcast and the bulb was low-watt, so we could barely see to pass around the hoods Láinez was getting out of his bookbag. His hands were trembling. What a jerk! He hadn't bothered to take any measurements, and it hadn't occurred to anybody that some had bigger heads. At the last minute I had to hand my hood over to García and use one that scratched my cheeks and made my eyelids burn. The other guys must have been uncomfortable too, but they didn't dare so much as peep. Once we had our hoods on, we crowded around the door and watched García leave with that springy step he had, like a boxer going into the ring.

The street was deserted, everybody must have gone down to Seventh Street to watch the march. We knew there were patrols on the corner of Twelfth Street and a riot squad at Bolívar Plaza, but there was nobody on our sidewalk but the usual pig. You could hear the yelling in the distance, down with the Minister of Education, slogans from Che and Camilo, people chanting Jalisco, here! Jalisco, here! because the name of one of the students from Cali that the troops had taken out was Jalisco. And then, yes, it was then, while we were all jammed in the doorway, that was when we heard a kind of a howl and something like a double meteor crashed into us. "Get his bayonet!" García yelled. Herrera and Daniel hit the floor. Láinez made a rush and I saw García hand him a pistol. Hurtado slammed the door and I pushed the table against it, still following the plan. I remember my knees were weak and my head was swimming. When I turned around, everybody was piled on top of the guy on the floor, squirming and grunting. I just stood there frozen, gasping for air. I barely saw them drag him into the corner where the table had been. Daniel had kicked over the chair and thrown the bayonet into a corner while García and Herrera held the Indian face down. They tied his hands together with a rope Láinez had remembered to put in his bookbag. I'd seen Láinez take out a bottle of booze when he was looking for the rope. I didn't care if the other guys were looking or not, I grabbed the bottle and took a belt. They weren't paying any attention to me, though. They were still piled on top of the pig, and he was wriggling like a snake and kicking to fight them off. He was no piker, that's for sure. Láinez was holding the gun to the pig's temple while Daniel tied the gag, cussing a blue streak. I saw Láinez's hand shaking. The agreement was that Hurtado and I wouldn't take part in the scuffle, because one of us had to see to the door while the other took care of the telephone. I was just standing there gawking like a moron. I had trouble seeing who was who in the pile-up because of the hoods, but I could practically feel them panting and taste the dryness in their mouths. And I could almost see the excitement or fear in their faces. Láinez would be losing his grip on the pistol. The veins would be standing out on García's forehead and neck, he'd skin his knuckles turning the Indian over, holding him down, jamming a knee into his neck. The poor sap's helmet had fallen off. All you could see above the gag was a pair of eyes popping out under a lot of messed-up black hair. Sweat was pouring down his forehead, along his sideburns. He groaned every time they kicked him. It sounded like he was saying "miamito, miamito."

"Shut up or I'll blow your head off, you fucking pig!" Láinez's voice was muffled by the hood.

The time had come. I took the slip of paper out of my pocket and went over to the telephone I'd left on the windowsill a few minutes before. My hands were shaking as bad as my jaw; I couldn't find the numbers to dial. All at once I heard my own voice, high and squeaky as the words tumbled out. "Hello, Las Aguas Police Station? Can I talk to the sergeant on duty?" Somebody said, "Hold the line." I grabbed the phone with my other hand, shifted it to the other ear. Somebody else said hello and I said, "Sergeant?" I didn't even stop to swallow my spit, just rasped out the speech I'd rehearsed a thousand times that morning. I rattled it off like a charm until I came to the number on the pig's badge. Hurtado ripped it off his shirt and stuck it under my nose. I read the number all right, but the last sentences came out in stammers, the part about it was wuh-wuh-one-ten in the afternoon and buh-before two-ten the suh-suh-students who'd been taken prisoner had to be fuh-fuh-freed, Sergeant, or else we'd execute the puh-policeman we were holding hostage. Nuh-nuh-no, it was no juh-joke, it was dead serious, Suh-Sergeant, we belonged to an organization that was muh-muh-making its eh-existence known in this fuh-fuh-first action, first ac-tion, first...

When I hung up, my hand was so sweaty I dropped the phone. I turned the chair over, collapsed into it, handed the badge to Hurtado, looked around. Nobody was saying anything, they were just watching me through the holes in their hoods: Herrera stooping over, Láinez pointing the gun at the pig, Daniel pinning him down with his feet, García driving a fist into his chest. All you could hear was people grunting and gasping. In the middle of it all, the pig was still twisting and kicking. His olive drab leggings were muddy. With the gag on he looked like a gargoyle. For some reason his eyes made me think of two coffee beans.

It was then that somebody started knocking on the door, not very loud at first. "Open the door, gentlemen!" Then louder, almost banging: "Open up!" The gatekeeper.

Daniel signalled us to keep quiet and stood up. We were all staring at that piece of rotting wood as if it were glass, as if we could see what was happening on the other side, why the blows were coming faster, then slower before they finally stopped.

When everything was quiet again we figured the guy had gone to give the alarm. "Quiet!" Daniel barked. But it wasn't easy. The room was cold and damp, but we felt overheated, claustrophobic. We tried to make ourselves comfortable: Hurtado on the table to take care of the bolt, Daniel and Herrera on the floor, one on either side of the pig. Láinez was standing with his back against the wall. García took out a bottle and passed it around. Whew! It was hard to breathe. The silence dragged on and on. We stared at each other through the hoods whenever we weren't rubbing our eyes (which was most of the time) and reached into our pockets every few minutes, but nobody had the guts to light up.

Noise at the door again, more knocking.

"Is this a joke? A practical joke?" The Scholastic Studies teacher sounded pretty near hysterical.

"They've locked it from inside!" The gatekeeper again.

More knocking, louder this time. "Open up in there!"

Daniel made a face. Láinez gave a nervous giggle and almost dropped the pistol. García jerked it out of his hand and stood with his feet apart like a soldier, aiming at the pig. Hurtado turned around to check the bolt and then looked toward the window. All you could see was dirt and a little patch of gray. Herrera picked up the bayonet from the corner and used it to make sure the window latch was still shut. I was paralyzed, numb; the cockroaches in my stomach had turned to worms. I felt like maybe I was going to get diarrhea.

More knocking: "Open up!"

We jumped when the telephone rang. I reached out to answer, but Daniel motioned to leave it alone. Better to let it ring. It couldn't be the police, they hadn't even had time to check if what we'd said was true; unless the pig's badge number, but not that quick, no way, and it kept ringing, pause, two rings, one-two, one-two. We stared at it like we expected it to explode. When it finally stopped we could hear a little scratching noise at the door, I mean in the lock. We had the key inside, so the gatekeeper was probably trying to pick the lock with a hook or skeleton key, something that made a gnawing sound. Then that stopped and the knocking started again, less patient, more aggressive. It was Scholastic Studies again. This time there had to be some other priests with him, because we weren't sure whose voices we were hearing, four or five of them, raising hell, thumping at the door, trying to force it, and it cracked and would have given way but for the double bolt and the safety plate. Finally it sounded like they got tired and Scholastic Studies yelled, "Open up or we'll call the police! Hurry up and get that door open now!"

That was when García, without warning, ripped his hood off and yelled back: "If you call the police, we'll blow away the one we've got tied up in here!"

Herrera and Daniel turned around to stare at him. I couldn't see their faces because of the hoods, but it looked like they thought he was some kind of hero. Nobody but me lifted a finger. I raised one hand to object, but I don't think anybody noticed.

"Open up this minute!" The priest insisted. He kept rattling the bolt as if he hadn't paid any attention to García.

Just then somebody blew a whistle in the street and we heard something that sounded like a jeep. We looked up at the window. We wanted to look out, but the window was too high and the glass was so dirty you could hardly even see the light from the street. Now the knocking had stopped and there were voices in the street: Scholastic Studies and the gatekeeper, mixed in with other priests and the crowd that was gathering. "They're going to talk to us through a megaphone, just like in the movies!" Daniel laughed.

Hurtado motioned for him to shut up. Láinez tried to jump high enough to look through the window. I offered him the chair, but he didn't want it.

García burst out, "This heat is killing me!" and threw the pistol on the table so hard we jumped again. The noise in the street was getting to all of us. García took a deep breath and blew it out, leaned against the wall, tore off his hood, took another deep breath, wiped the sweat off his face, put the hood back on. Meanwhile the hullabaloo outside was growing. Heavy military boots came thudding down the street, somebody started shouting orders.

García picked up the pistol. "We have to make a decision," he announced. His voice sounded like he was inside a cave.

The pig on the floor shuddered. He started to twist and struggle again, never taking his eyes off García. He drew up his knees. It looked like he was about to break loose.

"Quiet!" Daniel snapped at him and planted a foot on his chest.

Outside another car or truck pulled up outside, a pickup, maybe, and more people got out, probably more police. We heard the Scholastic Studies teacher's voice above the din and, for the first time that day, we heard the Monsignor's voice too. It sounded like they were objecting to something, arguing about something, but you couldn't understand what they were saying.

It was then—yes, exactly then, that García mumbled, "We have to blow him away. Now."

We all turned around and stared at him. Nobody could think of anything to say. On the floor, the Indian jumped and drew up his knees again, and when Daniel threatened him he started shivering, shivering and howling—squealing, actually. He was squealing, you could hear a high-pitched squeal even through the gag, he was squealing like a dog or a pig and shivering, and then, well, I think that was what got to me, that shaking and squealing, like an animal, I couldn't take it any more, I don't know, it was like I had a fit, I don't know why but I went berserk, jumped up and started yelling, yelling it wasn't fair, the damn Indian hadn't done anything, you can't do this, don't do it, no, don't, even though the other guys were looking at me like this through their hoods and García called me chickenshit and Daniel turned around and came at me but I tore off my hood and started to cry like a baby, like a hysterical female, blubbering, the poor pig shouldn't have to die, and I think Daniel would have decked me then and there, only that was when something exploded, the window panes blew and whammo! something hit the floor and exploded. Afterwards, I don't know. The room was full of smoke, we were all blind and coughing our guts out, everybody gagging, gasping like we were being throttled, our windpipes squeezed shut, smothering, choking, all of a sudden Herrera was on his knees, Daniel was tearing at his hood, Láinez was heaving, the last thing I remember was Hurtado pulling the table away from the door and García yelling, "Sons of bitches! They gassed us!"

That was it. It was all over. I never did find out what else happened. All I know is, when I came to I was on the floor, out of it, and they had to haul me away in an ambulance. So I never rode in the paddy wagon or went to the police station, and I never did find out what deal the judge cut with Monsignor after Hurtado's dad talked to him. Hurtado's dad was a lawyer.

Anyway, they hardly did anything to us. I was out of combat in the hospital and I think my folks decided to take pity on me when they saw what shape I was in. Only a child, that kind of thing. What about the others? Herrera never even lost his scholarship (they transferred it to El Carmen in Manizales for him), García's family sent him to the States, and Hurtado went to a boarding school in Medellín where they kept him plenty cool. Láinez, Daniel and I graduated from that same school; the priests put up with the three of us to the end, three black sheep. Well, they couldn't afford to lose that many students, either; they'd have wound up with a hell of a deficit! Aside from the fact that Láinez's dad and mine had put together a tidy little donation toward the new choirloft in the chapel. How could they kick us out? In fact, me they treated like I was glass from then on, probably because of the asthma. I've always thought the doctor must have warned them at some point, what I mean to say is he must have scared them shitless. Sometimes I think he passed a clue to Láinez and Daniel, too, after the tracheotomy, because when we saw each other at El Carmen later on, I don't know, it seemed to me they acted different around me. Maybe they felt uncomfortable because they knew I was in such godawful shape. Anyway, they both handled me with kid gloves from then on. And both of them avoided talking about the screw-up. If I tried to bring it up they'd look at their shoelaces or change the subject. And that was okay by me, incredible but true, I didn't want to talk about it either. Why? I don't know, we just never felt the same afterwards: we were always uneasy, afraid to talk out of turn, formal somehow. Maybe we missed the other guys. Anyway, after graduation we all went our separate ways.

That was almost ten years ago ... I wonder why I haven't thought about them in all that time, until now, in this office, on this couch. You say I add something new every time I tell the story, Doctor. Maybe so. Sometimes I get the details mixed up. But one thing I can tell you for sure: that was where I got the asthma. And another thing: whenever I have an attack I feel the same choking sensation, like I'm being strangled, suffocated. I swear to you, I never get relief until I land in the clinic and they punch another hole in my neck. Now they're saying it's dangerous because of the scars, I'm afraid I might beat them to it one of these days, just get my razor out and slit my own throat.

Translated by Catherine Rodríguez-Nieto

The Tree

María Luisa Bombal

The pianist sits down, coughs from force of habit and concentrates for a moment. The clusters of lights illuminating the hall gradually dim until they glow like dying embers, whereupon a musical phrase rises in the silence, swells: clear, sharp and judiciously capricious.

Mozart, maybe, Brígida thinks to herself. As usual, she has forgotten to ask for the program. Mozart—or perhaps Scarlatti ... She knew so little about music! And it was not because she lacked an ear or the inclination. On the contrary, as a child it had been she who demanded piano lessons; no one needed to impose them on her, as was the case with her sisters. Today, however, her sisters could sight-read perfectly, while she ... she had abandoned her studies after the first year. The reason for the inconstancy was as simple as it was shameful: she had never been able, never, to learn the key of F. "I don't understand—my memory serves me only to the key of C." And her father's indignation! "Would that I could lay down this burden: a miserable widower with children to educate! My poor Carmen! How she would have suffered with such a daughter! The creature is retarded!"

Brígida was the youngest of six girls—all endowed with different temperaments. She received little attention from her father because dealing with the other five daughters reduced him to such a perplexed and worn-out state that he preferred to ease his burden by insisting on her feeblemindedness. "I won't struggle any longer—it's useless. Leave her alone. If she chooses not to study, so be it. If she would rather spend her time in the kitchen listening to ghost stories, that's fine with me. If she favors playing with dolls at the age of sixteen, let her play." And so Brígida had kept to her dolls, remaining almost totally ignorant as far as formal education was concerned.

How pleasant it is to be ignorant! Not to know exactly who Mozart was—to ignore his origins, his influences, the particularities of his technique! To simply let oneself be led by the hand, as now ...

For in truth Mozart leads her—transporting her onto a bridge suspended above crystal water running over a bed of pink sand. She is dressed in white, tilting on one shoulder an open parasol of Chantilly lace, elaborate and fine as a spider's web.

"You look younger every day, Brígida. Yesterday I ran into your husband—I mean your ex-husband. His hair is now completely white."

But she makes no reply, unwilling to tarry while crossing the bridge Mozart has fabricated toward the garden of her youth.

Tall blossoming spouts in which the water sings. Her eighteen years; her chestnut braids that, unbound, cascaded to her waist; her golden complexion; her dark eyes so wide and questioning. A small mouth with full lips; a sweet smile; and the lightest, most gracious body in the world. Of what was she thinking, seated by the fountain's edge? Of nothing. "She is as silly as she is pretty," they used to say. But she did not mind being silly, nor acting the dunce at parties. One by one, her sisters received proposals of marriage. No one asked her.

Mozart! Now he conducts her to a blue marble staircase on which she descends between two rows of ice lilies. And now he opens a wrought-iron gate of spikes with golden tips so that she may throw herself on Luis, her father's intimate friend. From childhood, she would run to Luis when everyone else abandoned her. He would pick her up and she would encircle his neck between giggles that were like tiny bird cries; she would fling kisses like disorderly raindrops on his eyes, his forehead and his hair—which even then was graying (had he never been young?). "You are a necklace," Luis would say. "You are like a necklace of sparrows."

That is why she had married him. Because at the side of that solemn and taciturn man she felt less guilty for being what she was: foolish, playful and indolent. Yes—now, after so many years, she realizes that she had not married Luis for love; yet she cannot put her finger on why, why she left him so suddenly one day.

But at this moment Mozart takes her nervously by the hand, drawing her into a rhythm second by second more urgent— compelling her to retrace her steps across the garden and onto the bridge at a pace that is almost like fleeing. And after stripping her of the parasol and the transparent crinoline, he closes the door on her past with a note at once firm and sweet—leaving her in the concert hall, dressed in black, applauding mechanically as the artificial lights rekindle their flame.

Again shadows, and the prelude of silence.

And now Beethoven begins to stir the lukewarm tide of his notes beneath a summer moon. How far the sea has retreated! Brígida walks seaward, down the beach toward the distant, bright, smooth water; but all at once the sea rises, flowing placidly to meet and envelop her—the gentle waves pushing at her back until they press her cheek against the body of a man. And then the waves recede, leaving her stranded on Luis's chest.

"You have no heart, you have no heart," she used to say to him. His heartbeat was so faint that she could not hear it except in rare and unexpected moments. "You are never with me when you are by my side," she would protest in their bedroom when, before going to sleep, he would ritually open the evening paper. "Why did you marry me?"

"Because you have the eyes of a startled fawn," he would reply, giving her a kiss. And she, abruptly cheerful, would proudly accept the weight of his gray head on her shoulder. Oh, that silvery, radiant hair!

"Luis, you have never told me exactly what color your hair was when you were a boy. Or how your mother felt when you began going gray at the age of fifteen. What did she say? Did she laugh? Cry? And you— were you proud or ashamed? And at school—what did your classmates say? Tell me, Luis, tell me ... "

"Tomorrow. I am sleepy, Brígida. Very tired. Turn off the light."

Unconsciously, he would turn away from her in sleep; just as she unconsciously sought her husband's shoulder all night long, searching for his breath, groping blindly for protection as an enclosed and thirsty plant bends its tendrils toward warmth and moisture.

In the mornings, when the maid would open the Venetian blinds, Luis was no longer next to her. He had departed quietly without so much as a salutation, for fear the necklace of sparrows would fasten obstinately around his neck. "Five minutes, five minutes, no more. Your office will not disappear if you are five minutes late, Luis."

Her awakenings. Ah, how sad her awakenings! But—it was curious—no sooner had she entered her boudoir than the sadness vanished as if by an enchantment.

Waves crash, clashing far away, murmuring like a sea of leaves. Beethoven? No.

It is the tree outside her dressing-room window. She had only to enter the room to experience an almost overpowering sense of well-being.

How hot the bedroom always was in the morning! And what harsh light! By contrast, in the dressing-room even her eyes felt rested, refreshed. The faded cretonne curtains; the tree casting shadows that undulated on the walls like cold, moving water; the mirrors refracting foliage, creating the illusion of a green and infinite forest. How enjoyable that room was! It seemed a world submerged in an aquarium. And how that huge rubber tree chattered! All the birds in the neighborhood took refuge in it. It was the only tree on that narrow, falling street that sloped from one side of the city directly to the river.

"I am busy. I can't be with you ... Lots of work to do, I won't be home for lunch ... Hello ... yes, I am at the club. An engagement. Eat and go to bed ... No. I don't know. Better not wait for me, Brígida."

"If I only had friends!" she would sigh. But she bored everyone. "If I tried to be a little less foolish! Yet how does one recover so much lost ground at a single stroke? To be intelligent, you must start very young—isn't that true?"

Her sisters' husbands took them everywhere, but Luis—why had she denied it to herself?—had been ashamed of her, of her ignorance, her shyness, even of her eighteen years. Had he not urged her to pretend that she was at least twenty-one, as though her youth were an embarrassing secret they alone shared?

And at night—he always came to bed so weary! Never paying full attention to what she said. He smiled, yes—a mechanical smile. His caresses were plentiful, but bestowed absentmindedly. Why had he married her? To continue their acquaintance, perhaps simply to put the crowning touch on his old friendship with her father.

Maybe life for men was based on a series of established and continuous customs. Rupturing this chain would probably produce disorder, chaos. And after, men would stumble through the streets of the city, roosting on park benches, growing shabbier and more unshaven with each passing day. Luis's life, therefore, was patterned on keeping occupied every minute of the day. Why had she failed to see this sooner? Her father had been right: she was retarded.

"I would like to see snow sometime, Luis."

"This summer I will take you to Europe, and since it will be winter there, you shall have your snow."

"I am quite aware that winter in Europe coincides with our summer. I am not that stupid!"

At times, to rouse him to the rapture of true love, she would throw herself on him and cover him with kisses: weeping, calling, "Luis, Luis,

Luis ... "
"What? What is the matter? What do you want?"
"Nothing."
"Why do you cry out my name like that, then?"
"No reason. To say your name. I like to say your name."
And he would smile benevolently, pleased with the new game.

Summer came—her first summer as a married woman. Several new business ventures forced Luis to postpone the promised European trip.

"Brígida, the heat will be terrible in Buenos Aires shortly. Why don't you spend the summer on your father's ranch?"

"Alone?"

"I would visit you every week, from Saturday to Monday."

She sat down on the bed, primed to insult him. But she could not find the hurting words. She knew nothing, nothing—not even how to offend.

"What is wrong with you? What are you thinking of, Brígida?"

He was leaning over her, worried, for the first time in their marriage and unconcerned about violating his customary punctu ̄ ality at the office.

"I am sleepy," Brígida had replied childishly, hiding her face in the pillow.

For once, he rang her up at lunchtime from his club. But she had refused to come to the phone, angrily wielding a weapon she had discovered without thinking: silence.

That same evening she dined across from him with lowered eyes and nerves strung tight.

"Are you still angry, Brígida?"

But she did not answer.

"You know perfectly well that I love you. But I can't be with you all the time. I am a very busy man. When you reach my age, you become a slave to a thousand obligations."

...

"Shall we go out tonight?"

...

"No? Very well, I will be patient. Tell me, did Roberto call from Montevideo?"

...

"What a lovely dress! Is it new?"

...

"Is it new, Brígida? Answer me. Say something."

But she refused to break her silence.

And then the unexpected, the astonishing, the absurd. Luis rises from his chair and slaps his napkin on the table, slamming the door as he stomps from the house.

She, too, had gotten to her feet, stunned, trembling with indignation at such injustice. "And I ... and I ... " she stammered, "I, who for almost an entire year ... when for the first time I take the liberty of lodging a complaint ... ah, I am leaving—I am leaving this very night! I shall never set foot in this house again ... " And she jerked open the armoires in her dressing room, strewing clothes furiously in all directions. It was then that she heard a banging against the windowpane.

She ran to the window and opened it, not knowing how or from where the courage came. It was the rubber tree, set in motion by the storm, knocking its branches on the glass as though calling her to witness how it twisted and contorted like a fierce black flame under the burning sky of that summer night.

Heavy rain soon began to lash its cold leaves. How lovely! All night long she could hear the rain thrashing, splashing through the leaves of the rubber tree like a thousand tiny rivers sliding down imaginary canals. All night long she heard the ancient trunk creak and moan, the storm raging outside while she curled into a ball between the sheets of the wide bed, very close to Luis.

Handfuls of pearls raining on a silver roof. Chopin. Etudes by Frédéric Chopin.

How many mornings had she awakened as soon as she sensed that her husband, now likewise maintaining an obstinate silence, had slipped from bed?

Her dressing room: the window thrown wide, the odor of river and grass floating in that hospitable chamber, and the mirrors wearing a veil of fog.

Chopin intermingles in her turbulent memory with rain hissing through the leaves of the rubber tree like some hidden waterfall—so palpable that even the roses on the curtains seem moist.

What to do in summer when it rains so often? Spend the day in her room feigning sadness, a convalescence? One afternoon Luis had entered timidly. Had sat down stiffly. There was a long silence.

"Then it is true, Brígida? You no longer love me?"

A sudden joy seized her. She might have shouted, "No, no. I love you Luis, I love you," if he had given her time, if he had not almost immediately added, with his habitual calm, "In any case, I do not think it would be convenient for us to separate, Brígida. Such a move requires much thought."

Her impulse sank as fast as it had surfaced. What was the use of exciting herself! Luis loved her tenderly, with moderation; if he ever came to hate her, it would be a just and prudent hatred. And that was life. She walked to the window and placed her forehead against the cold glass. There was the rubber tree, serenely accepting the pelting rain. The room was fixed in shadow, quiet and ordered. Everything seemed to be held in an eternal and very noble equilibrium. That was life. And there was a certain grandeur in accepting it thus: mediocre, like something definite and irremediable. While underneath it all there seemed to rise a melody of grave and slow words that transfixed her: "Always. Never ... "

And in this way the hours, days and years pass. Always! Never! Life! Life!

Collecting herself, she realized that her husband had stolen from the room.

"Always! Never! ... " And the rain, secret and steady, still whispered in Chopin.

Summer stripped the leaves from its burning calendar. Luminous and blinding pages fell like golden swords; pages also of malignant dampness like breeze from a swamp; pages of furious and brief storms, of hot wind—the wind that carries the "carnation of the air" and hangs it on the huge rubber tree.

Some children used to play hide-and-seek among the enormous, twisted roots that pushed up the paving stones on the sidewalk, and the tree overflowed with laughter and whispering. On those days she would look from the window and clap her hands; but the children dispersed in fear, without noticing the childlike smile of a girl who wanted to join the game.

Alone, she would lean on her elbows at the window for a long time, watching the foliage swaying—a breeze blew along that street which sloped directly to the river—and it was like staring deep into moving water or the dancing flames in a fireplace. One could kill time in this fashion, no need for thought made foolish by peace of mind.

She lit the first lamp just as the room began to fill with twilight smoke, and the first lamp flickered in the mirrors, multiplying like fireflies eager to hasten the night.

And night after night she dozed beside her husband, suffering at intervals. But when her pain tightened so that it pierced like a knife thrust, when she was besieged by the desire to wake Luis—to hit him or caress him—she tiptoed to her dressing room and opened the window. Immediately the room came alive with discreet sounds and discreet presences, with mysterious footsteps, the fluttering of wings, the sudden rustling of vegetation, the soft chirping of a cricket perched on the bark of the rubber tree under the stars of a hot summer night.

Little by little her fever went down as her bare feet grew cold on the reed mat. She did not know why it was so easy to suffer in that room.

Chopin's melancholy stringing of one Etude after another, stringing of one melancholy after another, imperturbably.

And autumn came. The dry leaves hovered an instant before settling on the grass of the narrow garden, on the sidewalk of that sloping street. The leaves came loose and fell ... The top of the rubber tree remained green but underneath it turned red, darkened like the worn-out lining of a sumptuous evening cape. And now the room seemed to be submerged in a goblet of dull gold.

Lying on the divan, she waited patiently for the dinner hour and the improbable arrival of Luis. She had resumed speaking to him, had become his again without enthusiasm or anger. She no longer loved him. But she no longer suffered. On the contrary, an unexpected feeling of fulfillment and placidity had taken hold of her. Nothing, no one could hurt her now. It may be that true happiness lies in the conviction that one has irrevocably lost happiness. It is only then that we can begin to live without hope or fear, able finally to enjoy all the small pleasures, which are the most lasting.

A thunderous noise, followed by a flash of light from which she recoils, shaking.

The intermission? No. The rubber tree.

Having started to work early in the morning without her knowledge, they had felled it with a single stroke of the axe. "The roots were breaking up the sidewalk and, naturally, the neighborhood committee ... "

Dazed, she has shielded her eyes with her hands. When she recovers her sight, she stands and looks around. What does she see?

The concert hall suddenly ablaze with light, the audience filing out?

No. She is imprisoned in the web of her past, trapped in the dressing room—which has been invaded by a terrifying white light. It was as if they had ripped off the roof; a crude light entering from every direction, seeping through her very pores, burning her with its coldness. And she saw everything bathed in that cold light: Luis, his wrinkled face, his hands crisscrossed with ropy discolored veins and the gaudy cretonnes.

Frightened, she runs to the window. The window now opens directly on a narrow street, so narrow that her room almost brushes against a shiny skyscraper. On the ground floor, shop windows and more shop windows, full of bottles. At the corner, a row of automobiles lined up in front of a service station painted red. Some boys in their shirtsleeves are kicking a ball in the middle of the street.

And all that ugliness lay embedded in her mirrors, along with nickel-plated balconies, shabby clotheslines and canary cages.

They had stolen her intimacy, her secret; she found herself naked in the middle of the street, naked before an old husband who turned his back on her in bed, who had given her no children. She does not understand why, until then, she had not wanted children, how she had resigned herself to the idea of a life without children. Nor does she comprehend how for a whole year she had tolerated Luis's laughter, that overcheerful laughter, that false laughter of a man who has trained himself in joviality because it is necessary to laugh on certain occasions.

Lies! Her resignation and serenity were lies; she wanted love, yes, love, and trips and madness and love, love ...

"But, Brígida ... why are you leaving? Why did you stay so long?" Luis had asked. Now she would have to know how to answer him.

"The tree, Luis, the tree! They have cut down the rubber tree."

Translated by Richard Cunningham *and* Lucía Guerra

Culinary Lesson

Rosario Castellanos

The kitchen is resplendent with whiteness. A shame to have to dirty it with use. One should rather sit down to admire it, describe it, closing one's eyes, to evoke it. On examining this cleanliness, such beauty lacks the dazzling excess that makes one shiver in the sanatoriums. Or is it the halo of disinfectants, the cushioned steps of the nurses, the hidden presence of sickness and death that does it? What does it matter to me? My place is here. From the beginning of time it has been here. In the German proverb woman is synonymous with Küche, Kinder, Kirche. I wandered lost in classrooms, in streets, in offices, in cafés; wasting my time in skills that I now need to forget in order to acquire others. For example, to decide on a menu. How is one to carry out such an arduous task without society's and history's cooperation? On a special shelf adjusted to my height are lined up my guardian spirits, those admirable acrobats who reconcile in their recipes the most irreducible opposites: slimness and gluttony, decoration and economy, rapidity and succulence. With their infinite combinations: thinness and economy, swiftness and visual harmony, taste and ... What do you recommend for today's meal, experienced housewife, inspiration for mothers absent and present, voice of tradition, open secret of the supermarkets? I open a cookbook by chance and read: "Don Quijote's Dinner." Literary but not very satisfactory. Because Don Quijote was more of a crackpot than a gourmet. Although an analysis of the text reveals that, etc., etc., etc. Uf. More ink has run about this figure than water under the bridges. "Little birds of the face's center." Esoteric. Center of what? Does the face of someone or something have a center? If it had, it wouldn't be very appetizing. "Bigos, Rumanian Style." But who do you think I am? If I knew what tarragon and ananás were, I wouldn't be consulting this book, because I would know a heap of other things. If you had the slightest sense of reality, you or one of your colleagues would take the time to write a dictionary of culinary terms, with its prologue and propaedeutic, to make the difficult art of cooking accessible to the layman. But they start off with the assumption that we're all in on the secret and they limit themselves to enunciations. I solemnly confess that I for one am not in on it and have never been apprised of that game you seem to share with others, nor any other secret, for that matter. Frankly I have never understood anything. You can observe the symptoms: I find myself standing, like an idiot, in the midst of an impeccable and neutral kitchen, with a usurped apron to give a semblance of efficiency, which will be ignominiously, but justly, snatched away from me.

I open the refrigerator compartment that announces "meat" and remove a package, unrecognizable beneath its mantle of ice. I dissolve it in warm water and there appears a label, without which I would never have guessed its contents: beef for roasting. Wonderful. A simple and healthy dish. Since it doesn't offer the solving of an antinomy or the posing of an aporia, it doesn't appeal to me.

And it's not only the logical excess that turns off my hunger. There's also its appearance, rigidly cold, and its color that is clear now that I have opened the package. Red, as if it were about to bleed.

Our backs were the same color—my husband's and mine—after orgiastic tanning on Acapulco's beaches. He could allow himself the luxury of "behaving like a man," stretching out face down so that nothing would touch his skin. But I, submissive little Mexican woman, born like a dove for the nest, smiled like Cuautemoc on the rack when he said, "This is no bed of roses," and then fell silent. Face up I bore not only my own weight but his as well on top of mine. The classical posture for lovemaking. And I moaned, from excitement, from pleasure. The classical moan. Myths, myths.

Best of all (at least for my burns) was when he fell asleep. Beneath the tips of my fingers—not very sensitive because of prolonged contact with typewriter keys—the nylon of my nightgown slid away in a deceptive effort to simulate lace. In the darkness I played with the buttons and other ornaments that make one feel so feminine. The whiteness of my negligée, deliberate and repetitive, shamelessly symbolic, was temporarily nullified. Perhaps for a moment it had consummated its meaning in the light and beneath the gaze of those eyes now overcome by fatigue.

Eyelids closed and here once again in exile. I am not the dream that dreams, that dreams, that dreams; I am not the reflection of an image in the glass; I am not destroyed by the turning off of a consciousness or by any other consciousness. I will continue to live a dense, viscous, dark life, though he who is at my side and he who is far ignore and forget me, postpone me, abandon me, fall out of love.

I am also a consciousness that can turn off, abandon the other and expose him to ruin. I ... The piece of meat, now that it's salted has muffled the scandal of its redness and is now more familiar, more tolerable. It's the same piece I saw a thousand times when, without realizing it, I looked in to tell the cook that ...

We weren't born together. Our meeting was due to chance (a happy one?). It's too soon to decide that. We coincided at art exhibits, lectures, a film society; we bumped into each other in an elevator; he gave me his seat on a trolley; a guard interrupted our perplexed and parallel contemplation of a giraffe because it was time to close the zoo. Someone (he or I, it's all the same) asked the stupid but indispensable question: Do you work or study? Harmony of interests and of good intentions, indications of a "serious" purpose. A year ago I hadn't the slightest notion of his existence and now we lie together with our thighs intertwined, wet from perspiration and semen. I could get up without waking him and go barefoot to the shower. To purify myself? I'm not in the least disgusted. I prefer to believe that what unites me to him is something as easy to remove as a secretion and nothing as terrible as a sacrament.

So I remain still, breathing rhythmically to imitate peacefulness, perfecting my insomnia, the only unmarried woman's jewel that I have retained and am disposed to hang on to until I die.

Under the brief shower of pepper the meat seems to have gotten grey. I remove this sign of old age by rubbing it as if I were trying to get beyond the surface and impregnate the essential thickness within. Because I lost my old name and am still not accustomed to the new one, which isn't mine either. When an employee called me in the hotel lobby, I remained deaf, with that vague uneasiness which is the prologue to recognition. Who is that person that doesn't answer the call? It could be something urgent, serious, a matter of life or death. The one who calls becomes desperate, leaves without a trace, without a message, and any chance of a new encounter is gone. Is it anguish that presses on my breast? It's his hand that touches my shoulder. And his lips that smile with benevolent irony, more sorcerer than owner.

Well, I assent while we are walking toward the bar (my shoulder burns, it's peeling). It's true that in the contact or collision with him I have suffered a profound transformation; I didn't know, and I know; I didn't feel and I feel; I was not and I am.

I'll have to leave it there. Until it thaws to room temperature, until it becomes impregnated with those flavors I have showered on it. I have the impression that I didn't judge well and have bought too large a slice for the two of us. Out of laziness, I am not carnivorous; he, for aesthetic reasons, wants to keep his figure. Most of it will go to waste! Yes, I know I shouldn't worry; one of those spirits who hover over me will figure out what to do with the leftovers. At any rate, it's a false step. Married life shouldn't begin in such a slovenly manner. I'm afraid it shouldn't begin with such an ordinary dish as roast beef.

Thanks, I murmur, as I dry my lips with the tip of the napkin. Thanks for the translucent glass, for the submerged olive. Thanks for having opened the cage of a sterile routine so that I would close myself in the cage of a different routine which, according to all indications, will be fertile. Thanks for giving me the opportunity to show off a long and opulent gown, for helping me to walk forward in the church as the organ filled me with emotion. Thanks for ...

How long will it take to be ready? I shouldn't be concerned, since I won't have to put it in the oven till the last moment. The cookbooks say it's done in a few minutes. How much is a few? Fifteen? Ten? Five? Naturally the text is not precise. They assume that I have an intuition, which according to my sex I should possess but I don't, a sixth sense I was born with that will tell me the exact moment when the meat is done.

And you? Don't you have anything to thank me for? You've spelled it out with somewhat pedantic solemnity and with a precision you thought was flattering but to me was offensive: my virginity. When you discovered it I felt like the last dinosaur on a planet in which the species was extinct. I wanted to justify myself, to explain that if I came to you intact it wasn't because of virtue or pride or ugliness but simply a matter of adhering to a tradition, a style. I am not baroque. The tiny imperfection in the pearl is intolerable. My only other option is the neo-classic one and its rigidity isn't compatible with the spontaneity needed for lovemaking. I lack the agility of the oarsman, the tennis player, the dancer. I don't practice any sport. I consummate a rite and the gesture of surrender freezes on my face like a statue.

Are you waiting for my transition to fluidity, hoping for it, needing it? Or is this devotion that impresses you sufficient, so that you take it to be the passivity that corresponds to my nature? And if yours happens to be inconstancy, you may rest assured that I won't interfere with your adventures. It won't be necessary—thanks to my temperament—for you to stuff me, to tie me down with children, for you to smother me with the thick honey of resignation. I'll remain as I am. Calm. When you let your body fall on mine, I feel as if I am covered with a stone full of inscriptions, of names of others, of memorable dates. You moan inarticulate sounds, and I would like to whisper my name in your ear so that you may remember whom you are possessing.

It's me. But who am I? Your wife, of course. And that title is enough to distinguish me from past memories, from future projects. I bear a stamp of ownership, yet you observe me with suspicion. I am not weaving a net to catch you. Not a praying mantis. I'm glad you take stock in such a hypothesis. But it's false.

This meat has a hardness and consistency unlike that of beef. It must be mammoth. Those preserved since prehistoric times in Siberian ice that the peasants thaw and season for their meals. In the boring documentary they showed at the embassy, with its superfluous details, there was no mention of the time needed to make it edible. Years, months. And I am permitted a space of . . .

Is it a lark? A nightingale? No, our timetable will not be ruled by those winged creatures who warned Romeo and Juliet of the coming of dawn but by a stentorian and unmistakable alarm clock. And you won't descend today on the ladder of my tresses but by the steps of minor complaints: a button missing from your jacket, the toast is burnt, the coffee cold.

I will ruminate silently on my anger. I have been assigned the responsibilities and duties of a servant for everything. To keep the house impeccable, the clothing clean, the rhythm of mealtime infallible. But I'm not paid a salary, have no day off, can't switch employers. On the other hand, I am required to contribute to the maintenance of the household and I must efficiently carry out a labor in which the boss makes demands, the colleagues conspire and the subordinates are resentful. In my moments of leisure I am transformed into a society lady who prepares lunches and dinners for her husband's friends, who attends meetings, has a subscription to the opera, watches her weight, keeps up with the gossip, stays up late and gets up early, who runs the monthly risk of pregnancy, who believes in nightly meetings with executives, in business trips and the sudden arrival of clients; who suffers olfactory hallucinations when she senses the emanations of French perfume (different from hers) on her husband's shirts and handkerchiefs; who dur-

ing solitary evenings refuses to think of the whys and wherefores of such
anxiety, prepares a heavily loaded drink and reads a detective novel with
the fragile temperament of convalescents.

Isn't this the moment to turn on the oven? A low flame, to heat
the rack slowly "which should be coated with oil so the meat doesn't
stick." Even I know that, it wasn't necessary to waste space on such
recommendations.

As for me, I am clumsy. Now it's called clumsiness; it used to be
called innocence and that delighted you. But I was never delighted by
it. Before I was married I used to read things on the sly. Sweating with
excitement and shame. Fact is I never learned anything. My temples
throbbed, my eyes clouded over, my muscles contracted in a spasm of
nausea.

The oil is beginning to bubble. It got away from you, blunderer.
Now it's sputtering and leaping and you burned yourself. Thus I will
burn in hell for my crimes, for my guilt, for my immense guilt. But,
child, you're not the only one. All your school girl friends do the same
or worse, they accuse themselves in the confessional, are assigned pen-
itence, forgiven and then repeat it. Everyone. If I had continued to see
them, they would subject me to an interrogation. The married women
to reassure themselves, the unmarried ones to find out how far they can
go. Couldn't possibly disappoint them. I would invent acrobatic feats,
sublime fainting spells, "raptures" as they are called in the Thousand
and One Nights, records of endurance. If you were to hear me then,
you wouldn't recognize me, Casanova!

I drop the meat on the grill and instinctively retreat to the wall. What
a racket! It finally stops. The piece of beef lies quietly now, true to its
nature of cadaver. I still think it's too large.

But you haven't disappointed me. Certainly I didn't expect anything
special. Little by little we'll reveal ourselves, discovering our secrets, our
little tricks, learning to please one another. And one day you and I will
become a perfect pair of lovers, then in the midst of an embrace we will
vanish and there will appear on the screen the words *The End*.

What's happening? The meat is shrivelling up. No, I'm not having
hallucinations, I'm not mistaken. You can see the outline of its original
shape on the grill. It was larger. Fine! Now it'll be the size of our
appetite.

For my next film I would like a different part. White witch in a native village? No, today I don't feel like heroism or danger. Rather,
a famous woman (dress designer or something of the kind), indepen-

dently wealthy, lives alone in an apartment in New York, Paris or London. Her occasional affairs amuse her but are not troubling. She is not sentimental. After breaking up with her last lover she lights a cigarette and contemplates the urban landscape through the high windows of her study.

Ah, the color is more decent now. Only at the tips does it persist in recalling its raw state. The rest of it is golden and gives off a delicious aroma. Will it be enough for the two of us? Now it looks too small.

If I were to dress up right now, if I were to put on one of those models from my trousseau and go down to the street, what would happen then, huh? I might latch onto a mature man, with automobile and all the rest. Mature . . . Retired. The only type that can allow himself to go out cruising this time of the day.

What the devil is happening? This wretched piece of meat is starting to give off an awful black smoke. I should have turned it over! Burnt on one side. Well, at least there's another.

Miss, if you will allow me . . . Please, I'm married. And I warn you that my husband is jealous. Then he shouldn't let you go out alone. You're a temptation for any passerby. Nobody says "passerby." Pedestrian? Only the newspapers when they describe accidents. You're a temptation for any Mr. X. Silent. Sig-ni-fi-cant. Sphinx-like glances. The mature gentleman follows me at a prudent distance. Better for him. Better for me, because at the corner, wham! My husband, who's spying on me, who never leaves me alone, who is suspicious of everything and everyone, Your Honor. I can't go on living this way, I want a divorce.

And now what? Your momma forgot to tell you that you were a piece of meat and should behave as such. It curls up like a piece of brushwood. Besides I don't know where all that smoke is coming from, since I turned off the oven ages ago. Of course, Dr. Heart. What one should do now is open the window, turn on the air purifier and the odor will disappear when my husband arrives. I'll dress up to greet him at the door in my best outfit, my most ingratiating smile and my most heartfelt invitation to go out to eat.

Now that's a possibility. We'll examine the menu in the restaurant while this miserable piece of charred meat lies hidden at the bottom of the garbage can. I'll be careful not to mention the incident and will be considered a rather irresponsible housewife with frivolous tendencies, but not as mentally retarded. That will be the first public image I will project, and afterwards I'll need to be consistent, although it may not be exact.

There's yet another option. Not to open the window, not to con-
nect the purifier, not to throw away the meat. When my husband gets
here, let him sniff the air like the ogres in the fairy tales, and I'll tell him
that the air smells not of burnt human flesh, but of a useless wife and
housekeeper. I'll exaggerate my compunction in order to encourage
his magnanimity. After all, the incident is quite commonplace. What
newly-wed woman hasn't done the same? When we visit my mother-in-
law (who hasn't quite reached the stage of attacking me, because she
doesn't know my weak points) she will tell me about her own mishaps.
Like when her husband asked for a couple of dropped eggs and she took
him literally and ... Ha, ha. Did that stop her from becoming a fabulous widow, that is, a fabulous cook? Because the matter of widowhood
came about much later and for other reasons. From then on she let go
with her maternal instincts and spoiled her children rotten.

No, it won't strike him funny in the least. He'll say that I was distracted, that it's the height of carelessness. As for me, I will acquiesce,
accept his accusations.

But it's not true. I was carefully watching the meat, taking note of
the peculiar things happening to it. With good reason Saint Theresa
said that God may be found in the stew pots. Or, that matter is energy,
or whatever term is in vogue now.

Let's recapitulate. First of all, there's a piece of beef with a certain
color, shape, size. Then it changes and gets prettier and one is quite
pleased. Then it changes again and it is not quite as pleasing. And
it goes on changing and changing and one doesn't know how to put a
stop to it. Because, if I leave this piece of meat in the oven, it will be
consumed till there's not a trace left. And the piece of meat which gave
the impression of something real and solid will no longer exist.

The meat hasn't disappeared. It has merely suffered a series of
metamorphoses. And the fact that it is no longer visible to the senses
doesn't mean that it has completed a cycle, but that it has made a qual-
itative leap. It will go on operating at different levels: in my consciousness, in my memory, in my will, transforming me, determining me, establishing the direction of my future.

From this day forward I will be that which I decide at this moment.
Seductively scatterbrained, deeply reserved, hypocritical. From the start
I will impose, impertinently, the rules of the game. My husband will re-
sent the stamp of my domination that will widen like circles on a lake's
surface on the stone's impact. He will struggle to prevail, and if he gives

in, I will repay him with my scorn, and if he doesn't, I will forgive him for it.

If I assume another attitude, if I am a typical case, that is, femininity which seeks indulgence for its errors, the scale will tip in favor of my antagonist, and I will compete with a handicap which apparently will lead me to failure but which, at bottom, will guarantee my triumph by the same sinuous path my ancestors took, those humble women who only open their lips to assent and who won the other's obedience even for the most irrational of their caprices.

The prescription is an old one and its efficacy is well known. If I still have doubts, all I need to do is to ask my nearest neighbor, she will confirm my certainty.

Nevertheless, it repels me to behave in this manner. This description is not applicable to me, nor is the previous one, neither of which corresponds to my inner truth, neither of which saves my authenticity. Must I adhere to any of them and embrace their terms only because it is a commonplace accepted by the majority and perfectly clear to everyone? And it's not that I am a rara avis. You could say of me what Pfandl said about Sor Juana: that I belong to a class of cavilling neurotics. The diagnosis is easy, but what are the consequences of assuming it?

If I insist on affirming my version of the events, my husband will treat me with suspicion, will feel uncomfortable in my presence and will live with the constant expectation of my being declared insane.

Our relationship could not be more problematic. And he tries to avoid all kinds of conflicts. Most of all conflicts that are so abstract, so absurd, so metaphysical as those which I present. His home is the quiet cove where he seeks shelter from life's storms. I agree. I accepted this situation when I was married, and I was ready for any sacrifice on behalf of conjugal harmony. But I assumed that such a sacrifice, the utter renunciation of everything that I am, would only be required on the Sublime Occasion, at the Hour of the Grand Resolutions, at the moment of the Final Decision. Not with regard to what occurred today, which is something utterly insignificant, something ridiculous. And yet . . .

Translated by Julián Palley

The End of a Struggle

Amparo Dávila

He was buying the evening paper when he saw himself walk by with a blonde woman. He froze, non-plussed. It was he, no doubt about it. Not a twin or look-alike; he was the man who had walked by, wearing the English cashmere suit and striped tie his wife had given him for Christmas. "Here's your change, sir," the newsboy was saying. He accepted the coins mechanically and put them into his coat pocket. The man and the blonde woman were approaching the corner now. He hurried to follow them. He had to know who this other man was and where he lived, find out which of the two was the real one, whether he, Durán, was the actual owner of the body and the man who had walked by was the animated shadow, or if the other was real and he the shadow.

They looked happy, walking arm in arm. Durán couldn't catch up with them. At that time of day the streets were crowded and it was hard to make headway. When he turned the corner they were gone. Thinking he'd lost them, he felt the old anguish sweep over him. He stood there looking in every direction, not knowing what to do or where to go. Then he realized that they hadn't gotten lost, he had. Just then he saw them get on a streetcar. He was breathless, his mouth dry, when he got to the streetcar. He had trouble locating them in the crush of people. They were near the exit in the middle of the car, imprisoned like him, unable to move. He hadn't been able to see the woman very well when they passed by in the street, but she seemed beautiful. A beautiful blonde, well-dressed, arm in arm with him? He was impatient to be on the street again, where he could approach them. He knew he couldn't stand it much longer. As he watched, they moved to the exit and got off. He tried to follow, but when he was finally able to get off, they had vanished. He searched for hours along the neighboring streets, went into all the shops, peered in the windows of houses, lingered on the corners. It was all in vain; he couldn't find them.

Worn out and bewildered, he took the streetcar back. Always insecure, he was so shaken by the baffling encounter he could no longer be certain whether he was a man or a shadow. He went into a bar, not the one where he usually went for a drink with friends, but another one, where no one would know him. He didn't want to talk. He needed to be alone, to find himself. He had several drinks, but couldn't forget the encounter. When he got home, his wife was keeping dinner warm for him, as usual. He was too nervous to eat, there was a void inside him. Nor could he turn toward his wife as she lay beside him that night, or the following nights either. He couldn't deceive her. He was remorseful, disgusted with himself. Perhaps at that very moment he was possessing the beautiful blonde ...

From the afternoon he saw himself walk by with the blonde, Durán felt ill. He made mistakes in his work at the Bank, was nervous and irritable, spent as little time at home as he could. He felt guilty, unworthy of Flora. He couldn't get the encounter out of his mind. For several days he went back to the corner where he'd seen them and stayed there for hours, waiting. He needed to know the truth, to know if he was real or only a shadow.

One day they reappeared. The man was wearing the old brown suit that had been Durán's companion for so many years. He recognized it right away; he'd worn it so many times ... It brought a flood of memories. He was quite near them. That was his body, no doubt about it: the same half-smile, the graying hair, that way of wearing down the heel on his right shoe, his pockets always full of things, the newspaper under his arm ... no one's but his. He followed them onto the streetcar, caught a whiff of her perfume ... Le Galion's *Sortilege*. Lilia's perfume, the one she always used. He'd given her a bottle one day, even though it had cost him more than he could afford. Lilia had complained that he never gave her anything. As an impoverished student, he'd loved her for years, dying of hunger and of love for her. She despised him because he couldn't give her the things she liked: luxuries, expensive places, gifts. She went out with a number of men, hardly ever with him ... *He hesitated on his way into the store, counting the money to see if it was enough. "Sortilege is a lovely scent," the girl at the counter told him. "Your fiancée will be sure to like it." Lilia wasn't home when he went to give her the perfume. He waited for hours ... When he handed it to her she took it languidly, not even bothering to open it. He was horribly disap-*

pointed. That perfume was all he had to give her and more, and it had no importance for her. Lilia was beautiful, cold. She gave orders. He could never please her ... They got off the streetcar. Durán followed close behind. He'd decided not to speak to them on the street. They walked for several blocks. Finally they went into a gray house, 279. That was probably where they lived. He was living there with Lilia. He couldn't go on like this. He had to talk to them, find out all there was to know, put an end to this double life. He couldn't go on living with his wife and Lilia at the same time. His love for Flora was tranquil, serene. He'd loved Lilia desperately, always hurt, always humiliated by her. Now he was caressing both of them, possessing them both at the same time. And only one of them really had him; the other was living with a shadow. He rang the doorbell. Rang it again ... *He was patient, so patient, believing he could eventually win her over. He'd wait for her on the doorstep, content just to see her, to be allowed to take her wherever she was going. Then he'd leave and go back to the boardinghouse, at peace; he'd seen her, talked to her* ... As he rang the doorbell again he heard Lilia cry cry out. She was screaming desperately, as though someone were beating her. And he was beating her, cruelly, savagely. But he'd never had the courage to beat her, even though he'd often wanted to ... *Lilia was beautiful in her blue silk dress, beautiful and cold. "I'm going to the theater with my friend, I don't have time to see you now," she said. He had his diploma with him, had gotten it that very day, wanted her to be the first to see it. He thought she would congratulate him on his graduation with honors. He'd told his classmates Lilia was going to the graduation dance with him. "Wait a minute, Lilia, I just wanted to ask you ... "A car drew up in front of the house and Lilia stopped listening to him. He took her arm, trying to hold her just long enough to invite her to the dance. She broke away from him and ran to the waiting car. He watched her sit close to the man who'd come to pick her up, saw her kiss him, heard her laugh. He felt all the blood rush to his head, and for the first time he wanted to take her in his arms and tear her to pieces. That was the first time he drank himself into a stupor* ... He rang rang the doorbell again; no response. Lilia was still screaming. Then he began to beat on the door. He couldn't let her die at his own hands. He had to save her ... *"All I want is for you to leave me alone. I never want to see you again," Lilia told him that night. That was the last time he saw her. He'd been waiting to tell her goodbye. He couldn't go on living in the same city where she lived, putting up with her insults and the humiliation she heaped on him. Lilia got out of the car and slammed the door, furious. A man followed, caught up with her and began hitting her. He ran to rescue her. When the man drove away, Lilia was crying. He embraced her tenderly, protectively; she pushed him away and said she never wanted to see him again. Everything in him rebelled. He regretted having rescued her from the beating, having shown her his tenderness. It would have been his salvation if the other man had killed her. He left town the next day. He had to get away from Lilia, free himself once and for all from that love that was diminishing and degrading him. It hadn't been easy to forget her. He saw her everywhere, on streetcars, at the movies, in cafés. Sometimes he'd follow a woman down the street for blocks before he discovered she wasn't Lilia. He heard her speak, laugh. He remembered her phrases, the way she dressed, her walk, the warm lithe body he'd held in his arms so few times, the fragrance of her body tinged with Sortilege. His poverty grated on him; he often thought in desperation that she'd have loved him if only he'd had money. He spent years living on his memories of her. When Flora came into his life, he let himself drift toward her. He thought the only way he could be rid of Lilia was by having another woman near him. He married without passion. Flora was good, tender, understanding. She respected his reserve, his other world. Sometimes he'd wake up at night thinking it was Lilia who was sleeping at his side; then he'd touch Flora's body and feel something tear inside him. One day Lilia disappeared. He was finally able to forget her. He began to grow accustomed to Flora and to love her. Years went by ...* Lilia's screams were barely audible now. They were weak, muffled, as though ... He forced the door open and went in. The house was completely dark.

The struggle was long and silent, terrible. Several times, when he fell, he touched Lilia's body. She'd died before he could get there. He could feel her blood, still warm, sticky. More than once his hands were caught in her hair. He went on struggling in the dark. He had to endure until the end, until only Durán remained, or the other ...

Toward midnight Durán, badly wounded, staggered out of the gray house. He peered cautiously around him, like a man afraid of being arrested on sight.

Translated by Catherine Rodríguez-Nieto

In Heaven

Guadalupe Dueñas

The only bright spot in my youth was the abundance of perfumes, soaps and cosmetics teeming in the basement of our house. I spent my adolescence bathed in the effluvia of their exotic exhalations as sister after sister appeared each year—seven in all.

I was allowed one perfume each day of the week. Monday it was "Heliotrope," Tuesday, "Rumor," the day after, "Scandal," then "Arpege," "Intimate Hour," "Intermezzo" and on Sunday, "La nuit bleue." Each morning I would pick a different flower from the fantasy garden: it was like having the rainbow at my command. I was steeped in colognes and perfumes and I don't think there's a single one I haven't tried. I covered myself ankle to thigh in costly wrinkle creams; their softness still lingers.

When it was time for the powder, I covered myself from head to toe until I practically looked like a ghost. Even after I was dressed it would shower off me like pollen off wheat.

This magic garden compensated for many disappointments. I spent long hours eyeing the encased vials, absorbed in the diademed bottles and in exotic stoppers in the form of African princesses with jeweled necklaces. There were cut glass stoppers bigger than the bottles themselves, others shaped like prisms or tears, and a fascinating one encrusted with rubies and little silver cloverleaves with striped bubbles in the melted opal inside.

Essences of twilight! Avidly eyeing them, greedily unstoppering them! Mysterious, magical, debutantes in line.

There were perfumes that inexplicably hemorrhaged from untouched vials, stealing away like life itself. The unopened bottles yielded up their essence in short order and the prospect of their leaving chilled me, terrified me.

Our perfumes were popular throughout the region. Though this bothered some in the family, I was proud of it.

I was something of a celebrity at home—my friends were jealous. They were amazed that I had four different soaps: "Hiel de Toro" for my hair, "Grass of Pravia" from the neck to the waist, real "Lavender" from there to the ankles (I never put it on my feet) and, finally, "Rose" for my face and hands. It was the living end when, like some eccentric millionaire, I showed off the lotions I used every day, impressing them while I gave away a bunch of expensive perfume samples—I had such a good time I almost forgot the cheap, much-mended stockings I had on.

When some nice girl exclaimed, "You must be very rich!" I would hide my tacky shoes and coyly answer: "Oh, not really ... " There were also mean ones who tried to upset me, calling me "Miss Heavenly" and pretending to gag and vomit when my implacable vapors overtook them: they swore it gave them headaches.

But aside from those unpleasant moments, I was happy in the forest of fragrances that was all mine, like my tresses and my tears.

Luckily my parents never worried about what became of those samples. If they ever gave some away to a friend, they had to put up with my disconsolate and hysterical crying because I felt that they were mine.

They never realized how important that colorful paradise was for me, to my soul lost in the solitary rapture of that enchanted basement.

Translated by John Benson

Shoes for the Rest of My Life

Guadalupe Dueñas

Everything went sour the day my father went bankrupt in the shoe manufacturing business.

We could have gotten along fine somehow except for his brilliant idea of sorting out all the shoes by sizes and figuring out how many pair everyone in the family would need up till their dying day. Let's see, if I wore a size 19 when I was twelve, I would need 23's at twenty, and, after all was said and done, I would have enough shoes to last me forever.

The shoes for the rest of my life were boxed up in the corners of my room, piles of little coffins reaching up to the sky. I had plenty of time at night to feast my eyes on the bonds that would forever imprison my hapless feet.

Randomly I picked out a box, trying to avoid the collapse of my tower of Babel. And you can imagine my despair when I saw the curious sandals, hard as iron, invariably looking like women's shoes on a man and indubitably like men's shoes on women. Their abominable, iridescent color was the last straw. In another box I found some boots that might have aspired to goatskin but were actually made from canvas with rows of buttons on the sides, white with occasional black spots and miles of ribbon. There wasn't a single reasonable-looking pair—they were combat boots, iron-soled crypts for desperate feet.

I envied Indians and barefoot children, and dreamed of getting run over by a truck just so my father would have to atone for his sins. Luckily my feet weren't growing any and so I walked gingerly to make my red moccasins last.

Finishing off the pointy yellow shoes, all the sandals and funny little boots, tearing off the silk ribbons and ruining the finish in dirty water, mutilating straps and slippers, taking no hostages, leaving nary a pair to strangle my feet—this was the overriding obsession that dominated my life.

To carry out my plan I supplied myself with the right tools for the job: scissors, knives, sandpaper, a pumice stone and a couple of good spikes.

I went without sleep so I could continue wearing them out on both hands and feet in the hallways and the cobbled yard. I debuted a new pair twice a week. My friends were the beneficiaries of my largesse on their saint's day as well as on birthdays. I shod the local beggars. I often tried leaving one behind when visiting, but it didn't work: people kept returning the orphan shoe and I was punished for it. It was better just to forget about the newest ones that fit the children in the house.

I was so upset with the backstitched ones that a large number of them perished under the wheels of streetcars. I also collected bits of chewing gum from desks everywhere: it's very effective on satin and glossy finishes.

But it's getting to me. Sometimes I'll walk for miles harrassing the tough, charmed leather that neither yields nor changes, suffering immutably under my corns and blisters. I have come up with new steps that wear them out twice as fast, but it's killing me. Their malignant tongues and fiery soles mock me. There's no end of it. I try on six new pair a day and still only a few of the stacks have disappeared. The white boxes seem to band together as I writhe in agony.

It's hard sanding them down, hard jumping up and down trying to break them. I crack my nails and bloody my fingers in this unequal combat. The smell of cowhide precedes me wherever I go; I don't normally sweat much, but these instruments of torture could wring it out of anyone. Every day they get more and more out of date, it's embarassing. It would take seven lives to get through them all. There's just no end to it.

Translated by John Benson

The Child That Never Was

Maria Virginia Estenssoro

They were laughing on their way back from a spin in the car.

Out in the open country, the sky was jet black in the depths of the night.

Suddenly, Ernesto pointed at something: "Sirius!" And he recounted the affair in bitter-sad-cynical-mordant phrases.

"It was in New York. Her name was Caroline. I loved her. She arrived one afternoon at the park where I was waiting for her and she told me, 'It's all taken care of.' I was looking at Sirius, just like I am now, and replied, 'Yeah?' I was a little out of it. She was happy: 'Yes, I'm free now. What a relief! Aren't you happy?' 'Yeah, yeah ... "Well, what's wrong with you now? I'm going.' And I watched her stride away, pulling on her gloves, swallowed by the subway entrance. Sirius kept on shining like a sparkling diamond. I thought about God and the old curse: 'Be fruitful and multiply!' Nowadays nobody pays much attention to it, what with prophylactics and abortion. What do you think He thinks of his handiwork? What must God think about this anthropoid, this overgrown monkey that dares to be intelligent enough to invent things that abrogate his eternal laws, unchangeable laws, eternal and irresistable as God Himself?"

"Did you ever see her again?" asked Magdalena.

"No. I loved her a lot, almost as much as you. And that night I thought about how easy it is to lose someone in a city as vast as New York. So I looked up at Sirius—shining like a tear in the sky—and drummed on the window with my fingers, thinking about my son, the son that never was, that never became a ... a lawyer." Ernesto cut off suddenly with a short, sarcastic laugh.

Magdalena meditated on Sirius and on the moon that lit up the sky and seemed to bathe them in pearls. She slowly turned around, looked straight into his eyes and said, "But I will love your child."

Then he kissed her hand, all tenderness as in their best moments together, murmuring softly like a child about to break out in tears, "My God!"

Magdalena moaned monotonously on the operating table, "No more, please, no more."

The doctor stanched the blood with bits of sterilized cotton. She could smell the iodine, alcohol, disinfectant. The pain pierced her and she implored again, "Enough, for the love of God, enough!"

Suddenly the instrument drove home and, as she screamed, a muffled, babbled appeal came from within, "Mommy ... "

The doctor was drying his hands as he remarked, "That's all, ma'am. Rather squeamish, aren't we?"

"Please don't make fun of me."

And then she heard, "Mommy ... "

And then she left. Though she was still in pain, she lengthened her stride and tried to put some spring into her step as she walked along: Click, click, click, click, click, click. Mom, my Mom, my ...

A ragged, barefoot newsboy looked up at her imploringly. Magdalena bought a paper from him as she searched his face: "Mommy."

Her child was waiting for her at home, her boy, the one from her marriage. He came running out like always, little arms out, tripped and fell: "Mommy!"

Dejected, depressed, she lay down. Her little boy dozed happily at her side, his little brown-haired head nestled in the pillow. She looked at him, a lovely flower rooted in her heart. Now in that same heart she now felt another little one, something that could have bloomed forth in innocence, just like the first one which she had allowed the surgeon to cruelly uproot.

"Mommy."

But the dark head cut off in its beginning, torn from her, destroyed, sabred in her very womb, the little dark head had left it's imprint, a small, indelible trace, uneraseable, adorable. And in the mother's soul the little shade stretched forth his arms and cried: "Mommy! Mommy!"

"My poor baby!" Magdalena moaned, pressing the fair hand of the other son who slept on her breast, smiling and content. "My poor baby! You're half-frozen like a little bird. Come here and warm up, go to sleep. Poor dear, so cold, so unloved, little star, my little treasure. Poor baby, sleep, sleep."

And the little shadow kept on: "Mommy, Mommy ... "

She thought she was going crazy. The heart of the child sleeping next to her went "Mommy!"

The clock seemed to go "Mommy!"

She got up. Walking back and forth, she remembered the afternoon Ernesto mused about what God must think of his piteous creatures, and what Caroline said: "It's all taken care of."

She lay down again and dreamt.

The sky was jet black in the depths of the night. The tremulous light of a candle came and went up and down in the darkness. Wherever it passed, beads of light came to life like in electric signs: red letters, green letters and white ones.

"Mommy, Mommy, Mommy ... "

And then, a cold chill and everything went black again. Was it limbo? There was a stirring of shadows and wings. Were they newborns? Then, deep sighing and little sobs: "Mommy, Mommy, Mommy ... "

Suddenly a large figure hurried by, a skeleton in surgeon's costume and rubber gloves. Death/The Surgeon grasped a package that squirmed and cried: "Mommy."

She awoke in a cold sweat. She got up again. Striding around the estate, feverish, she peered inward in anguish.

"Does it take courage to raise a fatherless child?" she asked herself. "Does it?"

Yes, it does. But I have one already—my husband's; he never had any use for him, and all I have is love, love and instinct, tenderness and impulses. And happiness. And gratitude. I'm not courageous, not heroic. I'm happy. And what do I give him? Everything and nothing. He—weak, small, defenseless as he is—gives me his laughter, his happiness, the light in his eyes, the life I first gave him. He gives me back enchantment, fantasy, poetry. He transmutes even money—the filthy, worn bills I get I handle avidly, impatiently as though they were fine cloth or satin. It turns into his little shoes, toys, candies, his grabby little hands and his inquiring eyes excited at the prospect of a present. He is my supreme happiness, constantly renewed, hope, life itself. I'm not courageous, just happy.

Courage is something else. Terrifying, abominable. Magnificent yet infernal. Courage to forgo happiness, kill contentment, destroy the enchantment, rip the veil of fantasy, turn the knife to one's very bowels and against one's own life.

"But I will love your child."

"Mommy, Mommy, Mommy."

Mommy, I do love you so much! Mothers are supposed to sacrifice themselves for their children, but I will sacrifice myself for you. Mommy, dear Momma, I'll never bother you again. You'll never have to listen to me cry, although sometimes you'll wish you could. I'll never tear pages out of your books, never knock over and break a vase. You'll never have to worry about my getting sick, or fret over not being able to buy me a toy. I'll never be bad, or awkward or make you uncomfortable. I'm the nice boy, the good boy. I won't bother you with my noisy games and you'll never lose time dressing, washing or feeding me. Want me to go, Mommy? I'm the obedient one. No cradle, no Mother Goose, I'll disappear in the cold, in the night, out there somewhere ... Want me to go? All right, I'll go. But I do love you so much, dear Momma, Mommy, Mommy, Mommy ...

Translated by John Benson

A Poisoned Tale

Rosario Ferré

And the King said to Ruyán the Wise Man:
"Wise Man, there is nothing written."
"Leaf through a few more pages."
The King turned a few more pages, and
before long the poison began to course
rapidly through his body. Then the King
trembled and cried out: "This book is poisoned."

from *A Thousand and One Nights*

Rosaura lived in a house of many balconies, shadowed by a dense over-growth of crimson bougainvillea vines. She used to love to hide behind these vines, where she could read her storybooks undisturbed. Rosaura, Rosaura. A melancholy child, she had few friends, but no one had ever been able to guess the reason for her wistfulness. She was devoted to her father, and whenever he was home she used to sing and laugh around the house, but as soon as he left to supervise the workers in the cane fields, she'd hide once more behind the crimson vines and before long she'd be deep in her storybook world.

I know I ought to get up and see to the mourners, pass the coffee tray among my clients and the cognac tray among their unbearable husbands, but I feel exhausted. I just want to sit here and rest my aching feet, listen to my neighbors chat endlessly about me. Don Lorenzo was an impoverished sugarcane plantation owner, and only by working from dawn to dusk did he manage to keep the family in a suitable situation. First Rosaura, then Lorenzo. What an extraordinary coincidence. He loved the old plantation house, with its dozen balconies jutting out over

64

the cane fields like a windswept schooner's. He had been born there, and the building's historic past made his blood stir with patriotic zeal: it was there that the creoles' first resistance to the invasion had taken place, almost a hundred years before.

Don Lorenzo remembered the day well, and he would enthusiastically re-enact the battle scene as he strode vigorously through the halls and parlors—war whoops, sable, musket and all—thinking of those heroic ancestors who had gloriously died for their homeland. In recent years, however, he'd been forced to excercise some caution in his historic strolls, as the wood-planked floor of the house was eaten through with termites. The chicken coop and the pigpen that Don Lorenzo was compelled to keep in the cellar to bolster the family income were now clearly visible, and the sight of them would always cast a pall over his dreams of glory. Despite his economic hardships, however, he had never considered selling the house or the plantation. A man could sell everything—his horse, his shirt, even the skin off his back—but one's land, like one's heart, must never be sold.

I mustn't betray my surprise, my growing amazement. After everything that's happened, to find ourselves at the mercy of a two-bit writer. As if my customers' bad-mouthing wasn't enough. I can almost hear them whispering, tearing me apart behind their fluttering fans: "Whoever would have thought it; from charwoman to gentlewoman, first wallowing in mud, then wallowing in wealth. But finery does not a lady make." I couldn't care less. Thanks to Lorenzo, their claws can't reach me now; I'm beyond their "lower my neckline here a little more, Rosita dear, cinch in my waist a little tighter here, Rosita darling," as though the alterations to their gowns were no work at all and I didn't have to get paid for them. But I don't want to think about that now.

When his first wife died, Don Lorenzo behaved like a drowning man on a shipwreck. He thrashed about desperately in an ocean of loneliness for a while, until he finally grabbed on to the nearest piece of flotsam. Rosa offered to keep him afloat, clasped to her broad hips and generous breasts. He married her soon afterwards, and, his domestic comfort thus re-established, Don Lorenzo's laugh could once again be heard echoing through the house, as he went out of his way to make his daughter happy. An educated man, well versed in literature and art, he found nothing wrong in Rosaura's passion for storybooks. He felt guilty about the fact that she had been forced to leave school because of his poor business deals, and perhaps because of it he always gave her a lavish, gold-bound storybook on her birthday.

   This story is getting better; it's funnier by the minute. The two-bit
writer's style makes me want to laugh; he's stilted and mawkish and
turns everything around for his own benefit. He obviously doesn't sym-
pathize with me. Rosa was a practical woman, for whom the family's
modest luxuries were unforgivable self-indulgences. Rosaura disliked
her because of this. The house, like Rosaura's books, was a fantasy
world, filled with exquisite old dolls in threadbare clothes; musty ward-
robes full of satin robes, velvet capes, and crystal candelabras which
Rosaura used to swear she'd seen floating through the halls at night,
held aloft by flickering ghosts. One day Rosa, without so much as a
twinge of guilt, arranged to sell all the family heirlooms to the local antique dealer.

   The two-bit writer is mistaken. First of all, Lorenzo began pestering
me long before his wife passed away. I remember how he used to un-
dress me boldly with his eyes when I was standing by her sickbed, and I
was torn between feeling sorry for him and my scorn for his weak, sentimental mooning. I finally married him out of pity and not because I
was after his money, as this story falsely implies. I refused him several
times, and when I finally weakened and said yes, my family thought I'd
gone out of my mind. They believed that my marrying Lorenzo and taking charge of his huge house would mean professional suicide, because
my designer clothes were already beginning to earn me a reputation.
Selling the supposed family heirlooms, moreover, made sense from a
psychological as well as from a practical point of view. At my own home
we've always been poor but proud; I have ten brothers and sisters, but
we've never gone to bed hungry. The sight of Lorenzo's empty cupboard, impeccably whitewashed and with a skylight to better display its
frightening bareness, would have made the bravest one of us shudder.
I sold the broken-down furniture and the useless knicknacks to fill that
cupboard, to put some honest bread on the table.

   But Rosa's miserliness didn't stop there. She went on to pawn the
silver, the table linen and the embroidered bed sheets that had once
belonged to Rosaura's mother, and to her mother before her. Her nig-
gardliness extended to the family menu, and even such moderately epi-
curean dishes as fricasseed rabbit, rice with guinea hen and baby lamb
stew were banished forever from the table. This last measure saddened
Don Lorenzo deeply because, next to his wife and daughter, he had
loved these creole dishes more than anything else in the world, and the
sight of them at dinnertime would always make him beam with happiness.

Who could have strung together this trash, this dirty gossip? The title, one must admit, is perfect: the written page will bear patiently whatever poison you spit on it. Rosa's frugal ways often made her seem two-faced: she'd be all smiles in public and a shrew at home. "Look on the bright side of things, dear, keep your chin up when the chips are down," she'd say spunkily to Lorenzo as she put on her best clothes for mass on Sundays, insisting he do the same. "We've been through hard times before and we'll weather this one too, but there's no sense in letting our neighbors know." She opened a custom dress shop in one of the small rooms of the first floor of the house and hung a little sign that read "The Fall of the Bastille" over its door. Believe it or not, she was so ignorant that she was sure this would win her a more educated clientele. Soon she began to invest every penny she got from the sale of the family heirlooms in costly materials for her customers' dresses, and she'd sit night and day in her shop, self-righteously threading needles and sewing seams.

The mayor's wife just walked in; I'll nod hello from here, without getting up. She's wearing one of my exclusive models, which I must have made over at least six times just to please her. I know she expects me to go over and tell her how becoming it looks, but I just don't feel up to it. I'm tired of acting out the role of high priestess for the women of this town. At first I felt sorry for them. It broke my heart to see them with nothing to think about but bridge, gossip and gadflying from luncheon to luncheon. Boredom's velvet claw had already finished off several of them who'd been interned in mainland sanatoriums for "mysterious health problems," when I began to preach, from my modest workshop, the doctrine of Salvation through Style. Style is doubtless woman's most subtle virtue. Style heals all, cures all, restores all. Its followers are legion, as can be seen from the hosts of angels in lavishly billowing robes that mill about under our cathedral's frescoed dome.

Thanks to Lorenzo's generosity, I subscribed to all the latest fashion magazines, which were mailed to me directly from Paris, London and New York. I began to publish a weekly column of fashion advice in our local *Gazette*, which kept my clientele pegged as to the latest fashion trends. If the "in" color of the season was obituary orchid or asthma green, if in springtime the bodice was to be quilted like an artichoke or curled like a cabbage leaf, if buttons were to be made of tortoise or mother-of-pearl, it was all a matter of dogma, a sacred article of faith. My shop soon turned into a beehive of activity, with the town ladies constantly coming and going from my door, consulting me about their latest ensembles.

My shop's success soon made us rich. I felt immensely grateful to Lorenzo, who had made it all possible by selling the plantation and lending me that extra bit of money to expand my workshop. Thanks to him, today I'm a free woman; I don't have to grovel or be polite to anyone. I'm sick of all the bowing and scraping before these good-for-nothing housewives who must be constantly flattered to feel at peace. Let the mayor's wife lift her own tail for a while. I much prefer to read this vile story than speak to her, than tell her "how nicely you've put yourself together today, my dear, with your witch's shroud, your whisk-broomed shoes and your stovepipe bag."

Don Lorenzo sold his house and moved to town with his family. The change did Rosaura good. She soon looked rosy cheeked and made new friends, with whom she strolled in the parks and squares of the town. For the first time in her life she lost interest in her storybooks, and when her father made her his usual birthday gift a few months later, she left it half read and forgotten on the parlor table. Don Lorenzo, on the other hand, became more and more bereaved, his heart torn to pieces by the loss of his cane fields.

Rosa, in her new workshop, took on several seamstresses to help her out and now had more customers than ever before. Her shop took up the whole first floor of the house, and her clientele became more exclusive. She no longer had to cope with the infernal din of the chicken coop and the pigpen, which in the old times had adjoined her workshop and cheapened its atmosphere, making elegant conversation impossible. As these ladies, however, took forever to pay their bills, and Rosa couldn't resist keeping the most lavish couturier models for herself, her business went deeper and deeper into debt.

It was around that time that she began to nag Lorenzo constantly about his will. "If you were to pass away today, I'd have to work till I was old and gray just to pay off our business debts," she told him one night with tears in her eyes, before putting out the light on their bedside table. "Even selling half your estate, we couldn't begin to pay for them." And, seeing that he remained silent, with gray head slumped on his chest, and refused to disinherit his daughter for her sake, she began to heap insults on Rosaura, accusing her of not earning her keep and of living in a storybook world, while she had to sew her fingers to the bone in order to feed them all. Then, before turning her back on him to put out the light, she told him that, because it was his daughter whom he obviously loved more than anyone else in the world, she had no choice but to leave him.

I feel curiously numb, indifferent to what I'm reading. A sudden chill hangs in the air; I've begun to shiver and I feel a bit dizzy. It's as though this wake will never end; they'll never come to take away the coffin so the gossipmongers can finally go home. Compared to my client's sneers, the innuendos of this strange tale barely make me flinch; they bounce off me like harmless needles. After all, I've a clear conscience. I was a good wife to Lorenzo and a good mother to Rosaura. That's the only thing that matters. It's true I insisted on our moving to town, and it did us a lot of good. It's true I insisted he make me the sole executor of his estate, but that was because I felt I was better fit to administer it than Rosaura until she comes of age, because she lives with her head in the clouds. But I never threatened to leave him, that's a treacherous lie. The family finances were going from bad to worse and each day we were closer to bankruptcy, but Lorenzo didn't seem to care. He'd always been capricious and whimsical, and he picked precisely that difficult time in our lives to sit down and write a book about the patriots of our island's independence.

From morning till night he'd go on scribbling page after page about our lost identity, tragically maimed by the "invasion" of 1898, when the truth was that our islanders welcomed the Marines with open arms. It's true that, as Lorenzo wrote in his book, for almost a hundred years we've lived on the verge of civil war, but the only ones who want independence on this island are the romantic and the rich: the ruined landowners who still dream of the past as of a paradise lost; the frustrated, two-bit writers; the bitter politicians with a thirst for power and impossible ambitions and dreams. The poor of this island have always been for statehood, because they'd rather be dead than squashed once again under the patent leather boots of our own bourgeoisie. Each country knows what leg it limps on, and our people know that the rich of this island have always been a curse, a plague of vultures. All one has to do is look around and find out who built what: it was the Americans who built the schools, who paved the roads, who financed the hospitals and the University. Before they landed here, this island was an epidemic-infested hole, inhabited by a flea-bitten, half-starved, illiterate people, victim of the island's ten most powerful families. And today they're still doing it; those families are still trying to scalp the land, calling themselves pro-American and friends of the Yankees to keep their goodwill, when deep down they wish the Yankees would leave, so that these families could graze once more on the poor man's empty guts.

On Rosaura's next birthday, Don Lorenzo gave his daughter his usual book of stories. Rosaura, on her part, decided to cook her father's favorite guava compote for him, following one of her mother's old recipes. As she stirred the bubbling, bloodlike syrup on the stove, the compote's aroma gradually filled the house. At that moment Rosaura felt so happy; she thought she saw her mother waft in and out of the window several times on a guava-colored cloud. That evening, Don Lorenzo was in a cheerful mood when he sat down to dinner. He ate with more relish than usual, and after dinner he gave Rosaura her book of short stories, with her initials elegantly monogrammed in gold and bound in gleaming doe-heart's skin. Ignoring his wife's furrowed brow, he browsed with his daughter through the elegant volume, whose thick gold-leaf edges and elegant bindings shone brightly on the lace tablecloth. Sitting stiffly, Rosa looked on in silence, an icy smile playing on her lips. She was dressed in her most opulent gown, as she and Don Lorenzo were to attend a formal dinner at the mayor's mansion that evening. She was trying hard to keep her patience with Rosaura because she was convinced that being angry made even the most beautifully dressed woman look ugly.

Don Lorenzo then began to humor his wife, trying to bring her out of her dark mood. He held the book out to her so she might also enjoy its lavish illustrations of kings and queens all sumptuously dressed in brocaded robes. "They could very well inspire some of your fashionable designs for the incoming season, my dear. Although it would probably take a few more bolts of silk to cover your fullness than it took to cover them, I wouldn't mind footing the bill because you're a lovable, squeezable woman, and not a stuck-up, storybook doll," he teased her, as he covertly squeezed her derriere.

Poor Lorenzo, you truly did love me. You had a wonderful sense of humor and your jokes always made me laugh until my eyes teared. Unyielding and distant, Rosa found the joke in poor taste and showed no interest at all in the book's illustrations. When father and daughter were finally done admiring them, Rosaura got up from her place and went to the kitchen to fetch the guava compote, which had been heralding its delightful perfume through the house all day. As she approached the table, however, she tripped and dropped the silver serving dish, spattering her stepmother's skirt.

I knew something had been bothering me for a while, and now I finally know what it is. The guava compote incident took place years ago, when we still lived in the country and Rosaura was a mere child.

The two-bit writer is lying again; he's shamelessly and knowingly altered the order of events. He gives the impression the scene he's retelling took place recently, when it actually took place several years ago. It's true Lorenzo gave Rosaura a lavish storybook for her twentieth birthday, which took place only three months ago, but it's been almost six years since he sold the farm. Anyone would think Rosaura was still a girl, when in fact she's a grown woman. She takes after her mother more and more: she fiddles away her time daydreaming, refuses to make herself useful and lives off the honest sweat of those of us who work.

I remember the guava compote incident clearly. We were on our way to a cocktail party at the mayor's house because he'd finally made you an offer on the sale of your plantation. At first you were offended and rejected him, but when the mayor suggested he would restore the house as a historic landmark, where the mementos of the cane-growing aristocracy would be preserved for future generations, you promised to think about it. The decision finally came when I managed to persuade you, after hours of endless arguments under our bed's threadbare canopy, that we couldn't go on living in that huge mansion with no electricity, no hot water and no adequate toilet facilities; and where one had to move one's bowels on an antique French Provincial latrine which had been a gift to your grandfather from King Alphonse XII. That's why I was wearing that awful dress the day of Rosaura's petty tantrum. I had managed to cut it from our brocaded living room curtains, just as Viven Leigh had done in *Gone With the Wind*, and its gaudy frills and garish flounces were admittedly in the worst of taste. But I knew that was the only way to impress the mayor's high-flown wife and to cater to her boorish, aristocratic longings. The mayor finally bought the house, with all the family antiques and objets d'art, but not to turn it into a museum, as you had so innocently believed, but to enjoy it himself as his opulent country house.

Rosa stood up horrified and stared at the blood-colored streaks of syrup that trickled slowly down her skirt until they reached the silk embossed buckles of her shoes. She was trembling with rage, and at first she couldn't get a single word out. When her soul finally came back to her, she began calling Rosaura names, accusing her shrilly of living in a storybook world while she, Rosa, worked her fingers to the bone in order to keep them all fed. Those damned books were to blame for the girl's shiftlessness, and as they were also undeniable proof of Don Lorenzo's preference for Rosaura and of the fact that he held his daughter in higher esteem than his wife, she had no alternative but to leave him. Unless, of course, Rosaura agreed to get rid of all her books, which should immediately be collected into a heap in the backyard, where they would be set on fire.

Maybe it's the smoking candles, maybe it's the heavy scent of all those myrtles Rosaura heaped on the coffin, but I'm feeling dizzier. I can't stop my hands from trembling and my palms are moist with sweat. This story has begun to fester in some remote corner of my mind, poisoning me with its dregs of resentment. And no sooner had she ended her speech to Rosaura, Rosa went deathly pale and fell forward to the floor in a heap. Terrified at his wife's fainting spell, Don Lorenzo knelt down beside her and begged her in a faltering voice not to leave him. He promised her he'd do everything she'd asked for, if only she'd stay and forgive him. Pacified by his promises, Rosa opened her eyes and smiled at her husband. As a token of goodwill at their reconciliation, she allowed Rosaura to keep her books and promised she wouldn't burn them.

That night Rosaura hid her birthday gift under her pillow and wept herself to sleep. She had an unusual dream. She dreamt that one of the tales in her book had been cursed with a mysterious power that would instantly destroy its first reader. The author had gone to great lengths to leave a sign, a definite clue in the story which would serve as a warning, but try as she might in her dream, Rosaura couldn't bring herself to remember what the sign had been. When she finally woke up she was in a cold sweat, but she was still in the dark as to whether the story worked its evil through the ear, the tongue or the skin.

Don Lorenzo died peacefully in his own bed a few months later, comforted by the cares and prayers of his loving wife and daughter. His body had been solemnly laid out in the parlor for all to see, bedecked with wreaths and surrounded by smoking candles, when Rosa came into the room, carrying in her hand a book elegantly bound in red and gold, Don Lorenzo's last birthday gift to Rosaura. Friends and relatives all stopped talking when they saw her walk in. She nodded a distant hello to the mayor's wife and went to sit by herself in a corner of the room, as though in need of some peace and quiet to comfort her in her sadness. She opened the book at random and began to turn the pages slowly, pretending she was reading but really admiring the illustrations of the fashionably dressed ladies and queens. As she leafed through the pages, she couldn't help thinking that now that she was a woman of means, she could well afford one of those lavish robes for herself. Suddenly, she came to a story that caught her eye. Unlike the others, it had no drawings and it had been printed in a thick guava-colored ink she'd never seen before. The first sentence surprised her, because the heroine's name was the same as her stepdaughter's. Her curiosity kindled, she read quickly, moistening the pages with her index finger because the guava-colored paste made them stick to each other annoyingly. She went from wonder to amazement and from amazement to horror, but in spite of her growing discomfort, she couldn't make herself stop reading. The story began ... "Rosaura lived in a house of many balconies, shadowed by a dense overgrowth of crimson bougainvillea vines ...," but Rosa never found out how it ended.

Translated by Rosario Ferré *and* Diana Vélez

Blame the Tlaxcaltecs

Elena Garro

Nacha listened, motionless; someone was knocking at the back door. When again they persisted, she opened the door cautiously and looked out into the night. Señora Laura appeared, shushing her with a finger at her lips. She was still wearing the white dress, singed and caked with dirt and blood.

"Señora ... !" Nacha murmured.

Señora Laura tiptoed in and looked at the cook, her eyes puzzled. Then, feeling more assured, she sat next to the stove and looked at her kitchen as if she'd never seen it before.

"Nachita, give me some coffee. I'm freezing."

"Missus, your husband ... your husband is going to kill you. We'd already given you up for dead."

"For dead?"

Laura looked at the white tiles of the kitchen with amazement, put her legs up on the chair, hugged her knees. She grew thoughtful. Nacha put water on and watched her mistress out of the corner of her eye; she couldn't think of a single thing to say. The señora rested her head on her knees; she seemed so sad.

"You know, Nacha, you can blame the Tlaxcaltecs."

Nacha didn't answer; she chose to watch the pot, which hadn't boiled.

Outside, night had blurred the roses in the garden and cast shadows across the fig trees. The lighted windows of neighboring houses shone far beyond the branches. The kitchen was kept separate from the world by an invisible wall of sadness, by no more than a bar rest.

"Don't you agree, Nacha?"

"Yes, ma'am ... "

"I'm no different from them. I'm a traitor," Laura said, mournfully.

The cook folded her arms, waiting for the water to start bubbling.

"And you, Nacha, are you a traitor?"

She looked at her, hopefully. If Nacha shared with her this capacity for betrayal, then Nacha would understand her, and tonight Laura needed someone to understand her.

Nacha thought about it for a moment and went back to watching the water that now boiled noisily. She poured it over the coffee and its warm smell made her feel attuned to her mistress.

"Yes, I'm a traitor too, Señora Laurita."

She poured the coffee, happily, into a little cup, put in two cubes of sugar and set it in front of the señora. And she, in turn lost in her own thoughts, took a few sips.

"You know, Nachita, now I know why we had so many accidents on our famous trip to Guanajuato. At Mil Cumbres we ran out of gas. Margarita got frightened because it was getting dark. A truck driver gave us some gas to get us to Morelia. In Cuitzeo, when we were crossing the white bridge, the car stopped suddenly. Margarita was annoyed with me. You know how lonely roads and the eyes of Indians frighten her. When a car full of tourists came by, she went into town to look for a mechanic and I was stuck in the middle of the white bridge that crosses the dry lake and its bed of flat white rocks. The light was very white and the bridge, the rocks and the car began to float in it. Then the light broke into pieces until it became thousands of small dots and began to whirl until it was fixed in place like a picture. Time had entirely turned around, like it does when you see a postcard and then turn it to see what's written on the other side. That's how, at Cuitzeo Lake, I got to the child I'd been. The light brings about crises like that, when the sun turns white and you are in the very center of its rays. Thoughts, too, become thousands of small dots, and you get dizzy. At that moment I looked at the fabric of my white dress and, just then, heard his steps. I wasn't surprised. I looked up and saw him coming. In that same instant I remembered how serious my treachery had been; I was frightened and wanted to escape. But time closed in around me, it became singular and transitory, and I couldn't move from the seat of my car. When I was a child I was told, 'Some day you will find yourself faced with your acts turned to stones that are as irrevocable as that one,' and they showed me the statue of some god, though I can't remember now which one it was. We forget everything, don't we, Nachita, although we only forget for a time. In those days, even words seemed to be of stone, although of a stone that was liquid and clear. The stone hardened as each word was pronounced, and it was written for always in time. Weren't the words of your grown-ups like that?"

Nacha thought about it for a moment, then agreed, fully convinced.

"They were, Señora Laurita."

"The terrible thing is—and I discovered it that very moment—that everything that is unbelievable is true. He was coming, along the side of the bridge, sunburned and carrying the weight of defeat on his naked shoulders. His eyes shone. Their black sparks reached me from the distance and his black hair curled in the white light of our meeting. Before I could do anything about it, he was in front of me. He stopped, held on to the car door and looked at me. He had a cut in his left hand and the blood that spurted from the wound in his shoulder was so red it seemed black. He didn't say anything to me. But I knew he was escaping, and that he had been beaten. He wanted to tell me I deserved to die, and at the same time, that my death would bring about his own. As wounded as he was, he was looking for me.

"You can blame the Tlaxcaltecs," I told him.

He turned to look up at the sky. Then he focused his eyes on mine again.

"What are you doing to yourself," he asked, in a deep voice. I couldn't tell him I'd married, because I am married to him. There are things that just can't be said, you know that, Nachita.

"And the others?" I asked him.

"The ones who got out alive are in the same shape I am." I saw that each word pained his mouth and I hushed, realizing the shamefulness of my treachery.

"You know I'm frightened and that's why I betray you ... "

"I know," he answered, and bowed his head. He's known me since I was a girl, Nacha. His father and mine were brothers and so we are cousins. He always loved me, at least that's what he said and that's what we all believed. At the bridge, I was embarrassed. The blood kept on flowing down his chest. I took a small handkerchief from my bag and, without saying a word, began to wipe the blood. I always loved him too, Nachita, because he is the very opposite of me. He's not fearful and he's not a traitor. He took my hand and looked at it.

"It's very pale; it looks like their hands," he told me.

"I haven't gotten any sun for a while." He lowered his eyes and let my hand drop. We stayed like that, in silence, listening to the blood flow down his chest. He didn't reproach me for anything; he knows what I'm capable of. But the little threads of blood wrote a message on his chest, that his heart had preserved my words and my body. That's when I knew, Nachita, that time and love are the same thing.

"And my house?" I asked.

"We'll go see it." He held me with his hot hand the way he would hold his shield, and I realized he wasn't carrying it. "He lost it when he was escaping," I told myself, and I let him guide me. In the light of Cuitzeo, his footsteps sounded the way they had in the other light: muffled and soft. We walked through the city that blazed on the water's edge. I closed my eyes. I already told you I'm a coward, Nacha. Or perhaps it was the smoke and the dust that made my eyes water. I sat on a stone and covered my face with my hands.

"I can't walk any more," I told him.

"We're almost there," he answered. He knelt by me and caressed my white dress with his fingertips.

"If you don't want to see what happened, don't look," he told me, quietly.

His black hair shadowed me. He wasn't angry, only sad. I would never have dared to embrace him before, but now I've learned I don't have to be respectful of the man, so I embraced his neck and kissed him on the mouth.

"You've always been dearest of all things to my heart," he said. He lowered his head and looked at the earth, so full of dry stones. With one of them he drew two parallel lines and then lengthened them until they met and became one.

"These are you and me," he said without looking up. I was left at a loss for words, Nachita.

"There's only a little left for time to be over and for us to be one. That's why I was looking for you." I had forgotten, Nacha, that when time is all spent, the two of us will remain, one in the other, to enter true time as one. When he said that to me, I looked in his eyes. Before I had only dared to look in them when he was taking me, but, as I told you, I've learned not to respect the man's eyes. It's also true that I didn't want to see what was happening around me ... I'm such a coward. I remembered the shrieks and I heard them again, strident, flaming in the middle of the morning. I also saw the stones whizz over my head and heard them crashing. He knelt in front of me and raised his arms and crossed them to make a little roof over my head.

"This is the end of man," I said.

"That's true," he said, with his voice over mine. And I saw myself in his eyes and in his body. Could he be a deer come to carry me to its hillside? Or a star, flinging me out to trace signs in the sky? His voice traced signs of blood on my breast, and my white dress turned tiger-striped in red and white.

"I'll return tonight; wait for me," he whispered. He grasped his shield and looked at me from high above.

"Soon we'll be one," he added, with his usual politeness. After he left, I began to hear battle cries again and I ran out in the middle of the rain of stones and was lost all the way to the car, parked on the Cuitzeo Lake Bridge.

"What's the matter? Are you wounded?" Margarita shouted at me when she arrived. Frightened, she touched the blood on my white dress and pointed to the blood on my lips and the dirt that had matted in my hair. The dead eyes of the Cuzco mechanic stared at me from the other car.

"Indian savages! A woman can't be left alone," he muttered as he leapt from the car as if to help me.

"We arrived at Mexico City at nightfall. How it had changed, Nachita, I couldn't believe it! At noon the warriors had been there, but now there wasn't even a trace of them. There was no rubble left either. We passed the sad and silent Zocalo; nothing—nothing!—remained of the other plaza. Margarita watched me out of the corner of her eye. When we got home you opened the door. Remember?"

Nacha nodded her head, agreeing. It was quite true that, barely two months before, Señora Laurita and her mother-in-law had gone to Guanajuato on a visit. The night they returned they, Josefina the chamber maid and she herself, had noticed the blood on the dress and the señora's vacant gaze. Margarita, the older lady, motioned them to keep quiet. She seemed very worried. Josefina told her later that, at dinner, the master stared at his wife in annoyance and said, "Why don't you change your clothes? Do you enjoy returning to unpleasant memories?"

Señora Margarita, his mother, had already told him what happened and motioned to him, as if to say "Hush, have a little consideration." Señora Laurita didn't answer; she stroked her lips and smiled as if she knew something. Then the master went back to talking about President López Mateo.

"You know how he's always talking about that man," Josefina had added, contemptuously.

In their hearts, they were sure that Señora Laurita was bored with so much talk about the President and his official visits.

"How odd things are, Nachita, I'd never noticed until that night how bored I could be with Pablo," the mistress noted, hugging her knees affectionately, and subtly acknowledging that Josefina and Nachita were right.

The cook folded her arms and nodded in agreement.

"From the time I entered the house, the furniture, the vases and the mirror toppled over on me and left me sadder than I was. How many days, how many years will I have to wait before my cousin comes to fetch me? That's what I told myself, and I regretted my treachery. As we dined, I noticed that Pablo did not speak in words but in letters. I started to count them while I watched his thick mouth and dead eye. Suddenly, he was silent. You know he forgets everything. He stood there with his arms by his side. This new husband has no memory and all he knows are the day in, day out things."

"You have a troubled and confused husband," he told me, looking at the stains on my dress again. My poor mother-in-law got confused and, as we were drinking coffee, she got up to play a twist.

"To cheer you up," she told us, pretending to smile because she could tell trouble was brewing.

"We didn't talk. The house filled up with noise. I looked at Pablo. 'He looks like ... ' and I didn't care to say his name because I was afraid that they would read my mind. It's true that they look alike, Nacha. Both of them like rain and cool houses. The two of them look at the sky in the afternoon and have black hair and white teeth. But Pablo talks in fits and starts, he gets angry about anything, and is always asking, 'What are you thinking?' My cousin husband doesn't do or say anything like that."

"That's for sure. It's true that the boss is a pain in the neck," Nacha said with annoyance.

Laura sighed and looked with a sense of relief at her cook. At least she could confide in her.

"At night, while Pablo kissed me, I kept repeating to myself, 'When will he come for me?' And I almost cried, recalling the blood streaming from the wound in his shoulder. Neither could I forget his arms folded over my head that made a little roof for me. At the same time I was afraid that Pablo would notice that my cousin had kissed me that morning. But he didn't notice a thing, and if it hadn't been that Josefina had frightened me in the morning, Pablo would never have known."

Nachita agreed. That Josefina loved to start trouble; she was to blame. Nacha had told her, "Be quiet, be quiet, for God's sake. There must have been a reason they didn't hear us scream." But it was useless.

No sooner had Josefina come into the bosses' room with the breakfast tray than she told what she should have kept to herself.

"Missus, last night a man was peeking through your bedroom window. Nacha and I screamed and screamed!"

"We didn't hear anything," the master said. He was shocked.

"It was he," that fool of a mistress screeched.

"Who is he?" the master asked, looking at the señora as if he wanted to kill her. At least that's what Josefina said later.

The señora was really scared. She covered her mouth with her hand, and when the boss asked her the same question again—he was getting angrier and angrier—she answered, "The Indian, the Indian who followed me from Cuitzeo to Mexico City."

That's how Josefina found out the business about the Indian and that's how she told Nachita.

"We have to let the police know immediately!" the boss yelled.

Josefina showed them the window the stranger had been looking through and Pablo examined it closely. There were almost-fresh blood stains on the window sill.

"He's wounded," señor Pablo said in a worried tone. He took a few steps around the bedroom and stopped in front of his wife.

"It was an Indian, sir," Josefina said, just as Laura had said.

Pablo saw the white dress thrown over a chair and picked it up roughly.

"Can you tell me where these stains came from?"

The señora was silent, looking at the blood stains on the bodice of the dress while the master punched the chest of drawers with his fist. Then he went to his wife and slapped her. Josefina saw and heard all that.

"He's rough and his actions are as confused as his thoughts. It's not my fault he accepted defeat," Laura said disdainfully.

"That's true," Nachita agreed.

There was a long silence in the kitchen. Laura stuck the tip of her finger in the bottom of the cup to stir the black grounds that had settled, and when Nacha saw this, she poured her a nice fresh cup of hot coffee.

"Drink your coffee, Señora," she said, feeling sorry for her mistress' unhappiness. After all, what was the boss complaining about? You could see from miles away that Señora Laurita wasn't meant for him.

"I fell in love with Pablo on a road, during a moment when he reminded me of someone I knew, someone I couldn't remember. And later, just sometimes, I recaptured the moment when it seemed that he

would become the one he resembled. But it wasn't true. He became
absurd again, without a memory, and he only repeated the gestures of
all the men of Mexico City. How did you expect me not to notice the
deception? When he's angry, he doesn't allow me to leave the house.
You knew it's true. How many times has he started arguments at the
movies or at restaurants! You know, Nachita. On the other hand, my
cousin husband never gets angry at his wife."

Nacha knew what the señora was saying was true, and that was why
that morning when Josefina had come in the kitchen, scared and screaming, "Wake up Señora Margarita, the master is beating the mistress,"
Nacha, had run to the older woman's bedroom.

His mother's presence calmed Señor Pablo. Margarita was very surprised to hear the business about the Indian, since she hadn't seen him
at Cuitzeo Lake and had only seen the blood, as we all had.

"Perhaps you suffered from sunstroke at the lake, Laura, and had a
nosebleed. We had the top down on the car, you know, son." She talked
almost without knowing what to say.

Señora Laura flung herself face down on the bed and was lost in her
own thoughts while her husband and her mother-in-law argued.

"Do you know what I was thinking this morning, Nachita? Suppose
he saw me last night when Pablo was kissing me. And I felt like crying. Just then I remembered that when a man and a woman love each
other and they have no children, they are condemned to become one.
That's what my other father told me when I brought him a drink of water and he looked at the door behind which my cousin husband and I
slept. Everything my other father had told me was coming true. I could
hear Pablo and Margarita's words from my pillow and they were talking foolishness. 'I'm going to fetch him,' I told myself. 'But, where?'
Later, when you returned to my room to ask me what we were going to
do about dinner, a thought came to my head, 'Go to the Tacuba Café.'
And I didn't even know that café, Nachita, I'd only heard it mentioned."

Nacha remembered the señora as if she could see her now, putting
on her white, blood-stained dress, the same one she was wearing in the
kitchen now.

"For God's sakes, Laura, don't put that dress on," her mother-in-
law said. But she didn't pay any attention. To hide the stains, she put
a white sweater on over it, buttoned up to the neck, and left for the
street without saying goodbye. The worst came later. No, not the worst.
The worst was about to happen now in the kitchen, if Señora Margarita
happened to wake up.

There was no one in the Tacuba Café. That place is dismal, Nachita. A waiter came up to me. "What would you like?" I didn't want anything but I had to ask for something. "Some coconut nougat." My cousin and I ate coconut when we were small. A clock in the café told time. "In all the cities, there are clocks telling time; it must be wearing away bit by bit. When it only exists as a transparent layer, he will arrive and the two lines he traced will become one and I will live in the dearest chamber of his heart." That's what I told myself as I ate the nougat.

"What time is it," I asked the waiter.

"Twelve, Miss."

"Pablo arrives at one," I told myself. "If I have a taxi take me outside of town, I can wait a little longer." But I didn't wait and I went out on the street. The sun was silver. My thoughts turned into shining dust and there was no present, past nor future. My cousin was on the sidewalk. He stood in front of me. He looked at me for a long time with his sad eyes.

"What are you doing?" he asked me in his deep voice.

"I was waiting for you."

He was as still as a panther. I saw his black hair and the wound on his shoulder.

"Weren't you afraid to be here all by yourself?"

The stones and the shouts buzzed around us again and I felt something burn against my back. "Don't look," he told me.

He knelt on the ground and put out the flame that had started to blaze on my dress. I saw the despair in his eyes.

"Get me out of here!" I screamed with all my might, because I remembered I was in front of my father's house, that the house was burning and that my parents were in the back and my little brothers were dead. I could see everything reflected in his eyes while he knelt in the dirt putting out the fire on my dress. I allowed myself to fall on him and he gathered me in his arms. He covered my eyes with his hot hand.

"This is the end of man," I told him, my eyes still under his hand.

"Don't look at it!"

He held me against his heart. I could hear it pound like thunder rolling in the mountains. How long would it be before time was over and I would hear him forever. My tears cooled his hand, still burning from the fire in the city. The shrieks and the stones surrounded us, but I was safe against his breast.

"Sleep with me," he said in a very low voice.

"Did you see me last night?" I asked him.

"I saw you."

"We fell asleep in the morning light, in the heat of the fire. When we remembered, he got up and grabbed his shield."

"Hide until morning. I'll come for you."

"He ran off quickly, his legs still naked. And I slipped away again, Nachita, because I was frightened when I was alone."

"Are you feeling bad, Miss?"

"A voice just like Pablo's approached me on the middle of the street."

"How dare you? Leave me alone."

"I took a taxi that drove by the outskirts to bring me home and I got here."

Nacha remembered her arrival. She had opened the door herself, and it was she who gave her the news. Josefina came down later, almost diving down the stairs.

"Missus, the master and Señora Margarita are at the police station."

Laura stared at her, wordless in amazement.

"Where were you, Missus?"

"I went to the Tacuba Café."

"But that was two days ago."

Josefina had _Today's News_ with her. She read in a loud voice, "Mrs. Aldama's whereabouts remain unknown. It is believed that the sinister, Indian-looking man who followed her from Cuitzeo may be a psychopath. The police in the states of Michoacan and Guanajuato are investigating the event."

Señora Laurita grabbed the newspaper from Josefina's hands and tore it angrily. Then she went to her room. Nacha and Josefina followed her; it was best not to leave her alone. They saw her throw herself on the bed and start dreaming with her eyes wide open. The two had the very same thought and told each other so in the kitchen. "As far as I'm concerned, Señora Laurita is in love." When the master arrived they were still in their mistress' room.

"Laura!" he shouted. He rushed to the bed and took his wife in his arms.

"Heart of my heart," the man sobbed.

For a moment, Señora Laurita seemed to soften towards him.

"Señor," Josefina blustered. "The Señora's dress is completely scorched!"

Nacha looked at her, disapprovingly. The master checked over the señora's dress and legs.

"It's true. Even the soles of her shoes are singed. What happened, my love, where were you?"

"At the Tacuba Café," the señora answered calmly.

Señora Margarita twisted her hands and approached her daughter-in-law.

"We know you were there and that you had some nougat. What happened then?"

"I took a taxi and drove home past the outskirts of town."

Nacha lowered her eyes. Josefina opened her mouth as if to say something, and Señora Margarita bit her lip. Pablo reacted differently; he grabbed his wife by her shoulders and shook her violently.

"Stop acting like an idiot! Where were you for two days? Why is your dress burned?"

"Burned? But he extinguished it ... " The words slipped out of Señora Laura's mouth.

"He? That filthy Indian?" Pablo went back to shaking her in anger.

"I met him at the door to the Tacuba Café," the señora sobbed, half dead of fear.

"I didn't think you'd stoop so low," the boss said and pushed her onto the bed.

"Tell us who he is," her mother-in-law said, softening her voice.

"I couldn't tell them that he was my husband, could I, Nacha?" Laura asked, wanting the cook's approval.

Nacha approved of the señora's discretion and remembered how, at noontime, and, saddened by what her mistress' was going through, she had said, "Perhaps the Cuitzeo Indian is a witch man."

But Señora Margarita had turned towards her with her eyes blazing, to scream an answer, "A witch man! You mean a murderer!"

After that, they kept Señora Laura in the house for days. The master ordered them to watch the doors and windows. They, the maids, went in and out of the room continuously to check on her. Nacha never discussed the situation or the odd, surprising things she'd seen. But who could silence Josefina?

"Master, this morning at dawn the Indian was by the window again," she announced when she took in the breakfast tray.

The master rushed to the window and again found a trace of fresh blood. The señora began to cry.

"My poor little one, my poor little one," she sobbed.

It was that afternoon that the master brought a doctor. After that, the doctor came every afternoon.

"He asked me about my childhood, about my father and mother. But, Nachita, I didn't know which childhood he meant, or which father or mother he wanted to know about. That's why I talked to him about the conquest of Mexico. You understand me, don't you?" Laura asked, keeping her eyes on the yellow bowls.

"Yes, ma'am," and Nachita, feeling nervous, examined the garden through the window glass. Night was just beginning to announce its presence in the deepening shadows. She remembered the master's listless face and his mother's distressed glances at dinner.

"Laura asked the doctor for Bernal Díaz del Castillo's History. She said that that's the only thing that interests her."

Señora Margarita dropped her fork. "My poor son, your wife is mad."

"The only thing she talks about is the fall of the great Tenochtitlán," Señor Pablo added somberly.

Two days later, the doctor, Señora Margarita and Señor Pablo decided that locking Laura in made her depression worse. She should have some contact with the world and face her responsibilities. From then on, the boss sent for the car so his wife could take short rides around Chapultepec Park. The señora was accompanied by her mother-in-law, and the chauffeur had orders to watch them closely. Unfortunately the eucalyptus-laden atmosphere didn't improve her condition, and no sooner would Señora Laurita get back home then she would lock herself up in her room to read Bernal Díaz' *Conquest of Mexico*.

One morning, Señora Margarita came back from Chapultepec Park alone and frantic. "That crazy woman ran away," she shouted in a huge voice.

"Look, Nacha, I sat on the same bench as usual and told myself, 'He won't forgive me. A man can forgive one, two, three, four betrayals but not constant betrayal.' This made me very sad. It was very hot and Margarita bought herself some vanilla ice cream. I didn't want any and she got into the car to eat it. I realized that she was as bored of me as I was of her. I don't like being watched and I tried to look at other things so I wouldn't see her eating her cone and watching me. I noticed the grayish foliage that hung from the ahuehuete trees and, I don't know why, but the morning became as sad as those trees. 'They and I have seen the same crises,' I told myself. During the lonely hours, alone on an empty path. My husband had watched my constant betrayal through the window and had abandoned me to this path made of non-existent things. I remembered the smell of corn leaves and the hushed murmur of his steps. 'This is the way he walked, with the rhythm of dry leaves when the February wind carries them over the stones. At that time I didn't have to turn my head to know that he was watching me from behind.' I was meandering among those sad thoughts when I heard the sun spill and the dry leaves begin to shift. His breathing came close behind me, then he stood in front of me. I saw his naked feet in front of mine. He had a scratch on his knee. I lifted my eyes and found myself under his. We stood there a long time without speaking. Out of respect, I waited for his word."

"What are you doing to yourself," he asked me.

I saw that he wasn't moving and that he seemed sadder than ever. "I was waiting for you," I answered.

"The last day is almost here."

"I thought that his voice came from the depth of time. Blood still surged from his shoulder. I was embarrassed and lowered my eyes. I opened my bag, and took out a small handkerchief to wipe his chest. Then I put it away again. He followed, watching me quietly."

"Let us go to the Tacuba door ... There are many betrayals."

"He grasped my hand and we walked among the people, who screamed and moaned. Many bodies floated in the water of the canals. Pestilence rose up around us and children cried, running from here to there, lost and looking for their parents. I looked at everything without wanting to see it. The shattered canoes didn't carry anything but sadness. The husband sat me under a broken tree. He knelt on the earth and watched what happened around us. He wasn't afraid. Then he looked at me."

"I know you're a traitor and that you mean well. The good grows alongside the bad."

"The children were screaming so loudly I could hardly hear him. The sound came from far off, but it was so loud that it shattered the daylight. It seemed like the last time they would cry."

"It's the children," he told me.

"This is the end of man," I repeated, because I couldn't think of anything else to say.

He put his hands over my ears and then held me against his chest. "You were a traitor when I met you, and I loved you that way."

"You were born without luck," I told him. I embraced him. My cousin husband closed his eyes to keep the tears from flowing. We lay ourselves on the broken branches of the piru. The shouts of the warriors, the stones and the weeping of the children reached us even there.

"Time is almost over," my husband sighed.

"The women who didn't want to die that day were escaping through a crevice. Rows of men fell one after the other, as if clasping hands as a single blow felled them all at once. Some of them let out such loud cries that the sound echoed long after their death.

"It wasn't long before we became one that my cousin got up, joined some branches together and made me a little cave.

"Wait for me here."

"He looked at me and went back to the fray, hoping to turn aside defeat. I stayed there, curled up. I didn't want to see the people escaping, so I wouldn't be tempted, and I didn't want to see the bodies floating in the water, so I wouldn't cry. I began to count the little fruits that hung from the cut branches; they were dry and when I touched them with my fingers, the red husks fell from them. I don't know why I thought they were bad luck and decided to watch the sky as it began to darken. First it turned grey, then it began to take on the color of the drowned bodies in the canal. I recalled the colors of other afternoons. But the evening grew more and more bruised, swelling as if it would soon burst, and I understood that time was over. What would happen to me if my cousin didn't return? He might have died in battle. I didn't care what happened to him, I ran out of there as fast as I could, with fright on my heels. 'When he comes back to look for me ... ' I didn't have time to finish my thought because I found myself in the Mexico City dusk. 'Margarita must have finished her ice cream and Pablo is probably angry.' A taxi drove along the outskirts to bring me home. And you know, Nachita, the outskirts were the canals, clogged with bodies. That's why I was so sad when I got home. Now, Nachita, don't tell the master that I spent the afternoon with my husband."

Nachita arranged her arms on her purple skirt.

"Señor Pablo went to Acapulco ten days ago. He got very thin during all the weeks of the investigation," Nacha explained, feeling self-satisfied.

Laura looked at her without any surprise and sighed with relief.

"But Señora Margarita is upstairs," Nacha added, turning her eyes up to the kitchen ceiling.

Laura hugged her knees and looked through the window glass at the roses, blurred by the night shadows, and at the lights in the neighboring windows that had begun to go out.

Nacha sprinkled salt on the back of her hand and licked it eagerly.

"So many coyotes! The whole pack is in an uproar," she said, her voice full of salt.

Laura listened for a moment. "Damn animals! You should have seen them this afternoon," she said.

"As long as they don't get in the señor's path or make him lose his way," Nacha said, fearfully.

"Why should he be afraid of them tonight, he was never afraid of them before?" Laura said in annoyance.

Nacha drew closer to strengthen the intimacy that had suddenly sprung up between them. "They're punier than the Tlaxcaltecs," she told her in a soft voice.

The two women were silent. Nacha, licking bit by bit the salt on her hand, and Laura, who was worried, were both listening to the coyote howls that filled the night. It was Nacha who saw him arrive and opened the window to him.

"Señora, he's come for you," she whispered in a voice so low only Laura could hear.

Afterwards, when Laura had left with him for good, Nacha wiped the blood from the window and frightened away the coyotes, who had entered the century that was just then waning. Straining her ancient eyes, Nacha checked to see that everything was in order. She washed the coffee cup, threw the red lipstick-stained butts away in the garbage can, put the coffee pot away in the cupboard and shut off the light.

"I say Señora Laurita didn't belong to this time, and not to the master either," she said that morning when she took breakfast to Señora Margarita.

"I won't work at the Aldama house any more. I'm looking for something else," she told Josefina. And, because of the chamber maid's carelessness, Nacha left without even collecting her salary.

Translated by Ina Cumpiano

The Last Emigrant

Nora Glickmann

Old Leiserman is dead, the emigrant, Baruch Leiserman. The news shook loose memories of my hometown in the province of La Pampa. I remembered how much closer he was than my grandfather, or any uncle for that matter.

As the days grew longer, Mama would take me along on visits to see him and his wife, Sara. Around five, Dad might be engaging a customer in some interminable discussion about renewing an insurance policy and Mama would take advantage of the opportunity to escape from the office and would go to look for me at home.

It was just a few blocks away, we walked. Lanuse's bar exhaled it's beery and smoky breath that followed us as far as the corner. The Viners and the Shames would set up their wicker chairs next to the entrances of their respective stores to be able to kibitz with each other. The women seemed older than the men; they rocked slowly and chatted in Yiddish mixed with Spanish. Then we would pass Litner's bakery where a furry, dirty dog stretched out and blocked the sidewalk, undoubtedly para-lyzed by the languid, penetrating aroma of freshly-baked loaves. Or perhaps by age. Anyway, Mama would buy a few pastries there and Mrs. Litner would keep her posted on the rheumatism that was swelling her knees as well as on her mother who lay dying in the room in back. Mama always listened quietly: things seemed to worsen at a comfortable rate, and there would be months and months to enjoy the same pastries and same conversation.

Sara Leiserman would treat us to a tureen full of toasted sunflower seeds, with *leicash* and Russian tea, *prekuske*, and we bit on lumps of sugar as we drank the tea. I liked to dip the sugar a little bit at a time and watch it turn brown in the hot tea. Then Sara would take a nap.

She was always tired, and Mama stayed to chat with Baruch. I went
to the storehouse in back, cradling corn in my dress and feeding it to
the chickens around the patio. Sometimes I threw a handful as hard as
I could just to see them run and cackle a little. Other times I chased
them and plucked their feathers. Baruch's old roan always stood by the
water trough; he scratched his neck against it's rusty edge, though he
never cut himself. I would fill a bag full of grass for him and hang it on
his neck to see him through the night.

Mama would still be talking when I went back in the house. I listened to them while going through Sara's shoe-box full of yellowing
photographs. Baruch talked about the Russian Revolution, the ear in-
fection he inflicted on himself to avoid the draft—it still acted up now
and then—and the labor unrest in Buenos Aires. Mama commented
on articles from the Yiddish newspaper. She was big on Israel, Zionism
and the kibbutzes, although Baruch didn't see any advantage in a Jewish homeland. "It's better for them to hate us separately; a Jewish state
surrounded by Arab enemies won't last very long as a democracy." Just
to needle him, Mama would make me sing *Mir furn kain Eretz* and then
sing along even louder than me. Then it was *Zog mir shvester Leibn, vos
ich vel dir freign* where Leibn declares her intention to grow oranges in
Israel and forget about the Diaspora. Mama put everything into those
songs; she seemed to feel herself nearer to Israel, free of the burden of
the *golés*, the Diaspora.

Baruch made fun of her, grimacing with an impatient *Achhh*, waving away the songs with his thick and hairy hand. Then all of a sudden,
he would grab me around the waist and say *Danushka mains, zing mir
unter'n vigale',* which was his favorite song. I complied willingly and sang
that and other songs while they hummed along in time. Baruch had a
certain way of closing his eyes and arching his thick, bushy eyebrows,
creating a magic, irresistably appealing space in front of his forehead.
When he opened his eyes again, it was as if he had woken up with a
shudder. I don't know if it was pleasant or not, because he usually pre-
empted discussion with some mundane observation.

It was during these visits that Mom did Baruch's bookkeeping, and
there was always an argument. She would marshal two or three figures
and show how he could replace the carriage with a used pickup, how
if the outer hall were blocked off—the one leading to the grapevines—
the house wouldn't get so cold during the winter, how it was better to
have one laborer year-round rather than employ three just for the harvest ... Baruch would raise his hands to his cheeks, pressing them hard,

telling Mama how the plague of grasshoppers had ruined everything two years before, and how when the Perels' fields went up in smoke just before the harvest; his was saved only because the wind changed direction; how another fire like that, or perhaps hail, like in '51, could leave him penniless, and then, what would become of him? You always needed to keep something in reserve.

Mama would get exasperated: "My daughter is right—you're just an old tightwad and you'll never invest in anything, you old hardhead, you'll never get anywhere that way." Then, a few minutes of truce during which nothing could be heard except the crackling of the fire. Sunflower-seed husks piled up on the checkered tablecloth, or fell to the floor.

Back to the office, Dad would be grouchy, doing sums, tearing up sheets of paper and tossing them into the wastebasket—somehow he never missed, although he never seemed to try very hard. "You left Blanca alone at the cash register and she made some mistakes again . . . you left without posting the balance." "It's not as if I'm your employee," Mama replied. "Blanca gets paid to be a cashier, not me." Dad kept on crumpling paper into little balls and looking over his notes. There was no more discussion, though she stayed and worked until the evening. How could she just drop everything to go and see that *shlemazl*, that poor, lazy Baruch? What did she see in him? But she stood up for him—"He's got *seijl*. He thinks. He reads more than all of you put together, he should never have stayed in this crummy little town, this Bernasconi Bernashmoni." And then, *shohin*, that's enough! and the matter was closed.

But Dad did feel sorry for Sara. She was stuck with Baruch. She survived the pogrom in Russia, she lived through it all in Vilna by a miracle, though now, in Argentina, her luck had run out. She used to tell how she was the only one to hide in time when the Cossacks broke into her uncle's house; she saw everything and forgot nothing. The hooligans broke up the furniture with their sabers, tore up the comforters and the pillows and filled the room with feathers. They gutted Sara's uncle, a large man, and filled him with the feathers. Her aunt wailed and they tore her eyes out before killing her. I can't remember exactly what they did with the girls. Sara was an orphan and lived with them. After the pogrom my *zeide* brought her to Argentina, passing her off as her daughter. Sara was quiet and withdrawn. She seemed to rub her complaints off her veined hands by rubbing them into her apron. According to Dad, Baruch never even looked at her before taking her to wife—and probably never looked at her after, either. His first wife died while giving birth to her fourth child and the others were still small. It was clear that he couldn't handle them by himself, and there was Sara, available, submissive. Mama says that people are just the way they are, and if Sara wanted to be a martyr, she got what she wanted.

We had moved several years before to Bahía. Every summer we passed through the town, but just because it was on the way to the farm. Sometimes we dropped in to say hello to the Leisermans, but it just wasn't the same anymore. Dad came along with us, and the visits were always cut short so we could see as many friends and relatives—and offend the fewest—as possible.

Baruch's accident happened at his farm, a short distance from the town. He apparently saw the hurricane coming; nobody better than he could read the pinkish streaks in the clouds—like an old-time gaucho he understood the menace implicit in the motionless air, suspended like in a photograph. So Baruch must have anticipated the inexorable advance of the dark column that swallowed everything in its path and he, Baruch, the headstrong emigrant, had to thwart it, defeat it, just long enough to get his four panic-stricken cows into the barn; he went out alone to close the gates and protect his cattle.

The farmhand just happened to be in town that day. When he returned the following morning, he found Baruch among the wreckage, a hundred yards from the barn, in the middle of a huge puddle left by the storm. Baruch rolled into the mud, dragging with him all the plants he ever seeded during his life there. What would he have been thinking? About the cows that wouldn't make it? Whether he had enough supplies in reserve? The unfinished business? No: he probably just closed his eyes, just like when he liked a song, and then knitted his brow and let himself go, carried away in an enchanted cloak.

Translated by John Benson

The Virgin's Passion

Lucía Guerra

I am writing this only to fulfill a promise that I made long, long ago. Last night, after finishing the hem on Marita's skirt, I said to myself that if I have answered my duties to the family, surely I have the right to be dutiful to myself. Of course in that far-off time I didn't know that promises are little more than illusive pacts which give voice to hope. ("Oh Lord, I promise to pray four hours every day if Gustavo stops drinking!" I remember Aunt Adela whispering in every corner of the old house, without knowing, the poor thing, that her husband would die of cirrhosis—taking his untimely leave of her amid tears and horrifying screams.) My promise was also anchored in a hope. But being so young, how could I have known that some of us are born and yet do not truly exist until just before we die? In a movie I saw about ten years ago, or maybe it was fifteen, yes fifteen, because my nephew Jorge Javier had just graduated from high school, there appeared on the screen the image of an aborted child, which seemed to me the true reflection of myself: a body visible but without life.

A poor spinster you remain, without illusion, without faith; your heart grown sick with anguish; and today your mutilated life is but the setting of the sun. So goes the Tango that was so much in fashion in my youth, yet which still moves me—although it also makes me very angry. Mutilated life, yes (shouldn't I know!), but the real torment is that one never loses the illusion, nor the faith, or the hope that one day . . .

This is why I made the promise, which may sound ridiculous, especially at my age, but it was the most important thing in my life, and so it continues to be. The truth is that I do not recall when I stopped associating the word "virgin" with that statue cast in plaster and wrapped with Chantilly lace, wearing the crown of a queen on her head, that perfect profile tilted so tenderly toward the baby she never quite breast feeds, that tearful silhouette holding in her arms the wasted body of her son. Without knowing how or when "virgin" started to mean "not yet to be," and as I started accumulating details on the loss of virginity, I began to wish with all my heart for the pain and the blood. (Stains on nuptial sheets; hoarse cries of pain; a sharp storm penetrating so deep as to damage the uterus; newlywed young girls, victims of an oversized mate, bleeding and pale in an emergency clinic—these were some of the colorful patches that covered the quilt of my adolescence, handed down in whispers by the older girls in the family.) The sword the young prince ceremoniously receives from his father's hands seemed therefore a dull image when set beside this other initiation of vagina and vocal chords, this act of becoming with your whole body. And I was seized by the intense desire to become a woman through this rite of blood and kisses, to open myself like a flower under the penetrating ray of a man who would be forever after the solar star of all my constellations. That is why it seemed to me silly and even profane that my cousins and my sisters one night agreed (they even signed an oath!) to share all the details of their wedding night. To me, my passage into real life would be a written and sacred text, an intimate testimonial which, as years went by, I would re-read the way one re-reads sacred scripture, and thereby reenacting the ritual, resubmerging myself in that dark and bloody night of my true birth.

I and my sixteen years in front of the window naively making a promise that dragged inside me like a large snake with no head or tail. I, bent over this sheet of paper, giving form to this wet and scaly weight inhabiting my body. I, the young girl of marriageable age who thought it would be so easy to take pen in hand and write a tale faithful to reality. I, to the relatives of now three generations, the kind old maid, expert in making flan and sewing silk. I, the deflowered old woman trying to start a tale that lengthens the wished-for wedding night into a burning chain of hours, days and years ... Unlike the stories whispered by my cousins and my sisters, pregnant with details, and well-defined actions and sensations, I only have images, built up like barnacles inside me, not in my soul or my innocent heart, as they might think, but in this fiery box covered with hair as gray as ashes.

Tonight I see myself again in the back yard of the country house in that long-ago time of my childhood. Under the burning sun of a summer afternoon, I walk on a path of dry weeds, staring at the fruit of the trees which hide themselves among leaves covered with dust. We children of the house had already made off with the plums and apricots and figs that we could reach, but higher up, shiny as sin, hung a few that tempted my childish gluttony. Taking the long pole that supported the clothesline and climbing up onto two big stones, I started to hit at a plum growing between two branches. But the pole got stuck in the leaves, which fell on my freshly-cut hair, and in anger I began lashing out in all directions, and so fell to the ground. It was then that I heard a laugh from beneath the fig tree.

"No use swinging crazy like that. To grab fruit you gotta use tricks, same as with women!" said Antuco the gardener. "Come here, I'll pick you some ripe figs."

Happy and anxious, I parted the rough fig leaves which hung to the ground, and, putting my hands on my hips like the housekeeper did when she gave orders to the servants, I told Antuco to be quick about it. He took off his shirt, jumped onto a branch like a cat, and began crawling upward, filling his pockets with dark fruit.

"Didn't I tell you? You get what you want with tricks and strength. Look how fat and juicy they are! Melt in your mouth, they're so sweet. Only I don't know how the hell you're gonna carry them all. Listen, it'd be better to just eat them here, so's the other kids don't take them away from you." He jumped to the ground, landing nimbly on all fours. "Here, sit on my jacket, I always use it to take a nap about this time."

I sat down and he lay beside me, laughing. His face was full of mischief, and I, with my mouth stuffed with pink seeds and sweet juice, smiled gratefully back at him. Suddenly he put his hands between his legs and his smile faded.

"Shoot, kid, this old animal is getting hard again."

"What animal?" I asked, half curious and thinking it a game.

"A real nice little animal that rears up each time it sees a pretty girl," he said, closing his eyes.

And opening his pants, little by little he started showing me a piece of pink flesh that looked at first like a newborn mouse but then, as he stroked it, I saw it jump up furiously between his thighs.

"Lay down here beside me," he said, and I, still clutching two figs, obediently moved closer.

Rubbing my neck and back with his calloused hands, he led me into a lethargy of sun, fruit, and tenderness that recurred often throughout the rest of the summer.

I didn't know then that all the other suns in my life would prove to be so cruel, setting far too fast—callers who shone briefly and then went into an abrupt eclipse, leaving dark craters in my yearning soul. Now that time has taught me to know men, I think that I frightened them away with my eagerness, this passion for the other, angular body with its hard muscles which God ordained could only find rest and peace on the rounded spongy flesh of a woman. At this very moment I can see myself again, poring over movie magazines, cutting with frenzy the pictures of the famous actors of that era. Clark Gable smiling at me through cigar smoke! Tyrone Power in a bullfighter's costume, inviting me to enter the ring! Riding off into the sunset, Alan Ladd waves a reluctant goodbye! (Can still see myself, surrounded by all these irresistible men, trying to forget my sisters' trousseaus, their fussed-over pregnancies, and their children's birthday parties and First Communions.)

To this day I don't remember when I came to be considered the spinster of the family. In all honesty, I think that I was quite silly to allow them to dress me in garments which even now, at my age, seem foreign. The simple truth is that, through a kind of moral laziness, I allowed myself to become the kind and patient aunt who beat the eggs and embroidered the baby clothes, who with equal amounts of peroxide and love treated all the children's scratches. Poor little Inez, who irons clothes and sleeps alone, says another song; and that's what I was for them—the best housecleaner, a glorified maid who dreamed in her corner of a prince who never came. They didn't know, could not possibly have known that under those chaste garments, my body muzzled as it were, beat a primitive and tribal chant, a rhythm of horses running wild that made me moan in my sleep, tossing and tearing at my bonds like one lost at sea, pulled along by a tide as heavy as fruit ripening under the sun.

But Antuco came to save me. I cannot forget the day he arrived at our house. My father had just died, and my mother had gathered all of us together to distribute what she called the sentimental part of his legacy. On the dining room table she began to place his pocket watch, several pairs of fine French cuffs, tie pins he had collected on all his journeys, old postcards where radiant couples stood framed by violets, fountain pens, wooden chests which we had never seen opened. With an almost ritual seriousness, she started to parcel out our inheritance. Taking up a leather-bound photo album, she handed it to me, saying, "This is for you. We all know how much you like pictures." That night, half asleep, I began leafing through the sepia images of young men with walking sticks and derby hats, of gentlemen who stared back at me with solemn expressions made even more serious by the size of their thick

mustaches, ladies in white hats and high lacy collars. Suddenly I came
upon a photo that altered this landscape of solemnity, one taken at a
picnic: a row of well-dressed men stood at the rear; in front of them,
seated, a group of ladies holding parasols; before them crouched boys
in short trousers and little girls with ribbons in their braids; and in the
foreground, as though he were the center of all attention, lay Antuco,
holding up, with an amused and mischievous air, a demijohn of wine.
We looked at each other for a long time, my eyes on his even as I opened
the drawer of the night table and groped for a pair of scissors. "Many
things have happened during all these years, Antuco; but nothing has
happened to me," I told him as I rescued him from that bourgeois and
ornamental group of unrelaxed correctness. He lowered his eyes in sadness, then looked at me again with the same expression he wore when I
entered that lair of his within the overhanging branches of the fig tree.

With Antuco's arrival, it no longer irked me to wear the dark blue
and gray dresses my family liked to see me in (although of course they
never said so openly), and I ceased to grumble every time one of my sisters phoned me to ask that I stop by the San CamiloBakery to pick up
pastry, or to buy at the Cordonería Alemana the bronze buttons which
absolutely had to be ready for my nephew's school uniform the following
morning. All these mundane chores became as seaweed carried away
in the undertow of evening when, as I dozed, Antuco would caress my
back, and once again I tasted the ripe fruit of summer as he lulled me
to sleep ... Writing this, I cannot pinpoint the exact night when those
seeds soaked in sweetness started to descend like mysterious ants, moving from my palate to awaken my womb. Antuco's fingertips seemed to
multiply, roaming every inch of my skin while, face down and trembling
with pleasure, I bounced on the hard sheet, listening to the wet sound of
his thighs and picturing the pink flesh of his excited organ. In those moments my whole body became a huge wave about to break on the sand,
and I felt, if such a thing is possible, like a sealed volcano rumbling under the moon. And thus suspended on this wave, caught and held in an
impending storm that never burst, I would find myself watching the first
rays of dawn creep across my bed.

To my family's alarm, dark lines appeared under my eyes, and my
countenance took on that gray aspect of someone seriously ill. Dili-
gently, my oldest niece took me to various specialists, who examined me
in laboratories full of strange objects—slabs of lead, transparent tubes,
hidden screens, metallic devices they inserted down my throat. (And all
for nought—How could anyone have imagined my nocturnal torment?)

At dusk my hands started trembling, and my chin began to feel the tick-
ling that announced the Calvary of my body. In vain I would implore
Antuco to help me; only he could release this scream that was stuck in
my lips like a bloody wound. "I can't," he whispered one night. "I'd best
be off ... " And waving goodbye in the mirror, he vanished into air. I
sat up in bed with a start, and with my hands on my hips I ordered him
to return immediately. My heart heaving, I waited in vain until the sun
illuminated the window curtains, and then I felt that reptilian weight of
my promise coiling itself tight around my body.

They all thought I couldn't hear them criticizing me under their
breath. Naturally my hearing isn't what it used to be, especially in my
left ear—although this particular defect, as they well knew, was due not
to old age but to the ball my nephew Gustavo accidentally hit me with
when he was fourteen years old. They don't seem to need me anymore,
but I feel certain that should an emergency arise, they will all run in
search of their good old auntie.

It was Mercedes, the kindest of my sisters, who convinced me to take
a vacation. ("Inesita, my dear, it's been a long time since you've had a
real rest. Señora María's daughter tells me that in Puerto Montt there
is a wonderful boarding house with a very quiet atmosphere.") I was so
weary of their ill-concealed gossip about me, so tired of entering rooms
where the conversation suddenly ceased, that four days later I found
myself bidding goodbye to my niece Angélica and her children on the
boarding platform of the Estación Central.

The trip was very uncomfortable, but I didn't mind, because I had
already made up my mind to give Albertito a big surprise. I was going to
look for some shells to add to the precious collection he had started on
his fifteenth birthday. He always said that on the shores of Chiloé one
could find spectacular molluscs from long-extinct species, and that truly
fine fossilized clams lay on the sand like fallen fruit, ripe for the picking.
I would wait until we were alone to hand him this new treasure and,
picking me up in his strong arms, he would say, "Thank you, mamicha,
thank you!" Albertito was the only one who did not call me aunt. And
rightly so, for he is the only one who is like a true son to me. I was
already forty hears old when he was born, but I took him to live with
me barely six months later, and he did not return to his parents until he
entered grammar school. He was the only one who met Antuco, one day
during his fourth year of school when he stopped by for tea after football
practice. That afternoon I was sewing a button in his blue jacket, and I

asked him to hand me the thimble that I always keep in the drawer of my night table. When he saw Antuco, he asked me who he was, and I told him that Antuco was my secret fiancé. (There were so many secrets that I shared with Albertito!)

Immediately after settling into the boarding house I went to ask about the excursion boats that regularly visited the nearby islands. The following morning, after a leisurely and delightful journey down the coast, we docked at Chiloé. Once ashore, I stopped to ask an old fisherman about the shells. "The only one who keeps such things," he said, "is Ignacio, because he's a kind of witch, you know? He lives up there," he added, pointing over his shoulder. Under the mid-day sun I started walking toward a hut almost hidden among the trees on a nearby hill. Parting the waist-high weeds as I went, I arrived at the hut with my shoes covered with burrs. The door was made of upright logs, and I knocked on it with a rock I presume was the owner's doorstop.

"There's no bread in this house for beggars or curious people," shouted a voice from within. Shouting back, I told him that I had come to attend to very important business. I heard movement, and I had the impression of someone hurriedly washing his face, and then the door swung open.

"Come right on in, mam," said Antuco, much younger, and wearing a mustache.

The dark room was like a cave strewn with shells of all sizes and shapes and colors. The bone-white stalks of picoroco shells hung down from the ceiling like blunt stalactites. Large shells as deep as basins were attached to the walls like some growth, reflecting and refracting color, they shimmered in pink and gray as though alive. On a heavy wooden table slept enormous conch snails; clams that kept watch, opening and closing their slimy mouths; mussels sheltering small crustaceans in their thick black hair. "You shouldn't have disobeyed me, Antuco," I said. And, making the sign of the cross, he knelt and started to kiss my feet. "I am still the virgin girl who lay beside you under the fig tree," I added, taking off my black, cotton dress.

He nodded and said, "Holy Mary, mother of God." And then he began climbing my body with burning kisses that melted the scales of the long-hated snake. Solemnly he led me to a bed reeking of algae and sea water, and my thighs finally sheltered him in that pulsating ritual of blood and hot, spurting wax.

I returned to the continent at twilight, staring at the black clouds menacing the horizon, my hands folded on my placidly aching lap. At long last I was the owner of all dawns, and as I write the last words of the testimony of my true birth, I hear outside the steps of Antuco—returning, to stay with me forever.

Translated by Richard Cunningham *and* Lucía Guerra

Berkley or Mariana of the Universe

Liliana Heker

"How much longer till Mom comes home?"

It's the fourth time Mariana has asked that same question. The first time her sister Lucia answered that she'd be back real soon; the second time, that how the heck was she to know when Mom would be back; the third she didn't answer—she just raised her eyebrows and stared at Mariana. Following which, Mariana decided that things weren't going all that well and that the best thing to do was not to ask any more questions. *Anyhow*, she thought, *why do I want Mom to come back, if I'm here with Lucia* ... she corrected herself: *Why do I want Mom to come back, if I'm here with my big sister.* She blinked, deeply moved by the thought. *Big sisters look after little sisters*, she said to herself as if she were reciting a poem; *how lucky to have a big sister.* Lucia, with large guardian angel wings, hovered for a second over Mariana's head. But in a flash the winged image was replaced by another, one which returned every time their mother left them on their own: Lucia, eyes bulging out of their sockets, hair in a furious tangle, was pointing at her with a gun. Sometimes there was no gun: Lucia would pounce on her, trying to rip Mariana's eyes out with her nails. Or strangle her. The reason was always the same: Lucia had gone mad.

It is a well known fact that mad people kill normal people, which meant that if Lucia went mad when they were alone together, she'd kill her, Mariana: that was obvious. Therefore Mariana decides to abandon her good intentions and asks again, for the fourth time: "How much longer till Mom comes home?"

Lucia stops reading and sighs.

"What I'd like to know," she says, and Mariana thinks: *she said "I'd like to know"; does one say "I would like to know" or "I should like to*

101

know"?—"What I'd like to know is why in God's name you always need Mom around."

"No." *Now she'll ask me "No what?" She always manages to interfere,* but Lucia says nothing, and Mariana continues, "I was just curious, that's all."

"At twelve."

"What do you mean, at twelve!" Mariana cries out. "But it's only ten to nine now!"

"I mean at twelve, six and six," Lucia says.

Mariana howls with laughter at the joke; she laughs so hard that for a moment she thinks she'll die laughing. To tell the truth, she can't imagine there being anyone on earth as funny as her sister. *She's the funniest, nicest person in the world, and she'll never go mad. Why should she go mad, she, who's so absolutely terrific?*

"Lu," she says adoringly, "let's play something, Okay? Let's, Okay?"

"I'm reading."

"Reading what?"

"Mediocre Man."

"Ah." *I bet now she'll ask me if I know what mediocre man means, and I won't know, and she'll say then, "Why do you say 'Ah,' you idiot?"* Quickly she asks, "Lu, I can't remember, what does mediocre man mean?"

"The mediocre man is the man who has no ideals in life."

"Ah." This puts her mind at rest, because she certainly has ideals in life. She always imagines herself already grown up, when all her problems will be over, and everyone understands her, and things turn out fine, and the world is wonderful. That's having ideals in life.

"Lu," she says, "we, I mean, you and I, we're not mediocre, are we?"

"A pest," Lucia says, "that's what you are."

"Lucia, why is it that you are so unpleasant to everyone, huh?"

"Listen, Mariana. Do you mind just letting me read in peace?"

"You're unpleasant to everyone. That's terrible, Lucia. You fight with Mom, you fight with Dad. With everyone." Mariana lets out a deep sigh. "You give your parents nothing but trouble, Lucia."

"Mariana, I wish you'd just drop dead, okay?"

"You're horrible, Lucia, horrible! You don't tell anyone to drop dead, not your worst enemy, and certainly not your own sister."

"That's it, now start crying, so that afterwards they scream at me and say that I torture you."

"Afterwards? When afterwards? Do you know exactly when Mom will be back?"

"Just afterwards." Lucia has gone back to reading *Mediocre Man*. "Afterwards is afterwards," lifting her eyes and frowning as if she were meditating on something very important. "The future, I mean."

"What future? You said Mom would be back very soon."

Lucia shakes her head with resignation and goes back to her book.

"Yes, of course, she'll be back very soon."

"No. Yes, of course, no. Is she coming back very soon or isn't she coming back very soon?"

Lucia glares at Mariana; then she seems to remember something and smiles briefly.

"And anyway, what does it matter?" she says and shrugs her shoulders.

"What do you mean, what does it matter? You don't know what you're saying, do you? If someone comes home very soon, it means she comes home very soon, doesn't it?"

"If someone comes home, yes."

"What?"

"I just said that if someone comes home, then yes. Will you please let me read?"

"You're a cow, that's what you are! What you really want is for Mom never to come home again!"

Lucia closes the book and lays it down on the bed. She sighs.

"It has nothing to do with my wanting it or not," she explains. "What I'm saying is that it simply doesn't matter if Mom is here or there."

"What do you mean, there?"

"Just there; anywhere; it's all the same."

"Why the same?"

Lucia rests her chin on both her hands and stares gravely at Mariana.

"Listen, Mariana," she says, "I've got something to tell you. Mom doesn't exist."

Mariana jumps. "Don't be stupid, okay?" she says, trying to look calm. "You know Mom doesn't like you saying stupid things like that."

"They're not stupid things. Anyway, who cares what Mom says, if Mom doesn't exist?"

"Lu, I'm telling you for the last time: I-don't-like-you-say-ing-stu-pid-things, okay?"

"Look, Mariana," Lucia says in a tired tone of voice. "I'm not making it up; there's a whole theory about it, a book."

"What does it say, the book?"

"What I just said. That nothing really exists. That we imagine the world.":

"What do we imagine about the world?"

"Everything."

"You just want to frighten me, Lucia. Books don't say things like that. What does it say, huh? For real."

"I've told you a thousand times. The desk, see? There isn't really a desk there, you just imagine there's a desk. Understand? You, now, this very minute, imagine that you're inside a room, sitting on the bed, talking to me, and you imagine that somewhere else, far away, is Mom. That's why you want Mom to come back. But those places don't really exist, there is no here or far away. It's all inside your head. You are imagining it all."

"And you?"

"I what?"

"There's you, see?" Mariana says with sudden joy. "You can't imagine the desk in the same, same place that I imagine it, can you?"

"You've got it all wrong, Mariana sweetheart. You just don't understand, as usual. It's not that both of us imagine that the desk is in the same place: it's that you imagine that both of us imagine that the desk is in the same place."

"No, no, no, no. You got it all wrong. Each of us doesn't imagine things on our own, and one can't guess what the other is imagining. You talk about what you imagine. I say to you: how many pictures are there in this room? And I think to myself: there are three pictures in this room. And exactly at the same time you tell me that there are three pictures in this room. That means that the three pictures are here, that we see them, not that we imagine them. Because two people can't imagine the same thing at the same time."

"Two can't, that's true."

"What do you mean?"

"I'm saying that two people can't."

"I don't understand what you're saying."

"I'm saying that you are also imagining me, Mariana."

"You're lying, you're lying! You're the biggest liar in the whole world! I hate you, Lucia. Don't you see? If I'm imagining you, how come you know I'm imagining you?"

"I don't know, I don't anything. You are just making me up, Mariana. You've made up a person called Lucia, who's your sister, and who knows you've made her up. That's all."

"No, come on, Lu. Say it's not true. What about the book?"

"What book?"

"The book that talks about all this."

"That talks about what?"

"About things not really existing."

"Ah, the book ... The book is also imagined by you."

"That's a lie, Lucia, a lie! I could never imagine a book like that. I never know about things like that, don't you understand, Lu? I could never imagine something as complicated as that."

"But my poor Mariana, that book is nothing compared to the other things you've imagined. Think of History, and the Law of Gravity, and Math, and all the books ever written in the world, and aspirins, and the telegraph and planes. Do you realize what you've done?"

"No, Lucia, no, please. Everyone knows about those things. Look: if I bring a lot of people into this room and I say, when I count to three, we all point at the radio at the same time, then you'll see: we'll all point in the same direction. Let's play at that, Lu, please, come on, let's play at pointing at things. Please."

"But are you stupid or what? I'm telling you that you are the one who's imagining all the people in the world."

"I don't believe you. You say that just to frighten me. I can't imagine all the people in the world. What about Mom? What about Dad?"

"Them too."

"Then I'm all alone, Lu!"

"Absolutely. All alone."

"That's a lie, that's a lie! Say that you're lying! You're just saying that to frighten me, right? Sure. Because everything's here. The beds, the desk, the chairs. I can see them, I can touch them if I want to. Say yes, Lu. So that everything's like before."

"But why do you want me to say yes, if anyway it will be you imagining that I am saying yes?"

"Always me? So there's no one but me in the world?"

"Right."

"And you?"

"As I said, you're imagining me."

"I don't want to imagine any more, Lu. I'm afraid. I'm really frightened, Lu. How much longer till Mom comes home?"

Mariana leans out the window. Mom, come back soon, she begs. But she no longer knows to whom she's begging, or why. She shuts her eyes and the world disappears; she opens them and it appears again.

Everything, everything, everything. If she can't think about her mother, she won't have a mother any more. And if she can't think about the sky, the sky. And dogs, and clouds, and God. Too many things to think about all at once, all on her own. And why she, alone? Why she alone in the universe? When you know about it, it's so difficult. Suddenly she might forget about the sun, or her house, or Lucia. Or worse, she might remember Lucia, but a mad Lucia coming to kill her with a gun in her hand. And now she realizes how dangerous all this is. Because if she can't stop herself thinking about it, then Lucia will really be like that, crazy, and kill her. And then there won't be anyone left to imagine all those things. The trees would disappear, and the desk, and thunderstorms. The color red would disappear, and all the countries in the world. And the blue sky, and the sky at night, and the sparrows, and the lions in Africa, and the earth itself, and singing songs. And no one will ever know that, once, a girl called Mariana invented a very complicated place to which she gave the name Universe.

Translated by Alberto Manguel

Knight, Death and the Devil

Vlady Kociancich

A Gentle Knight was pricking on the plaine,
Y cladd in mightie armes and siluer sheilde ...
... on his brest a bloudie Crosse he bore,
the deare remembrance of his dying Lord ...

SPENSER, *The Faerie Queene*

I stopped at the first turning of the path that crossed the forest. The moon, after shredding its way through the treetops, appeared suddenly full, above my head, violently illuminating my coat of armor, turning me into the ghost of a knight whose only real features were his weariness and low spirits. Even in the dim light that came from the heavens my eyes were burning. I did not allow myself the time to dwell on the annoying sweat crawling, multiplying itself along my body, beneath the weight of my armor, down the barely curved line of my back. I remembered the long day in the sun and, as all men have done sometime, I blessed the darkness and the night. I was riding towards my father's castle. Something stronger than impatience, perhaps the delight of a return so long desired, made me loiter foolishly on the road to admire a tree carved with my initials, to discover in the hieroglyphics of its branches and leaves the lost steps of my childhood. I was in no hurry, and as I basked in the calm of knowing myself home again, night came upon me.

When a boy casts aside the sweet protection of the walls which surround his birthplace and steers away from the familiar voices and faces to test his mettle in war, to leave his blood on foreign ground or to return victorious, then that boy becomes a man. And when the man returns not knowing well what it is he has won in the Name of the Lord, what

107

it is that weighs so heavily on his soul, that man wants once again to be the boy he was. These were my thoughts, when my horse's hooves no longer sounded muffled on the soft earth and made instead a hollow, metallic sound. Water. A barely moving thread of water, more mud than anything else. I halted and looked carefully around me. At night the world does not seem the same, but even though I could not see more than the narrow strip of road, I knew they were waiting for me. I pulled the reins and led my horse towards where I felt the meeting would take place. Until the moment of entering the clearing I doubted its very existence. The moon had faded the greenery and the delicate web of forest flowers. This was a silver field inside the forest, and in the middle of the field was yet another circle of light that seemed to spring mysteriously from the ground. I dismounted and stared at the pond while a nostalgic yearning grew voluptuously inside me. I took off my helmet and touched for the first time my sweat-sodden head. With difficulty I knelt among the reeds which broke without a sound, and I wet my face. Fresh water, crystal-clear, pure, innocent water. An idea more dangerous than sin, the heretic conviction that Nature is innocent, suddenly took hold of me. Patiently (there was no other way) I lifted off my armor. It was a bothersome and ridiculous task because there was no one there to help me, and the heat that had built up during the day stifled me. Before entering the water I intended to ask God His forgiveness for this fault and for the risk I was taking, promising that I would pay for it by increasing the ranks of the enemies of Christ in the underground army of Satan, but I decided not to compound my sin by adding to it a blasphemy. In the water, the shirt I had kept on hindered my swimming, so I took it off and threw it onto the shore. Now I could enjoy myself with no cares, diving in, stretching full length, turning around in the coolness of the pond that had known me as a boy and now received me as a man, a man victorious and a transgressor beyond repentance. As I came out of the water, naked, throwing my hair back and drying it with my hands, a vague unease came over me. I dressed myself, feeling ashamed, beneath the moon, very clumsily because my happiness had made me tired. I was about to climb back onto my horse when I felt my right hand touch a skin, a serpentine dampness. Before seeing what I was to see, I realized two things: that it was dark and that I was alone. I could not scream although fear or surprise rose to my throat. The creature looked like several things at once, and yet fully like none, like no creatures that seemed even more horrible because they were common, familiar beasts: a wolf, a goat, a serpent. Disproportionate, absurd, his laugh was the laugh of a man. I saw him lean towards me, I smelled the stench Our Lord has marked him with to warn us and which I was not to recognize even in my dreams—that is, if what was happening to me was not itself a dream. With a hand which I was not able to close completely I clutched my sword and lifted the cross-shaped hilt in front of the Devil's mad eyes. He neither backed away nor drew nearer. In the tortuous silence of nightmares, I mounted my horse. The Devil was not coming after me, but I could sense him growing vaster in the shadows.

It took me a great effort to calm down. I was still trembling, shamelessly—because the fear of the unknown does not taint a man's courage—when I saw, as a bird sees his nest, the powerful bastions of my home, taller than the tallest branches in the wood, appearing and disappearing before my eyes at every turn of the road. Now it was as if nothing had happened. There was my home, my family expecting me, my mother, my proud father, and my friend Guy, the Frenchman, younger than I and still learning the art of battle. Nothing had taken place. Neither the beautiful war nor the miseries of war, neither the splendors of the sea nor the misfortunes of travel. I no longer remembered my brave comrades, the pure, the strong, the sometimes hateful soldiers of God. Neither did I remember the doubts I had felt. Only in the moment of triumph or in the heat of the battle half lost or half won, had I felt towards those comrades a brotherly love. The rest of the time, during the long pauses that opened my eyes to the corruption and deceit, to the horrible discoveries of rape, starving children, mutilated bodies, I had been separated from the others. Between the ruin and the plunder of victory, my thoughts had drawn me apart, made me resentful. One single thought had torn me away from my doubts and allowed me to carry on: the certainty of fighting for the right cause, with no other purpose than that of defending what was best in this world, in spite of mankind and of myself.

The German knights took exception to my friend Guy. They said that he was closer to Hell than to salvation, closer to the everlasting fire than to Paradise, a foreigner who had not yet been ordained and who did not belong to any known brotherhood in his homeland. But what did they know of Guy? Perhaps it was his lax chastity which allowed him to be humble and generous with the weak. Intelligent, brave, deft with his sword—my friend Guy. Next time we would ride together.

When I reached the castle's drawbridge I could think of nothing except my distant and perfect past, the marvellous days without doubts or responsibilities, almost without sorrows. I spurred my horse to cross the bridge when a troubling thought crossed my mind. The bridge had been lowered. Why? There were no guards about. The habit of war made me stop and look cautiously around. Then suddenly, in the moonlight, on that both brilliant and cloudy night, a figure ran towards me. My hand, not I, gripped my sword. But it was only a woman: I heard her laughter.

We met in the middle of the bridge. She was dancing. She moved her arms around madly, first to the left, then to the right, her skirts flying about in a sudden gust of wind. I stared at her curiously, not knowing what to do or what to say. The plump dancing body barred my way: a peasant woman, her eyes wide open, as if she were listening carefully, her laughter shrill and vulgar. I asked her, "Is there a feast at the castle?"

She lifted her face towards me, but neither answered nor stopped dancing. I saw her stretch a trembling hand towards the reins, but I did nothing to stop her. "Perhaps," I thought, "all this is part of a new game, a ceremony," and I allowed her to lead the horse towards the gateway.

"Woman, do you know who I am?"

Without a word, without stopping her dance, she led me on. As soon as we crossed the bridge, I noticed the glimmer of a fire in the dark.

"So there is a feast!" I shouted.

The peasant woman laughed convulsively, pointing a finger at me as if she were accusing me in front of nobody, and then she left me, dancing and shaking and finally disappearing down an ill-lit corridor.

I would have followed her, but a cry made me turn my head towards the fire. A group of men and women formed a haphazard circle around the crackling flames. Missing something I could not well define, perhaps the customary etiquette, I drew near them. On the bonfire—I could now see it was a bonfire—a body was writhing in pain. Terrified and unable to believe my eyes, covering my nose and mouth with my hands, I drew nearer. Among the billows of smoke and disfigured by the torture, I recognized the face of my friend Guy. I wanted to throw myself on the flames to free him, but countless arms held me back.

"Guy, Guy!" I cried. "What have they done to you?"

The eyes of the dying boy opened to stare at me.

"Hermann ... "

The beloved face grimaced and managed to smile a familiar smile, fighting the pain. I made out his words perfectly, in spite of the clamor and my own cries.

"It is nothing ... " he said.

Even my despair was insufficient to fight the weight of the crowd that made my metal prison even heavier. When they let go of me it was too late. Guy had become one single flame.

They drew me away from him firmly, respectfully explaining something I failed to understand. In between fits of coughing and of nausea, I allowed them to take off my armor, I allowed solicitous and repugnant hands to dress me in a silken shirt, a velvet jacket, a cape. Astounded and horrified, I let them lead me up to the room where my parents were resting. I advanced among people I did not know and who contaminated the painful welcoming ceremony. I no longer heard the voices that kept on explaining; only the voice of my friend Guy: "Hermann, it is nothing ... " Neither did I notice the upheaval along the corridors and hallways, the absence of the usual servants, the presence of a disorderly and mixed crowd. They opened the door that separated me from my mother, and in a daze, I looked for her. She was next to the bed of my father who seemed asleep. I reached out for her and she turned her face towards my voice. Her pale face grew paler.

"Mother, it is I."

She answered in a tone I had never heard before.

"Go away, Hermann, go away! Oh, why did you have to come back now?"

"What has happened? I've seen Guy ... "

"They found him guilty of the plague."

I understood that my father was dead and that Guy had been condemned by the terror. I learned that my mother would die and that I would die as well. I caught her in my arms as she fainted. I lay her next to my father as if she were sleeping.

Later I walked down the deserted hallways. Sometimes the remains of polite manners in the midst of the panic would make a head bow in homage as it recognized me, and then drift away. I wished for war, for the clean death on the battlefield. I wished for a visible enemy who would lend worth to this body already condemned, to this other armor. I wished not to be where I was: unable to do anything, barely witnessing the end of all I had loved.

In the courtyard I saw Guy's body burn. The pile of corpses was growing. I fetched my horse and mounted. I did not want to escape, I simply wanted to leave. It made me despair not to understand the stupid death of those for whom I had fought in the East, fought to honor them with my own honor and with the clear proof of my courage. A dog ran after me, whining. But I was not alone. I carried the mournful following of my lost family, of Guy's useless torture—Guy whom I knew to be innocent. I carried the denied embrace of my mother, the false sleep of my father, my absent or dead cousins.

During that long and splendid summer's morning I rode in circles followed by my dog and by the painful memory of what had happened. That afternoon I let myself fall on the harsh ground in the woods, without the strength to eat or sleep. Human vanities never seem as vain as when we are about to lose them—so precious, so fragile, so incomprehensible. Night fell without my realizing it. Stretched out on the ground I could see my friend Guy's eyes, and hear his voice again: "Hermann, it is nothing ... "

Again I would see my mother's pale face among the shadows, and the Duke's body seemed to decompose by my side. All night long I watched alone over my dead, waiting for my death and for the death of my dog who at length had fallen asleep. Dawn came as quickly as the night that had passed.

And I was not dead. My skin felt clean, my face refreshed. God had spared my life. In despair, in anger, I cried, still surrounded by the bleak circle of my people. The pride of pain made me stand up with a cry, and clench a fist at heaven on this morning so radiant it seemed the very first morning of the world.

"If you have not forgotten me, I want a proof," I shouted. "I have no reason to live. I need something to believe in, other than this senseless destruction, these useless horrors, this emptiness."

I said no more; even the birds were silent. Not a sound, not a leaf rustling in the wind. I walked aimlessly towards my horse. The dog shook itself and trotted happily after me.

Once mounted, I suddenly noticed that I was in the same clearing of the woods where I had stopped two nights ago. Next to the edge of the water were two figures. One was the Devil. The other was inconceivable Death, the dirty, bedraggled death of the flesh, smiling at me with a lipless smile, staring at me without eyes, spurring its horse in my direction. I looked around me. My mother, my father, Guy were no longer there.

I thanked my compassionate God, my generous God. I did what I was supposed to do. Accompanied by my dog, by the Devil, by Death, I turned back towards my castle. We crossed the bridge and I placed myself at the head of a group of fleeing peasants laden with parcels, men and women who had abandoned their children, their parents, their brothers and sisters. I said to them, "I am your master, the Duke."

I gave the order and the bridge was raised.

Translated by Alberto Manguel

The Cove

Luisa Mercedes Levinson

In the midst of the cove, or clearing, already half-overrun by brambles and underbrush, at the Mendihondo country place, you can see the remains of two sheds girded by side porches, and a zinc roof where the sun buttresses its rage. The cove barely three miles in all, is surrounded by the Missions jungle which, like a running knot, could well strangle it at any given moment. The cove is a dried up island to which monkeys or ostriches occasionally come, or once in a while a wanderer, like myself, who for some motive of want, ventures to cross the jungle and the barren plains of ruddy earth.

At one time, the ruins of the cove were whitewashed and the little camp populated by a few cattle. An old well with a mule tied to a water wheel provided the only source of water. A Paraguayan hammock hung suspended from the rafters of the porch. On it, a dark complexioned woman, short and round of limb, was stretched out and fanning herself with a rush fan. In spite of the dark tint of her skin, she did not appear to belong; the exaggerated darkness around her eyes hinted at kohl, mascara of the Orient. She was wearing a thin transparent dress which distinctly revealed the prominent features of her body. The hammock rocked under the weight of this small, solid figure. She appeared to be enveloped in a spray of vapor, like a fringe or a halo. Perhaps it was merely the pulsating cloud of flies and mosquitos.

Don Alcibiades had brought her from Obera one night and she had stayed. He did not call her by name, but addressed her as: hey, tell me, come see. She had a name hard to pronounce. She had really believed that this fast-moving bearded man with the dead eyes and the thick silver-embossed belt was going to take her places—to cities with fairs where ferris wheels fly through the air, to camps where fanfares are heard for miles around and where the rum rolls from one mouth

114

to another, squirted from flasks kept swollen by the secret schemes of men at nightfall. She stayed with nary a guitar or dog. Later El Ciro, the peon, was hired. He, in addition to driving the animals to the water trough, neutered them, butchered them from time to time, prepared the meals, and occasionally did the laundry. He also transferred the hammock from one porch to another in search of a little shade, with or without the woman in it. He barely spoke and at night shut himself off, an obscure figure against the last pillar of the porch. Since he did not smoke, it was rare to perceive the brilliance of his shimmering eyes. The stars glittered in the magnificent night far off in open space.

Don Alcibiades, now wrapped in darkness, tossed away his cigar and made his way to the hammock. After remaining for quite a while, he suddenly seized the woman and carried her off to the room.

El Ciro was preparing the mate tea in the early hours of the morning. The woman was already in her accustomed place in the hammock, as if she had never moved, fanning herself eternally, her eyes shadowed with kohl. The expression on her face was no different from that of a great many women one meets in towns or cities: a mask of melancholy or tedium, and behind the mask, nothing.

El Ciro squatted when he served the mate, the pot slightly removed on ruddy earth. Squatting, he offered corn husk cigar, a fruit perhaps, a partridge brought in from the lagoon fifteen leagues away. The patrón fastened his silver buckle, his eye keen, his dry lips pursed. The boy was a good worker and able. He was becoming more and more dependable.

One morning while the woman was eating the fruit of the invisible palm trees, El Ciro spotted a snake in the distance; he shot at its head as he had done so many times with the revolver there in the hammock. Don Alcibiades came out of the room.

"Hey, good shot! Damn good aim! You'll be rewarded. I'm off to the fair with the young bulls and I'll bring you back a shirt."

"Don't you want me to go with you, boss?" asked El Ciro.

"No."

Turning to the woman, Don Alcibiades added, "There's one bullet left. It's enough for you," and he left.

The ambiguous mask on her face was unchanged.

El Ciro mounted the mare to make his rounds of the camp and as ever, cordoned three wild steer from the forest, treated a flea-bitten calf and cleaned the maggots and ticks from others; he adjusted the twigs and branches used as fences. When he returned to the house, he began his domestic chores; he lit the fire for the asado amid dust and wind.

Crouching as he always did, he viewed the woman out of the corner of his eye. She stretched and then undid her blouse; it was as though the buttons were hurting her chest. Stretched out on the hammock, fanning herself, her face impassive, it was only her body that moved, undulating over the netting, multiplying its flutterings like thousands of brilliant underwater fish disputing among themselves in an unnatural environment, to no end; all a bit monstrous. There was a remote and trenchant beauty in this. El Ciro approached slowly, noiselessly and on his knees; he began to stroke the hand hanging from the netting. His hand then reached her breast and caught her other hand. El Ciro bounded on to the netting, beguiled, desperate, like a storm unleashed. His hot sweat merged with fathomless salts and finally the secret of the whole world unfolded before him. The woman half-parted her lips. A white corporeal peace spread over the ruddy earth where there were no birds. The woman's outcry startled her very self. A shot rang out and El Ciro, rigid with the last death rattle, fell over the rolling earth, beneath the hammock.

"So you weren't expecting me so soon, eh?" And then, "I didn't let him fall on top of you, you've no cause for complaint, eh?"

Alcibiades approached, returning the revolver to his belt. He seized the edges of the hammock, starting from the top, closing it over her and braiding it with his lasso. The woman was still, silent, her unseeing eyes open under the rope that was closing her in, first her face, then the entire length of her body. Skilled in the use of the lasso, he worked conscientiously. He finished with a big double knot at the top, on the side of the feet.

She still was not aware of what had happened. The rope covered her face, her breasts. Something sticky had spashed over her thighs and one arm. An odor was rising from the rolling earth, a mixture of gunpowder and love, things distant and profound—the seas perhaps. In one twist, the hammock overturned and she was face down. She saw a dead man and it was El Ciro; his disjointed nose followed upon a shattered forehead, his sweet grateful lips hopelessly bruised, lips earlier kissed by a child.

The woman was still numbed by a peace already flown. She knew nothing of fear. She could not imagine anything worse. For some time now she had touched bottom; happiness could be just a befuddled, fleeting memory, or a moment without a future. She had drunk deeply of it for the first time and despite all else, she was invaded by a sense of well-being; she bathed in it and it counted more than anything that had happened; it moved time around and kept her in a present which had already passed. In Doña Jacinta's house, she had known the urgencies of many men, but never had she experienced this feeling of well-being. It enabled her to retrieve memories that were distant: her childhood, a boat, a haunting song. She felt her breasts and belly weighing upon her, the center of the universe. She suddenly opened her eyes. El Ciro was there, on the ground below, motionless, in all his measure. She twisted inside the hammock; a hard-grey hatred generated within her, coming as it were from the very bowels of the earth, a clay-like hatred seeping through her, vanquishing her. Skinning and bruising her hips, she managed to turn on her side. Her hate had nothing to do with anguish or weakness or that she was there, a prisoner, tied up in ropes. It was calloused hatred against a man who wielded power, the boss Alcibiades, over there against the pillar on the very spot where hope had stood before—hope, forbearance, poverty and love; all part of El Ciro.

As always, the mask on the woman's face expressed nothing more than ambiguity. But she was now reliving a scene from her past when the bearded man entered Doña Jacinta's patio one afternoon, the creak of his shoes tearing at the daylight with each step. She saw the passing parade of the girls: La Zoila, so terribly thin, seemingly ready to crack, and La Wilda with her kinky hair, her swollen lips and green eyes ... and the others. He had chosen her and made her spread out with her arms around his neck. A wave of nausea had risen to her throat; this had never happened before. He promised to show her cities, offered her corn husk cigars, so she forgot the initial repulsion. She went off leaving the others chained to their fate. Briefly, he had bought her new dresses, even a sky-blue suit. They arrived at the cove; days passed, always the same, just as they had in the patio, dawn turned to dusk, night to day, one heat wave followed another.

She was choked by rancor. It welled up from her stomach in mouthfuls. It was the same fearful retching she experienced when Alcibiades had kissed her for the first time. Something dormant within her, like a stagnant pool, began to course through her body and mind, overflowing and dragging broken reflections impregnated with newly-come images, both fatuous and alarming. And when the past was washed away, there was lucidity; it was perfectly clear that she seek retribution. The comings and goings of the boss man could be heard from his room; he was counting his silver coins, opening his valise to pack his clothing and his poncho from the bed. This meant he was taking off, leaving her to be consumed by the sun to the very end, a sun already on its way to the porch amid a cloud of furry green flies buzzing upwards in her direction from the shattered head of the dead man. In the distance, the buzzards and crows were on the watch.

Her tongue, dry, stuck to her palate; her stomach hardened with a hundred nails bearing down. It never occurred to her she was hungry, more so, thirsty. Her hatred exceeded her needs. A mild odor wafted up from below, a fragrance sweet as the blended fragrance of the two of them, like the palms he had brought her from afar and the watering hole where the mule drank.

Alcibiades, suitcase in hand, stopped near her, his lips protracted and tight, in a kind of smile. Perhaps what he had done made him feel wonderful; it transcended him. He was proud of himself, proud of his resolution. He had killed a man, the boy. He had clearly liberated himself from something that had nagged at him. Now he had to flee and that was nagging at him too. He didn't know what to do. It was hot and it was siesta time.

The woman was like a puma, a wild cat, her limbs short, her belly and bosom prominent; her skin was patched with red splotches under the oppressive net of the sun. She began to twist and turn, the sun first on her right shoulder and hip, then covering all of that side. She positioned herself face-up like a dead one. The sun beat down on her heavy breasts right under the rope; a purple nipple protruded through a small square in the netting. Her black hair was dishevelled and covered her face, the entire mass of hair barely agape to allow her expression to wither. A moan, barely perceptible and monotonous, accompanied the swaying of the hips, like the cooing of a wild beast, if indeed a wild beast does coo; the sound emanated from the depths of her being and penetrated the narrow brow as ancient folk wisdom; it was a brow depressed under the hair falling over it. If she knew how to call to him, entice him to come to her, he would pounce upon her, untie the knot and lasso and release the edges of the hammock. It would mean triumph for the woman; the female would have achieved dominance, life, power and finally retribution.

Alcibiades seemed ill-at-ease standing next to the pillar. He set his suitcase on the ground and took one step forward. He stopped again.

"Hey, you look as if you're burning up there in the sun," he said this in an unusually dulcet voice.

She twisted and moaned a little. The man then spoke again, this time in a deep voice, as if it were costing him to speak: "Now, nobody's going to bother you, only the sun."

He was coming near, approaching slowly, pausing and then taking another step. He seemed to loom large before her. At any moment he would pounce and take her. His impatience might even make him cut the rope with his knife.

The rhythm of the woman's trembling changed; she trembled and shook, and he didn't notice. The retching waves of hatred were overtaking her small talents, her sloth, her desire and all that she had been until then, invading her in undulating ebb and flow. Her entire being was an undercurrent of hot hate and it hardened her. Her hatred was more impatient than his desire, more urgent. Now vengeance was devoid of meaning, as was life. Her hatred was making its rightful claim in a tyranny born of ferocious majesty. It swelled within her, strained at her and she could no longer contain it. A shot rang out ...

"Bitch," the man muttered between his teeth. He somersaulted falling on his back to the ground. One hand was over his chest and he was still cursing.

The revolver, now of no account and empty, remained in the hammock; she too remained in it. She had used the last bullet; she had produced the last sound that broke the murmurs, the boredom and the longing. For her, it was the last sound on earth. The man, Alcibiades, lay there, obscure as an obstinate shadow, contorting against the light and cursing in death. And finally there was just death under the pillar and close to the worn, swollen suitcase. A thread of blood sketched lines on a not very white shirt under a very black beard.

The woman surrendered herself to the sun; it took total posession of her. Her hatred, now sated, left her, just as a man does and she felt swaddled in a dense opaque peace which had little to do with what had earlier brought love. That, at least, was enduring.

All the sunshine destined for the ruddy-earthed cove was concentrated on the moist naked body beneath the netting and the body was drying out. The luxuriant strings of passing flies in the shadow of the sun, their outstretched wings and little feet were making round trips from the bodies of the men to hers, not distinguishing at all between the ravaged head, the chest still dripping blood and her longing. She nourished hatred at the expense of craving; she had fulfillment; she was satiated. She was drowsy for a while, motionless. All at once the hammock netting began to come apart, first one little square and then another. Her skin, her lips, her eyes burned. Everything in her was burning even though night was slowly approaching and weighed heavily, the weight of a hundred men. Now the jungle was beginning to stretch out in the distance, first dragging, then at a furious gallop, narrowing the bounds of the cove and strangling it. It dimmed the radiance of the lagoons and the treacherous advance of the river's flight ... Night, sun, and again night, and eating away at the threads of cold, fear and solitude. Her own screams engendered others taking form and encircling her; they thundered away bewilderingly through the night. Then silence wrapped itself around her and the knot on the lasso, there above and over her feet, expanded in the air, unreachable, all-powerful. The jungle gallop redoubles. Shadows, squawks, sticky wings buffet her face, sting her eyes, her hips, and spray her with darkness and death. La Wilda and La Zoila are asleep under a mosquito netting. The men are on their way. Doña Jacinta is going to be angry. The seams on my stockings are crooked and the men are squeezing the girls' breasts with their hands, breasts which yield the sour milk yellow milk to shortchange man's lust. The midwife burning out your insides! Palm leaves and snakes aflame! Down deep, very deep in the rolling earth, silver coins burn, the black beard burns; everything reduced to blackened liquid now ...

Round and round turn the wheels throughout the cities. Ciro! Ciro! Unloose me from the wheel! Below in the patio of jasmines, are soldiers with their fanfare and handsome blue uniforms. Angels fly through the air singing. Bring silken blouses for the girls. Let us all pray to the Virgin for a miracle; a petticoat trimmed with thick knotted lace and a man who never leaves you. The jungle covers me. It hides me among its leaves, its luxuriant growth inside itself ... Dear Virgen, hovering, borne on the air, do not blind me with your light ...

The hammock, in space, like a bridge or yet a whispering dream, was rocking over death, when I, the poor wanderer, arrived.

Translated by Sylvia Ehrlich Lipp

Looking For Some Dignity

Clarice Lispector

Mrs. Jorge B. Xavier simply couldn't say how she'd gotten in. It hadn't been by one of the main gates. She seemed to have entered in a vague dreaminess through some kind of narrow opening past some construction work debris, as if she had crossed obliquely through some opening made just for her. The fact is that when she looked up she was inside.

And when she looked up she saw that she was inside, very much so. She walked endlessly through the underground passages of the Maracana Stadium which seemed to be narrow caverns leading to rooms which occasionally opened out onto the arena through a single window. The stadium, at that scorchingly deserted hour, shimmered beneath the noonday sun, uncommonly hot for the middle of the winter.

So the woman continued down a somber corridor. This one led her to another even more darker. The ceilings of the passages seemed low.

And that corridor there took her to another which in turn took her to another.

The deserted corridor turned. And there she came to another intersection, which took her to another corridor which took her to another intersection.

So she continued mechanically entering corridors which always led to other corridors. Where could the meeting room for the first class be? She had agreed to meet some people there. The lecture might have begun already. She was going to miss it. She didn't allow herself to miss anything "cultural," since this way she stayed young inside. No one on the outside would have guessed she was almost seventy years old. Everyone thought she was around fifty-seven.

But now, lost in the internal dark windings of Maracana, the woman dragged her feet heavily.

It was then that in one of the corridors she suddenly ran into a man who seemed to have sprung from thin air. She asked him about the lecture, but he knew nothing of it. But he did try to find out from another man who suddenly appeared at the turn of the corridor.

The second man said that near the bleachers, on the right in the middle of the open stadium, he'd seen "a gentleman and two ladies, one dressed in red." Mrs. Xavier doubted that these were the people she was to meet before the lecture and, to tell the truth, she had lost sight of the reason she was taking this endless walk. In any case, she followed the man toward the naked, disgorged stadium where she stood bleary-eyed in the empty space, in a vast light and a boundless silence, no soccer game, not even a ball. Above all, no crowd. A crowd that made its presence felt through its complete absence.

Had the two ladies and the gentleman already disappeared down some corridor?

The man then said with exaggerated resolve, "I'm going to help you look, and some way or another I'll find those people. They couldn't have just vanished into thin air."

In fact they saw them from way off. But a second later they disappeared again. It seemed to be a child's game whose laughter bit into Mrs. Jorge B. Xavier.

Then she and the man passed through some more corridors. But then this man also disappeared at an intersection.

The woman gave up on the lecture which after all was not very important; not very important, that is, as long as she could finally get out of that scramble of endless paths. Could there not be some exit? She felt as if she were in an elevator stuck between floors. Could there not be some exit?

But all of a sudden she remembered the directions her friend gave on the telephone: "it's fairly near the Maracana Stadium." Remembering this, she understood the hare-brained, distracted way she only half-listened, with her other half immersed somewhere else. Mrs. Xavier was very inattentive. So, the meeting was not inside Maracana but near it. Meanwhile her little destiny had willed her to be lost within the labyrinth.

Yes, and the battle resumed, even worse now. She really wanted to get out and had no idea which way to go. And once again that man who was looking for the people appeared in the corridor, and once again he guaranteed that he would find them because they could not have disappeared. He said precisely that: "People just don't vanish into thin air."

And the woman said, "You don't need to bother looking any more, all right? It's all right. Thank you very much. The place I'm supposed to meet the people isn't in Maracana."

The man stopped immediately to look at her, with wonder. "So what are you doing here?"

She wanted to explain that her life was just like that, but she did not know what she meant by "like that" or "her life," and she said nothing. The man repeated the question, feeling curious and at the same time wishing to be discreet: what was she doing there? Nothing, she answered to herself, about to drop from fatigue. But she did not answer him. Instead she let him think she was crazy. Besides, she never explained herself to anyone. She knew that the man thought she was crazy—and who wouldn't? Wasn't she shamefully feeling what she just referred to as "that"? She felt this even though she knew how to keep her mental health on a par with her physical health. Her physical health now exhausted, she shuffled through the labyrinth on high-mileage feet. Her way of the cross. She was sweating and suffocating, dressed in very heavy wool during the unseasonably severe summer heat, that summer day misfiled in the winter. Her legs hurt; they hurt under the weight of the old cross. By now she had, in a sense, resigned herself to never leaving Maracana and dying there from her weak heart.

Then, as always, it was only after giving up our dreams that they come true. Suddenly an idea occurred to her: "What an old dummy I am!" Why, instead of looking for people who aren't here, didn't she find that man and find out how to get out of those corridors? All she really wanted was to get out and not run into anyone.

Finally, she found the man coming around a corner. And she spoke to him in a voice turned somewhat tremulous and hoarse from fatigue and the fear that everything was in vain. The discreet man agreed immediately that it was certainly better that she go home and told her carefully, "You seem to be a little confused. Perhaps it's this terrible heat."

Saying this, the man then simply turned with her into the first corridor and at the corner they saw the two large open gates. Just like that? Was it so easy?

Just like that.

Then it occurred to her that she was the only one who could not find the exit, although she did not go on to draw any further conclusions. Mrs. Xavier was just a little frightened and at the same time accustomed to this. There's no doubt that each one of us has an endless road to travel, making this a part of our destiny, something she wasn't sure she believed in.

A taxi was passing by. She hailed it and told the driver with a controlled voice that she was getting older and more tired.

"Driver, I'm not sure of the address. I've forgotten it. But what I do know is that the house is on some street or another that has something to do with Gusmao, and it intersects a street which if I'm not mistaken is called Colonel-what's-his-name."

The driver was as patient as if he were with a child. "Well, don't you worry about a thing. We're calmly going to find a street that has Gusmao in the middle and Colonel at its end," he said turning around with a smile and a conniving wink of his eye that seemed indecent. They drove off with such a bouncing that her belly shook.

Suddenly she spotted and joined the people she was looking for on a sidewalk in front of a large house. It was, however, as if the aim were just to get there and not to listen to a talk which she had forgotten altogether by that time. Mrs. Xavier had lost sight of her objective. And she did not know why she had walked so far. She saw that she had worn herself out beyond her limits, and she wanted to get out of there. The lecture was a nightmare. She then asked an important and vaguely known woman who had a car with a driver to take her home, because she was not feeling good with all this unusual heat. The driver would be there an hour from then. Mrs. Xavier then sat down in a chair they had placed for her in the corridor. She sat there stiffly in her tight girdle, removed from the culture which was unfolding in the closed hall, from which there came not a sound. Now "culture" meant little to her. And there she was in the labyrinths for sixty seconds and for sixty minutes which would lead her to an hour.

The important woman arrived and told her her ride was waiting outside, but that since she was feeling so bad and the chauffeur would take a long time, she had stopped the first taxi that passed by. Why hadn't Mrs. Xavier herself had the idea of calling a taxi, instead of submitting to the vagaries of waiting? Mrs. Jorge B. Xavier thanked her with exaggerated courtesy. The woman was always very courteous and well-behaved. She got into the taxi and said, "Leblon, if you please."

Her mind was blank. It seemed her brain was fasting.

After a while she noted that they drove and drove but once again they kept returning to the same plaza. Why didn't they get anywhere? Once again, was there no way out? The driver finally confessed that he didn't know the south side of Rio and that he only worked in the north. And she didn't know how to tell him the way. The cross she bore for years weighed more and more, and absence of an exit simply revived the black magic of the Maracana corridors. There was no way to get free from the plaza! Then the driver told her to take another taxi, and he even beckoned one over to their side. She thanked him coolly; she observed the social graces, even with those she knew well. More than this, she was very kind. In the next cab she said fearfully, "If it's all right with you, could we go to Leblon?"

And they simply left the plaza and drove through other streets.

It was on opening the door to her apartment with her key that she imagined that she wanted to cry out loud. But she wasn't one to sob or complain. She informed the maid in passing that she wouldn't take any telephone calls. She went straight to her bedroom, removed all her clothes, took a pill with no water and waited for it to take effect.

In the meantime she smoked. She remembered that it was the month of August, and they say that August is bad luck. But September would come one day, like a way out. And September was in some ways like the month of May: a lighter and more transparent month. She was vaguely thinking about this when drowsiness finally came, and she fell asleep.

Hours later, when she woke up she saw that a fine, cold rain was falling; the cold was like the edge of a knife. Naked in bed, she was freezing. And she thought how an old naked lady was quite odd. She recalled that she had planned to buy a woolen shawl. She glanced at the clock: she'd still find businesses open. She got a cab and said, "Ipanema, if you please."

"What's that? The Botanical Garden?" the man asked.

"Ipanema, please," the woman repeated, quite surprised. It was the absurdity of the complete lack of communication: after all, what did the words "Ipanema" and "Botanical Garden" have in common? But again she vaguely thought that "that's just how her life was."

She made another purchase quickly and saw herself in the street, now dark, with nothing to do, since Mr. Jorge B. Xavier had traveled to Sao Paulo the day before and wouldn't return until the day after.

Then, again at home, between taking another sleeping pill or doing something else, she opted for the second, remembering that she could return to look for the lost bill of exchange. What little she understood of it was that that piece of paper represented money. Two days ago she searched the whole house carefully, including the kitchen, but in vain. Now it occurred to her, why not under the bed? Perhaps. She kneeled on the floor. But being on her knees quickly tired her out, and she bent down and leaned on her two hands.

She then noticed that she was on all fours.

And so she stayed for a while, perhaps meditating, perhaps not. Who knows, Mrs. Xavier might have tired of being human. She was a dog on four feet. With no dignity whatsoever. Her pride a thing of the past. On all fours, a little pensive perh aps. But under the bed there was just dust.

She stood up with some effort, caused by her stiff joints, and saw that there was nothing more to do but consider realistically—and it was only with painful effort that she could view reality—that the letter was lost and that to continue looking for it would be the same as never getting out of Maracana.

And just as always, as soon as she stopped looking, as she opened her hanky drawer to pull one out—there was the letter of exchange.

Then the woman, tired from the effort of being on all fours, sat on the bed and for no apparent reason began to cry softly. It seemed more like a monotonous Arabian chant. She hadn't cried for over thirty years, but she was so tired now. If this was indeed crying. It wasn't. It was something. Finally she blew her nose. Then she thought that she would take her fate in hand and improve it somehow. "Where there's a will there's a way," she mused (without actually believing it). And all this about being a slave to a destiny occurred to her because without wanting to, she'd already begun thinking about "that."

But it happens that the woman also thought: it was too late to have a destiny. She thought that any kind of switch with another human being would do her good. It was then that it occurred to her that there was no one else with whom she could trade places. Despite what she would wish, she was who she was and couldn't become another. Each one was unique. Mrs. Jorge B. Xavier was unique too.

But everything that occurred to her was preferable to being "that." And that came from her long exitless corridors. "That," now with no sense of decency, was the painful hunger of her insides, the hunger of being possessed by the unattainable television idol. She never missed his television program. Now that she couldn't stop thinking about him, the trick was to allow herself to think about and recall the girlish face of Roberto Carlos, my love.

She went to wash her dusty hands and saw herself in the wash basin mirror. Then Mrs. Xavier thought, "If I want him a lot, really a lot, he'll be mine for at least one night." She believed vaguely in the force of the will. She got tangled up again in choked and twisted desire.

But, who knows? If she gave up on Roberto Carlos, then things between him and her would happen. Mrs. Xavier meditated a bit on the matter. Then she cleverly pretended to give up on Roberto Carlos. But she knew well that the magical abandonment only gave positive results when it was true, and not just a trick as a means to an end. Reality required a lot of the woman. She examined herself in the mirror to see if her face would turn hideous under the sway of her feelings. But it was a quiet face which long ago had ceased revealing her feelings. Besides, her face never expressed anything but good upbringing. And now it was just the mask of a seventy year old woman. Then her lightly made-up face seemed clown-like to her. The woman made a half- hearted attempt to smile to see if it would help. It didn't.

On the outside—she saw it in the mirror—she was dry, like a dried fig. But inside she wasn't parched. On the contrary. Inside she was like moist gums, soft like toothless gums.

She then pursued a thought that might spiritualize her or dry her up once and for all. But she'd never been spiritual. And because of Roberto Carlos the woman was wrapped up in the darkness of the matter where she was profoundly anonymous.

Standing in the bathroom she was as anonymous as a chicken.

In a split second she unconsciously glimpsed that everyone was anonymous. Because no one is the other and the other didn't know the other. Then—then that person is anonymous. And now she was tangled in that deep and mortal well, in the body's rebellion. Body of invisible depths in which the rats and lizards of her instincts scurried about veiled in malignant shadows. And was everything out of time, fruit out of season? Why hadn't the other old women advised her that this could happen until the end? In old men she had seen many lecherous eyes. But not in old women. Out of season. And she was alive, as if she were someone, she who was no one.

Mrs. Jorge B. Xavier was no one.

And she wanted to have beautiful romantic feelings about the delicacy of Roberto Carlos's face, but she couldn't. His delicacy just took her to a dark corridor of sensuality. And the damage was lasciviousness. It was a vulgar hunger. She wanted to consume the mouth of Roberto Carlos. She wasn't romantic, she was ill-informed on the subject of love. There, in the bathroom, before the wash basin mirror.

With the indelible mark of age.

Without even one sublime thought to serve as a rudder and ennoble her existence.

Then she began to undo her French knot and to comb her hair slowly. She had to dye it soon; her white roots were showing now. Then the woman thought: never in my life have I had a climax as in the stories you read. The climax was Roberto Carlos.

She thought. She concluded that she was going to die as secretly as she had lived. But she also knew that every death is secret.

From the bottom of her future death she imagined she saw the coveted image of Roberto Carlos in the mirror, with that soft curly hair of his. There she was, a prisoner of desire as out of season as a summer day in midwinter. A prisoner in the tangle of corridors of Maracana. A prisoner of the mortal secret of old women. It's just that she wasn't used to being almost seventy years old. She lacked practice and didn't have the least bit of experience.

"My dear little Roberto Carlos," she said loudly and quite alone.

And she added: my love. Her voice sounded strange to her as if with no sense of decency or shame it were the first time she were confessing that which after all should have been shameful. The woman imagined that it was possible that little Roberto might not wish to accept her love because she herself was aware that this love was silly, saccharinely voluptuous and gluttonous. And Roberto Carlos seemed so pure, so sexless.

Would her lightly colored lips still be kissable? Or would it, perhaps, be repugnant to kiss the mouth of an old woman? Showing no emotion, she examined her lips carefully. And still showing no emotion, she softly sang the refrain from Roberto Carlos's most famous song: "Warm me this winter night, and everything else can go to hell."

It was then that Mrs. Jorge B. Xavier abruptly doubled over the sink as though she were going to vomit out her viscera and she interrupted her life with an explosive silence: there!—has!—to!—be!—a!—way!—out!

Translated by Leland Guyer

In the Family

María Elena Llano

When my mother found out that the large mirror in the living room was inhabited, we all gradually went from disbelief to astonishment, and from this to a state of contemplation, ending up by accepting it as an everyday thing.

The fact that the old, spotted mirror reflected the dear departed in the family was not enough to upset our life style. Following the old saying of "let the house burn as long as no one sees the smoke," we kept the secret to ourselves since, after all, it was nobody else's business.

At any rate, some time went by before each one of us would feel absolutely comfortable about sitting down in our favorite chair and learning that, in the mirror, that same chair was occupied by somebody else. For example, it could be Aurelia, my grandmother's sister (1939), and even if cousin Natalie would be on my side of the room, across from her would be the almost forgotten Uncle Nicholas (1927). As could have been expected, our departed reflected in the mirror presented the image of a family gathering almost identical to our own, since nothing, absolutely nothing in the living-room—the furniture and its arrangement, the light, etc.—was changed in the mirror. The only difference was that on the other side it was them instead of us.

I don't know about the others, but I sometimes felt that, more than a vision in the mirror, I was watching an old worn-out movie, already clouded. The deceaseds' efforts to copy our gestures were slower, restrained, as if the mirror were not truly showing a direct image but the reflection of some other reflection.

From the very beginning I knew that everything would get more complicated as soon as my cousin Clara got back from vacation. Because of her boldness and determination, Clara had long given me the impression that she had blundered into our family by mistake. This suspicion had been somewhat bolstered by her being one of the first women dentists in the country. However, the idea that she might have been with us by mistake went away as soon as my cousin hung up her diploma and started to embroider sheets beside my grandmother, aunts and other cousins, waiting for a suitor who actually did show up but was found lacking in one respect or another—nobody ever really found out why.

Once she graduated, Clara became the family oracle, even though she never practiced her profession. She would prescribe painkillers and was the arbiter of fashion; she would choose the theater shows and rule on whether the punch had the right amount of liquor at each social gathering. In view of all this, it was fitting that she take one month off every year to go to the beach.

That summer when Clara returned from her vacation and learned about my mother's discovery, she remained pensive for a while, as if weighing the symptoms before issuing a diagnosis. Afterwards, without batting an eye, she leaned over the mirror, saw for herself that it was true, and then tossed her head, seemingly accepting the situation. She immediately sat by the bookcase and craned her neck to see who was sitting in the chair on the other side. "Gosh, look at Gus," was all she said. There in the very same chair the mirror showed us Gus, some sort of godson of Dad, who after a flood in his hometown came to live with us and had remained there in the somewhat ambiguous character of adoptive poor relation. Clara greeted him amiably with a wave of the hand, but he seemed busy, for the moment, with something like a radio tube and did not pay attention to her. Undoubtedly, the mirror people weren't going out of their way to be sociable. This must have wounded Clara's self-esteem, although she did not let it on.

Naturally, the idea of moving the mirror to the dining-room was hers. And so was its sequel: to bring the mirror near the big table, so we could all sit together for meals.

In spite of my mother's fears that the mirror people would run away or get annoyed because of the fuss, everything went fine. I must admit it was comforting to sit every day at the table and see so many familiar faces, although some of those from the other side were distant relatives, and others, due to their lengthy—although unintentional—absence, were almost strangers. There were about twenty of us sitting at the table every day, and even if their gestures and movements seemed more remote than ours and their meals a little washed-out, we generally gave the impression of being a large family that got along well.

At the boundary between the real table and the other one, on this side, sat Clara and her brother Julius. On the other side was Eulalia (1949), the second wife of Uncle Daniel, aloof and indolent in life, and now the most distant of anyone on the other side. Across from her sat my godfather Sylvester (1952), who even though he was not a blood relative was always a soul relation. I was sad to see that Sylvester had lost his ruddiness, for he now looked like a faded mannequin, although his full face seemed to suggest perfect health. This pallor did not suit the robust Asturian, who undoubtedly felt a bit ridiculous in these circumstances.

For a while we ate all together, without further incidents or problems. We mustn't forget Clara, however, who we had allowed to sit at the frontier between the two tables, the equator separating what was from what was not. Although we paid no attention to the situation, we should have. Compounding our regrettable oversight was the fact that lethargic Eulalia sat across from her so that one night, with the same cordiality with which she had addressed Gus, Clara asked Eulalia to pass the salad. Eulalia affected the haughty disdain of offended royalty as she passed the spectral salad bowl, filled with dull lettuce and grayish semi-transparent tomatoes which Clara gobbled up, smiling mischievously at the novelty of it all. She watched us with the same defiance in her eyes that she had on the day she enrolled in a man's subject. There was no time to act. We just watched her grow pale, then her smile faded away until finally Clara collapsed against the mirror.

Once the funeral business was over and we sat back down at the table again, we saw that Clara had taken a place on the other side. She was between cousin Baltazar (1940) and a great-uncle whom we simply called "Ito."

This *faux pas* dampened our conviviality somewhat. In a way, we felt betrayed; we felt that they had grievously abused our hospitality. However, we ended up divided over the question of who was really whose guest. It was also plain that our carelessness and Clara's irrepressible inquisitiveness had contributed to the mishap. In fact, a short time later we realized that there wasn't a great deal of difference between what Clara did before and what she was doing now, and so we decided to overlook the incident and get on with things. Nevertheless, each day we became less and less sure about which side was life and which its reflection, and as one bad step leads to another, I ended up taking Clara's empty place.

I am now much closer to them. I can almost hear the distant rustle of the folding and unfolding of napkins, the slight clinking of glasses and cutlery, the movement of chairs. The fact is that I can't tell if these sounds come from them or from us. I'm obviously not worried about clearing that up. What really troubles me, though, is that Clara doesn't seem to behave properly, with either the solemnity or with the opacity owed to her new position; I don't know how to put it. Even worse, the problem is that I—more than anybody else in the family—may become the target of Clara's machinations, since we were always joined by a very special affection, perhaps because we were the same age and had shared the same children's games and the first anxieties of adolescence ...

As it happens, she is doing her best to get my attention, and ever since last Monday she has been waiting for me to slip up so she can pass me a pineapple this big, admittedly a little bleached-out, but just right for making juice and also a bit sour, just as she knows I like it.

Translated by Beatriz Teleki

Symbiotic Encounter

Carmen Naranjo

We were lovers. My name is Ana. His is Manuel. We did not meet casually. Someone had told Manuel about me. About my unusual way of living. About my liking street cats, about my dreams of a different world, about how night opens my eyes and makes me beautiful, about how I say very little at times, and how, at other times, no one can get me to keep quiet, about how I get carried away by expressive faces and write novels with interminable monologues. That same someone had told me about Manuel, about his disastrous love affairs, his loneliness, his neurotic habit of thinking seriously about the commonplace, that unremitting affliction that wore him down through his pathological sensitivity. Later, that someone arranged an accidental meeting.

I arrived first. That damned habit of punctuality that makes me feel out of step.

I knew he had arrived. I recognized his voice and his manner of greeting with a cheerful hello. He was not one of those who embrace without enthusiasm, who give cold and inexpressive slaps on the back or who approach your cheeks with a loud and distant kiss.

When I thought the gathering should be over, I left without seeing him, without speaking to him. I said goodbye to the group of people close by, the group with which, among other things, I spoke about recipes and how to enhance one's profile with dark earrings. Someone shouted at me close to the door: "How can you leave when things are just getting started!" I replied without seeing him that I had something else to do and that they should have a good time, and I said goodbye. I was glad to maintain my reputation as a party-pooper, and to make sure from the conversation that I hadn't even made his acquaintance, in spite of the advance preparations. "I will introduce him to you, and

133

I know you will both hit it off, that's easy to see."

Once in the street, I breathed easy—what a pleasure. I felt mono-logue was preferable to dialogue, sentiment to sensation, choosing to being chosen. When I was almost at the street corner, he stopped me. "You were trying to get away from me, but I came because of you, and I don't want to miss the opportunity. Can we have a cup of coffee to-gether?"

His voice was imposing and convincing. It left no alternative. In the café, sitting face to face, our feet touched and I felt that overwhelming energy, I was ready, definitely ready. I saw his mouth, and words and kisses ran together. He kissed me, smelling of coffee and cigarettes. I kissed him until the edge of the table made my waist hurt.

We walked holding hands, kissing at each step until we reached my apartment. We spent an entire week there, unable to differentiate be-tween night and day, until we got tired of the crumbs in the bed, the smell of tuna cans and the need to answer the telephone which, at the beginning, we did not hear but which finally became a jarring obsession.

I loved you, and I still love you, Manuel. You must understand that. Of course things changed because of the natural effect of mutually ap-proved variations which are also part of human relations. All agree-ments come to an end and linger in the memory .... .

We started cutting down to just weekends. At first, glorious ones, as if we had hungered ever so long; then they were more routine and less prolonged, and, finally, almost unremarkable because they had become predictable: *Well, what are we going to do this weekend?*

We exhausted all the possibilities: surprise, forcible abduction, se-duction, comedy, play-acting, jealousy, suspecting infidelity, even bring-ing the rival lover.

You remember what we talked about. We always talked about our-selves, about how honest we were, how happy and fortunate, about our marvellous affinity, how different we were from the rest, about needing a special world of our own, and how nobody understood our politics because we still believed that utopia was within reach if we just made the right changes. In literature our attention was riveted by the odd and unexpected.

One day, a friend asked me about the color of Manuel's eyes. I replied quickly that they were blue, a beautiful, naive blue, sensitive and steady. Then I was unsure. Sometimes they were almost green, the blue turns greenish when you look at mountains a lot. I was struck by the realization that I didn't know the color of his eyes. I had never really seen him eye to eye, our caresses having left us lost in a world of mist.

At that time we would argue about who was giving more in the relationship. I said that providing the furnished apartment, rent, electricity and phone was enough to ensure my independence and freedom. He asserted that between the meals, the vodka, cigarettes, gasoline and the extras for eating out, he was left with just pennies, which would soon disappear in tips. *This can't go on, I've never had it so bad. With free lodging, free woman and free conversation. What kind of mortgaged man did I get? Praise be to God for his ingenious benefactions. In raffles, I only win the junk.*

You told me I know nothing of austerity and thrift, that I was, by and large, a spendthrift. I really don't understand the anal-retentive obsession with savings, that vestige of chewing over again what has already been digested. It's the result of teaching that you can double your money without either sowing or harvesting.

What arguments we had! I saw you clearly. Your eyes on mine. Yes, yours on mine. I don't know how long we were looking at each other intensely and curiously. I discovered the color: a dirty yellow, which reflects and changes everything, with fits of passionate looks and a profound coldness that freezes everything in sight. Too many details, one caught up completely in details, down to savings and inveighing against waste. We kept on looking at each other as sweetness, surprise, reproach and resentment filed through our eyes. That was the last time we made love. When we finally averted our intense and penetrating eyes, we were trembling, sweaty, the orgasm past.

I recovered my voice long enough to be able to say that we had been mired in trivia. He begged forgiveness, *it will never happen again, today things went sour for me.* We decided to separate for a week, afterwards things would be different, because absence and missing each other give real substance to human relationships. When the week was up, he arrived with his suitcase and dirty clothes, hungover and with bad breath. He felt sick, and I missed him. I could neither lie nor tell the truth, so I kept quiet.

We each retired to our separate corners. Each one in his space, just like animals measuring each other. At night I heard him vomiting. He could not keep anything down. He took to eating prunes, and so, bits of half-digested prunes decorated the toilet seat cover and the bathroom. He had the same reaction to guavas, cubaces, fried beans, tortillas with cheese, macaronia la bolognesa and combination pizzas.

I came to detest his trifles, their abundance: some niggling, some affected, many effeminate.

He was thin, which was why he was surprised to see his breasts growing and abdomen swelling. Six months later, poor Manuel of my perplexity, the most horrible body one could imagine for a man: a belly almost protruding to a point, enormous, drooping breasts, a slow, tired gait, hunching over to hide himself. The nausea persisted, interrupting breakfasts, lunches, dinners, conversations.

I suggested a visit to the doctor. The poor man did not want to go out, or work, he did nothing but knit incessantly. He knitted scarves and sweaters, since his low blood pressure made him tremble terribly and nothing could keep him warm.

Repugnant as he was, I put up with his mannerisms, trifles and conversations that all boiled down to the same things: *I am dying, I am no longer good for anything, this is a case of precocious senility.* He tried to indulge in sex, but I could not stand it. As he started to touch me, I pushed his hands away, I told him it filled me with revulsion, and I started to vomit too.

We went to the doctor; after examining him nude, abdominal auscultation and seeing water run out when the breasts were squeezed, he asked if we were transvestites. I told him we were not, that it hadn't yet come to that. Then he replied: *the baby is fine, it will be delivered in December by Caesarian section, and if you give me exclusive research rights I won't charge you anything.*

Me? The mother of Manuel's baby? Or father to a child of his? That just couldn't be. We both decided against it, for in addition to being unheard of, it was ridiculous, we would be the laughing-stock of acquaintances and strangers alike. By common agreement, we proposed an abortion. The doctor said that would be suicide on Manuel's part, and murder with respect to the child, and that I, the surviving member, would be responsible for both consequences. Ultimately, a child does not come about just like that, I had a great deal invested in it.

We asked for time to think it over.

We scrutinized our actions, our genitals, the different positions we had tried, attitudes, the games we played. And there was nothing that could explain our bizarre situation. Witchcraft? Perhaps. There is always that possibility, although we may not believe in it. The realization became clearer and clearer: that opthalmic orgasm in which we exposed each other laid bare the truth and some horrible demon maliciously deranged the scheme normally regulated by the division of the sexes.

After fretting over it interminably and consulting a library of strange phenomena and unbelievable occurrences (which made us experts on these subjects without helping us at all), we decided to cross the border so as to amuse only strangers.

Did he complain during the trip! He was such a nuisance! He didn't fit anywhere, what with his nine months being almost up. If I detested him before, now I simply wished he would go away. I was tempted to open the car door and throw him out on some deserted stretch of the highway.

Finally, we arrived. I left him at the door of the hospital to manage as best he could. The next day, I got in line with the other visitors. I reluctantly approached the maternity ward. I asked for Manuel, yeah, Manuel the freak. No one could tell me anything about him. They had never treated a pregnant man at the hospital. I looked for him everywhere, in the morgue, at the cemetery, in hotels, boarding houses, private clinics, bars. I was desperate: after all, it was my child. That *my child* came out in a husky voice. I started to feel the presence of a moustache as I talked. I went to see crones, quacks and charlatans. Nothing. I was convinced that my child had been stolen. This I said in the bass voice of an opera singer while I felt burdened with a beard that swayed in the wind.

I returned to my apartment, manifesting all the signs of a defrauded father. The loneliness was overwhelming because I felt mutilated; someone was walking around somewhere with a part of me. I was hardened by the loneliness, just like my face— scourged as it was by the razor— which now needed shaving twice a day.

Translated by Cedric Busette

The Midgets

Olga Orozco

"I don't want it. It has eyes," Laura said again.

"It has eyes," I repeated in a weak echo.

"Chicken eyes," Laura added.

"Blind chicken eyes," I stated further, with more enthusiasm, sensing the game.

Laura's foot touched mine under the table. I understood. Any secret sign indicated the start of her being the leader and me the follower. Something was about to happen, and as always, I should obey the order to follow her.

She looked at Maria de las Nieves, who had dedicated her sixteen years of life to a surprisingly unsuccessful attempt to mature, and who now, in the absence of all the adults, was presiding over the table. Then she smiled, pursed her lips, and jutting out her lower jaw in a funny imitation of a skunk—that unusually sneaky grimace that destroyed any solemnity, that face she made that would later have to be erased from all the photographs—she started saying rapidly, in a tone between defiant and a musing: "Ox eye, eye of a spring, eyes of a lamb's chopped-off head, the keyhole eye of lock; out of sight, out of mind; an eye for an eye, a tooth for a tooth; an eye, an eye ... " Her inspiration began giving out. The first words had sounded sharp, accusing; the last like a weak, reluctant, rote prayer. She looked at me, insisting I hurry.

"Watch the birdie," I said, making a silly association.

Laura loved it. Then, as though it had been prearranged, we threw ourselves into the game unflinchingly, between giggles, in an overpowering dialogue, one after the other:

"I see, I see."

"What do you see?"

"Eyes, eyes, eyes."

"Do good, and look not to whom."

"Look, but don't touch."

"God is watching you."

"See no evil, hear no evil, speak no evil."

"See Rome and die ... "

"Veni, vidi, vici," shouted the parrot, Nanni, in a sharp, triumphant voice from behind the door.

The string had been cut. We were quiet.

From the start, Maria de las Nieves had been rapping her pale knuckles on the table lightly, as a sign of reproach. The rapping increased. It became a furious drumming. We picked up our spoons.

The chicken soup lay untouched in our plates. The large and small oily eyes floating on its surface were already covered by a thin protective film, whitish, like drops of stearing. Now it would surely be impossible to drink it. I was almost nauseated.

The spoons skimmed the surface, without stopping, moving those filthy sightless eyes about. But they just sat there, not looking up.

"I can't. It's made with melted candlewax," Laura complained.

"A candle for every saint," I said timidly, just in case it was time to go on, just in case the game could be prolonged until who knows when.

"Watch for a candle in the window. Watch for the watchman. The sailor's watch. Watch over the wake of the little angel and watch the dance of the seven veils," Maria de las Nieves shouted.

The first few words had excited us. We supposed that she too was getting into the game. But she was not. This wasn't the game. Her pale face kept getting redder, and the corners of her dark, almond eyes were stretched toward her temples, angry and sparkling, like the glint of a weapon through the jungle.

"Idiots!" she added through her clenched teeth, which appeared to conceal another weapon, the ultimate weapon. She opened her mouth and slowly took a breath of air, of the mean air that would avoid her years later when it would have to cross an area of thick, malignant vegetation to reach her lungs, a zone choked by suffocating growth, like the forest on a summer night.

"Idiots!" she repeated.

For Laura and me the enjoyment had ceased, but our smiles persisted, ashamed, not knowing how to disappear graciously from our faces.

"What do I care if you eat your soup or not! It isn't as though you're going to grow if you eat it. Enough stupid stories! It isn't true that you would grow, even if you did eat it. You are never going to grow, because you are midgets. Real dwarfs, both of you, and old. Two old, foolish dwarfs, and it's best you know it once and for all."

She pushed her chair back, got up brusquely and left the dining room with that majestic air that she was now rehearsing, so that one day it would really become the demeanor of a great Roman lady.

It was a blow right on the back of the neck.

Laura and I looked at one another like two confused birds. Any gesture would have seemed a desperate beating of wings, any word like an insufferably shrill cry. No, even though we might be the same, it was a revelation too monstrous to begin to share it.

Almost simultaneously we tore out of our chairs and ran from the dining room, through separate doors. That's the way it always happened. Great moments always led us to different doors. That's also the way it happened later. My moments would take me toward that succession of doors that always opened to the light for an instant, toward the open air, until others appeared, hidden like traps; the ones that aspired to shut me up alone with a desperate, almost lamentable fate. Her doors were, on the other hand, few, and open onto a peaceful happiness.

This time I did not seek refuge under the oak tree. It was night, and besides, I needed timeless, permanent, perhaps decisive help. I threw myself face down on the bed and cried. I cried until the sand (I wonder from what arid, unknown depth those sands arose?) under my eyelids began to hurt. Only then did I begin to think. Before I had done no more than cry over my own unfortunate, invariable, tiny image of a midget condemned to being a midget.

I was a midget. I only knew two midgets: Felicitas and Chico Dick. I had seen them in the circus, posted at the entrance to the tent, one on each side, with their red suits fringed with looped silver and gold ribbon and cord, in their shiny boots and shakos with black visors shading their tired, resentful eyes.

"Good evening, children," he said as Grandmother, who could see very little, passed by stretching out both arms to the sides of their heads to pull their ears jokingly. But those irate faces turned up to her, those tight-jawed, stolid, confident faces that in no way looked like children's faces. They did not look like our faces, either. They looked as though they had been painstakingly stuffed from above, then their sides pressed to distribute the stuffing along their short bones. That procedure had marred them; it had produced bags under their eyes, around their wrists, and on various areas of their bodies. Their steps were short, and the flabby movements of their limbs were shorter than those of any child. They dragged their bodies stiffly, as though something impeded their play, as though they had uncut membranes or stitches between their fingers and in their joints. They turned this way and that, like tops rotating slowly.

There were also the other dwarfs, the magical ones, those who made their homes among the sudden mushrooms, lichens and mosses, in the depths of the forest, in those regions that turn a bloody or saffron color when evening falls. But they were all men and had white beards. No, that was not our situation.

I was a female midget, and I was old, too. Nevertheless, I had no distant memories, nor did I know how to measure backwards to calculate my age. I had no trunks with dresses and objects from other times, nor did I know of things that counted as having happened many years ago. Momma, Poppa, Grandmother, Maria de las Nieves, Aunt Adelaida, Alejandro—whom they had told me I would not see again until much later, unless I got a ride in Elias's car (I thought that Elias would have a black mustache, blue-black skin covered with green tattoos and a noisy little cheap car)—all of the family had always looked the same. I had not seen them grow up or age. Of course there was the family album with the formal pictures and the snapshots among which Laura pointed out those blank erasures that replaced her unexpected skunk faces, saying with pride, "I am always the same. I'm the one who changes the least, as well as being the palest." I remembered the photographs one by one. But that shed no light on the matter. I knew nothing of the implacable tedium of time. What's more, perhaps dwarfs forgot everything. On the other hand, I was now discovering the meaning of many other things: interrupted conversations, embarrassed silences, concealed signals, phrases loaded with allusions and mysteries, and above all, Momma's laughter when I asked if I had been present at her wedd ing. But why had they said to me, time and again, at times as a promise, at times as a warning, "When you grow up?" No. Now I would not grow. I would not be able to be a saint, nor a diver, nor a circus rider. Goodbye to marine phosphorescences, white coral and sunken ships where there are always terrible secrets to discover. Goodbye to the high stage lights, to the diaphanous dress that twists and turns and turns, and to the white horse upon which I would stand on only one foot while taking a last lap around the arena of my triumph.

I sobbed over all of the turned-off lights, over all of the broken windows.

Someone took my hand, squeezed it lovingly and held it between hers. They were warm hands, but small, those of another midget.

I hardly raised my head, glancing sidelong at her, slowly, through my wet hair. She didn't nauseate me, nor make me afraid or apprehensive; she made me feel only trust and love.

Laura was seated on the edge of my bed. She seemed calm, but preoccupied.

"I have found out everything," she said in the sad, low voice she affected to reveal any news. Told in that voice, births, visits, rains became something ominous, extremely vulnerable.

"I asked Maria de las Nieves. She told me that many, many years ago, when the grandparents came to live in this house, there was a tree here that has now dried up. On one of the lower limbs, which was high up because the tree was so tall, they found a nest with two white eggs in it. They had wreaths around them made of pink flowers, like sugar flowers, and some letters that spelled out "Remembrance." Around each one there was also a pink velvet ribbon with a bow. They looked like Easter eggs, but they weren't (Maria de las Nieves's generosity had not even extended that far). At that time the circus was in town. Then the grandparents made a deal with Felicitas and Chico Dick to sit on the eggs until they hatched. After the midgets climbed the tree, they took away the ladder so that the midgets couldn't move from their place. They sat on the nest, in their Hussa costumes for forty days and forty nights. (This coincidence with the same number of days and nights as the Deluge gave the situation prestige, as though the nest, the eggs, and the midgets had all actually been transported in the Ark.) Seen from afar they looked like two enormous red birds, but they did not sing. Every day they would take them whole trays of fried potatoes and tureens of chocolate mousse, as well as dates and champagne. Then they would take the ladder away again. During the day Grandmother sat at the foot of the tree and told them children's stories, ghost tales, and even accounts of the lives of the saints. At times Grandfather posed riddles or played ball with them. When it seemed they were becoming distracted, Grandfather would poke them with his cane and Grandmother threatened them with her fist so they would warm more to their task. At night, after supper, the municipal band came and played them 'The March of the Giants' (I never understood that particular bit of hostility), until Felicitas and Chico Dick would fall asleep. On Sundays and holidays, Father Indalecio made them pray. He would climb the ladder to a higher branch ten meters over their heads to give them the impression that he was in the pulpit, and from there he preached to them. He too looked like a bird, an immense black bird cawing and beating his wings. At times he became enthused with his sermon, with the wrath of God, with the punishment of sinners, and he would shake the branches violently. Leaves and acorns rained down upon the attentively upturned faces of Felicitas and Chico Dick.

"One morning they announced that it was done, that all was in order, and that it was a job well done. When they came down from the tree it could be seen that there were two infants in the nest: you and I newborn. We have lived in the house since then. Later Momma was born, then Aunt Adelaida and later on all the rest."

She was quiet, gazing blankly at the wall, lost in a thoughtful daydream.

So that was the story, the cruel, secret, humiliating story?

"I don't believe it," I cried, "it can't be so. Grandmother did not recognize them as her own. Besides, why didn't they leave them to rot? Why didn't they put them on the chicken nests? Why did they have to call Felicitas and Chico Dick?" I asked between sobs, my voice choking, hoping that Laura had thought about it as much as I had, hoping that she had found something useful in all that review of albums, of remembrances, of people, and that she would now offer it to me as a possibility for salvation, although the most obscure, the smallest possibility.

But she, having already undressed, put on her night gown and gotten into bed, seemed to have no answer to this desperate questioning of destiny's injustice.

"Don't be miserable. Be calm," she said after an interminable silence. And then, with a voice like someone figuring accounts, "It is probably not so serious. Maybe we can go on a trip. There must be places where they all live together ... all those ... all those ... " She was not able to say "dwarfs." "We could go there. We would be able to wear silver high-heeled shoes, green hats with shoulder-length pink feathers from the Amazon, fitted spangled dresses. We could go to the theatre every night in stork feather fans and masks, dance in golden ballrooms amidst confetti, balloons, and little Japanese lanterns; read novels about crimes, kidnappings, many crimes, many kidnappings," her voice was drifting off, "smoking, drinking rum, pillage the enemy," she was mixing everything up. She was talking about pirate life, as when she wanted to be a pirate, "Buried treasures, maps, on the island, the parrot ... here comes Robinson Crusoe, Friday, Friday, Saturday, Sundays, Mondays-s-sh-sh," and off to sleep she went, on that shushing sound that asked for and ordered silence, that showed that dwarfs also sleep with slumber grasped in one hand, like a stone that they can throw at the face that tries to wake them.

Once again I went back over all the years I could remember, to the first image, the one that kept slipping away like a fish among the moving sands and murky waters at the bottom of my memory. Starting from there, I would go forward. And then backwards again, and forward. Forty, sixty times.

I did not care if I had arrived from Paris in a celestial cabbage, in a white basket, or in an almost Easter egg. The important thing was that I had no parents. Were my parents Felicitas and Chico Dick, or perhaps the grandparents, or who?

But what was insufferable, the thing that made me chew the edge of the bedsheet, was my monstrous, wretched, repugnant condition as a midget forever condemned to being a midget.

Dawn. One could make out the car at a distance. One could already hear the humming of the motor. A distant automobile horn sounded. It was getting closer. In that celestial chariot, wrapped in that seraphim's song, announced by those trumpets played by the angels, Momma was coming back.

I knelt next to my bed and I prayed: "Please don't let a jackrabbit or a quail get in the way. Let the wind part the thistles. Let those who have to cross the road leading cattle sleep a little longer. Let them go on sleeping in peace. Let nothing detain or slow down that march. Let nothing retard Momma's arrival. Let her come now, soon, and let Momma be Momma, please."

At that moment the door opened and in came Maria de las Nieves. Her face was like a mosaic formed by tiny bits of guilt, amusement, mockery, remorse, compassion, and even fear.

Translated by Gustavo V. Segade

A Gentleman on the Train

Antonia Palacios

Delia is looking out the train window. She watches the land going by, so different, so much the same. The passing landscape, flat although slightly tilted, upturned in the inclines, in the unavoidable curves, bunched up high in gigantic promontories. She watches the green and distant prairies go by, and the windows of a house already passed. She is sitting very still in the train as the countryside parades by her. Opposite her, a gentleman is reading his paper. Maybe he doesn't know a thing about the landscape, the landscape on parade. He is reading the newspaper which is raised above his knees, level with his hands.

"Are you comfortable, Miss?"

"Yes, thank you. And you?"

Delia continues to watch animals passing by, a fat white cow lying by the rails which the train almost carries off. Delia would like to be a cow, as white as the one left behind, a cow comfortably settled into a fertile field with all sorts of aromas, chewing the green grass, and, chewing them over time and again, with large, unworried melancholy eyes and soft pink udders, just like the cow. A harmless cow, lying on the ground, indifferent to it, the ground passing by with men, women and children. Passing by without them.

"Do you smoke, Miss?"

"No, thank you. Do you?"

There is an enormous silence, then the train strains forward. The countryside in review makes a show of its luxuriant hair and its spotted pelt. The train rolls along and Delia watches with her hands folded over the pleated skirt. Her beautiful hands, so smooth and golden. The train rolls along and Delia watches.

"Are you going to Quietzco?" the gentleman asks.

"To Quietzco?" she echoes.

And she thinks of a faraway Quietzco, a Quietzco ... she does not know, whose name she never heard ... and wonders where it is. Maybe it is just a dot by the sea in some old atlas or a brown stain on the calcined earth.

"I know a street in Quietzco where there is a small bar. You're welcome to have a few drinks with me by the sea."

Delia imagines the streets of Quietzco to be different, twisted, where one gets lost easily. And she imagines that its people are also different, easy to talk to, and easy to be quiet with just looking at the sea. The sea of Quietzco—if there is one—will be peaceful, with never-ending shores, a smooth sketch on very fine sand. A sea with seagulls flying to almost touch the sea spray and then shooting away and disappearing over the water. Delia imagines Joaquín waiting for her in Quietzco ... —"You are welcome to have a few drinks with me by the sea"—he will hold her very close while they cross the streets, those streets that Joaquín knows so well. Is Quietzco small? Is Quietzco big? Quietzco is endless ...

"Please don't worry, this is a brief stop. Would you like something to drink? Coke, Pepsi, something cold?"

"No, thank you."

"Have a soda, or a Seven-Up?"

"No, thank you. How about you?"

"I think I'll have a soda. It'll have to be quick, the stop is very short."

Delia watches the gentleman drinking from the bottle. The train has stopped. The child selling the drinks has also stopped, as have the fields and the big wire fences from which green and yellow branches hang. Delia, also at rest, observes the gentleman as he stands up and stretches his long, long arm covered by the brown sleeve. The bottle tumbles, the train has started. Everything returns to its appointed place and the countryside resumes its procession. Now the people and the animals go by very fast, the ground with its varied planes pulled by strange, different speeds, the fastest and the slowest. Delia closes her eyes and watches her own internal parade, that of the people who live with her on earth. Soldiers, captains, colonels, high-ranking officers, prostitutes and nannies, priests, beggars, presidents and vice-presidents, men in bare feet and men in shining boots, the hungry and the sated, men with gorged stomachs and high-society women with long, undulating dresses, ladies and gentlemen with calling cards, their names, degrees, titles and ancient lineage delineated in a line of the white card. The parade continues with deposed queens and kings, their crowns fallen to the ground where a child snatches them up and waves them above his head. Delia opens her eyes and looks at the dawn.

Summer is warm when the day is being born, the first light peeping out from a hidden place as if still walled in by night. The summer is warm with an inner warmth and light not yet full new, not yet through, before following its course which is also the flow of time. The summer is warm in that decisive instant when the night goes out and the beams of light float in the air, torn from nothingness at that instant that seems to be prolonged forever, forever, forever ...

"This world has gotten so horrible, so ugly!"

"Which world?" Delia asks.

"This very world," the gentleman answers, "in which we both live."

"Which world?" she repeats.

Delia doesn't know the world. Maybe there are several worlds or just one ... maybe ... She thinks of a hidden, very wide world where many people live happily. Delia doesn't know the world. She probably knows her world: walls that rise up, a middle-sized wall, a small wall and a wall grown taller than the others. One wall behind another. They are closing in, forming circles, squares, long angular corridors. Some have roofs; others without them reveal up high a clear summer's sky. Delia knows her world, oh, so small and narrow! Where the walls touch each other. She knows her world: a wardrobe, a sofa-bed, two tables, some chairs and a wide couch where Joaquín sits. A large crystal vase with a red flower, a sweet flower Delia watched grow. There are books everywhere, on the chairs, against the walls, in heaps on the floor. There are creased papers, ballpoint pens of several colors and a dry inkwell that belonged to her grandmother. Delia imagines her grandmother writing long letters to her beloved, dipping the fine nib attached to the penholder in the black ink and filling the white pages in her tiny longhand, telling her lover perhaps the same things Delia says to Joaquín. She thinks back in that time of infinite distance—everything so far away, the seas were lost and the skies untouched!—in that time of infinite distance, where lovers were united in spite of the separation.

"This world is in a bad way. Have you seen the horrors in today's paper? A mother strangled her son, a boy of twelve jumped off a tall building, a child molester raped two girls ... What do you think of this awful world?"

"Which world?" Delia whispers.

"What disgusting times we live in! No more peace, or love, or anything ... "

Is this man very old? Delia wonders. Maybe not so old ... He just dressed old. Delia dresses him up differently: tight blue jeans, a wine-colored polo shirt. That's a lot better! As if he were somebody else ... Delia dresses him as a hippie with long hair and a thick beard, faded pants with frayed cuffs and a lot of medallions dangling on long chains around his neck. Oh no! He's not a hippie. Such an outfit! She dressed him in white. Oh yes, white does suit him! Anyone would think him young, as young as Joaquín. With an open-neck shirt showing his chest. The gentleman's hairs ... and suddenly she thinks of Joaquín's hairs, so stiff and curly. She rests her cheek on Joaquín's chest and his smell envelops her. His own, particular smell! Of cut wood, of recently sawn trees, wafted by the breeze and imbibed by Delia, an aroma that wraps itself around her like a sweet somnolence. The summer is burning in the brilliance of the day, in the exploding exuberant light. The summer is white, with a colorless luminosity and the earth does not remember that almost invisible shadow folded within itself. The summer is vibrant halfway through the day, as if everything were in a vibrant suspense, as if the sun, in the midst of that incredible brilliance, were stopped in the middle of the day, stopped forever, forever, forever ...

"Are you comfortable, Miss?"

"Very."

"Why don't you come and sit over here?"

"Thank you, I'm fine here."

"I'm fine here too, but it would be better with you next to me."

"Thanks, I'm all right here."

"I'm sure you'd feel better here. We'd be closer and could talk more comfortably."

"What's being comfortable?" Delia asks as she looks at the gentleman. He looks so serious!

"One doesn't argue about it, one gets comfortable, that's all."

Yes, the gentleman is very serious, but his eyes dwell on Delia's beautiful legs, so fine and nicely turned. Her legs are crossed under the pleated skirt while Delia looks at the countryside parade through the window. But is not the earth passing in front of Delia's eyes? It is the sky and clusters of clouds and birds in it, flying up to almost touch the clouds. Delia would like to be a bird, with feathered skin, smooth and shiny feathers that would shed the rain. She would like to be a lark, or a woodpecker, always probing the hidden heart of the trees with its beak. She would like to be a hummingbird, an iridescent humming-bird turning round in mid-air, held up in space by a mysterious force, turning around a flower, drinking drop by drop love's essence from the calyx. Delia would like to be as free as the birds. Are they really free? She thinks of migrant birds in their long journeys along the same route, she thinks of the exhaustion of crossing the enormous distances in the obligatory flight from frost, hail, and wind in a winged search for shelter, warmth and a feeling of protection and welcome ... No, birds are not free. They are prisoners dragging invisible chains through the skies. Delia feels free, tied to Joaquín. Free in his high, high flights, free possessing the earth sky, seas and stream. Delia feels free in Joaquín's arms that surround her tenderly, that hold her strongly and Delia would love to be held, embraced, sustained forever in his arms.

"I tell you, Miss, we live in an awful world!"

Delia looks at her world—such a small world!—which fills with light when Joaquín is in it. Lying on the sofa-bed, Delia very close to him while Joaquín sits up, and his hands ... his own extra-special hands ... strong and tender, subtle and wise ... those hands caressing her body, lingering on her round breasts and sweetly pressing her nipples. Those hands that travel along her body, now on her belly, now between her legs. And Joaquín's lips right next to hers and his teeth touching hers, mouths together, and within her mouth that thing alive and trembling, a naked fish caressing the innermost corners of her mouth, so deeply ... and Joaquín's weightless weight on her body ... and Joaquín penetrating her and reaching her most hidden being, that most distant being ... and Delia feels fulfilled, frightened with a fulfillment and abandon that leaves her she knows not where ... Delia forgets her name, her birthdate, her fingerprints, those shallow curving designs on her fingertips ... And Delia is moving, moving with the earth alongside Joaquín with an inebriating and all-enveloping sensation and feels lifted and detached from this earth, projected to those infinite heights she may not reach; or maybe descending, slowly, to those depths beyond the subsoil, beyond the seas, beyond the bottoms of the seas ... Delia loses her memory and all notion of time, hours or minutes, seconds or centuries. Delia forgets yesterday's memories and tomorrow's ... Delia loses herself to find herself panting and wet with different dampnesses, of sweat and of her innermost being. And through half-open lids her eyes perceive a semidarkness where the same old things, though apparently different, are waking up ... and Delia sees Joaquín, asleep with his head on her bare breast.

"Relax, young lady, we'll see what happens. Take it easy. What's the matter with this train?"

The train seems to be stunned, dragging its own weariness. Things go by frighteningly slowly and inadvertently Delia thinks about death, not knowing why. Maybe because, unknowingly, she is looking backward in time, into her world in shadows, no longer illuminated by Joaquín. His books are closed, the sofa-bed is empty, the pens dusty and untouched, and grandmother's inkwell reveals a dark hollow ... Delia thinks that when somebody leaves you it is like a death and if nobody looks at things, they die ... and ... Joaquín left her. Delia saw him in the streets, his arms around Valentina, so close together their figures became one, Valentina cheek-to-cheek with him, his arm tight around her waist—no, not Delia's, but Valentina's—that night when Delia saw her ... that afternoon? morning? dark night? ... walking slowly, pressed close to Joaquín. And Delia didn't know what to do. She wanted to scream, loudly, and could not, to call for help, shout out loud through the immense, bottomless void. She tried to scream, shout, make somebody hear her, hold her up—was Delia falling?—to hear anybody's voice or feel their shadow. And Delia kept on looking without realizing what she was seeing, watching Joaquín going away, close to Valentina, along a little street which Delia sees as long, infinitely long, dark and empty ... only Joaquín getting further away, smaller ... until there is nothing left, not even his shadow.

"This is a very strange train and there is nobody we can call. I wonder what's the matter?"

Delia watches the gentleman who is very close to her, already on his feet, his head out looking at the tilted train. Is the train tired out? Delia understands if the train feels like that. What an enormous effort to perform hour after hour, each minute of each day and night! How exhausted it must be! The same old red flags waved by the same hands, the same green lamps piercing the darkness to illuminate the rails. The same route, back and forth, back and forth, the same people harvesting the same wheat, plowing the fields, making scratches in the earth. But maybe the train discovers the small and large differences that distinguish one thing from another. It is true that nothing is the same ... people or things, streets or mountains. People are all different ... and most of all ... Joaquín. He doesn't resemble anyone. He is above everybody. Nobody is comparable to him. His laughter is different, his voice is different. Joaquín says "Good evening!" and he makes the day begin.

"Okay, it's beginning to move. Look here, lean forward and you'll see the wheels starting to roll. You see, everything is okay. The train has started again."

The gentleman returns to his seat. He is already opening the newspaper he himself folded up a few seconds before. The paper is raised above his knees, level with his hands, and Delia cont inues to look at the earth's procession. The earth is not naked anymore, it is covered with layers of different substances: cement, granite, waxed floors. Covered by bricks, mats and large stone blocks. One can no longer see the sky, the roofs reach up to the clouds. Many people crowd the streets without even turn ing their heads to watch the passing train.

Summer is sweet at sunset before the impenetrable night. Summ er offers a dying sweetness with long, oblique rays, a golden, ethereal light. Summer is sweet when late afternoon traces a curved line and suddenly becomes still, as if the dusk, the dying day could last forever, forever, forever ...

"Are you going to Quietzco?"

"Quietzco?" Delia asks.

"You don't know what it is to be in Quietzco. It's a magic place. The people are different there. They only think of love. Quietzco's streets love, squares love, the towers love ... Did you know that Quietzco has seven towers? They are not very tall, but they shine as if they were near the stars. And what a sea Quietzco has! ... difficult to describe how its waves climb high and then calmly recede to sleep on the shore. Quietzco has a rainbow every afternoon, joining all the towers from end to end. You'll see ... We're near Quietzco now."

How nicely the gentleman speaks! Nobody would have imagined it. Will Quietzco be as pretty as he describes it?

"How long to Quietzco?" Delia asks in a small voice. "Not long now, you can feel Quietzco in the air. Can't you smell the fragrance of roses, of honeysuckle in bloom? Can't you feel the air getting lighter, the sun getting drowsy, everything getting smooth and restful? ... Can't you feel that peace is certain and that love is sweetness, impossible sweetness? ... "

How beautifully he says what she feels and cannot express herself! How he has changed! He has dropped the newspaper on the floor and with it the world, the awful world he mentioned before. Delia is already forgetting the newspaper world: the mother who strangled her son, the youthful suicide, the sadistic rapist of the two girls ... Now she wants to sit very near the gentleman to hear what he has to say about Quietzco. To hear him without straining, restfully. Delia doesn't look anymore at the countryside going by and thinks of a distant Quietzco, the gentleman's Quietzco ... Delia imagines that Joaquín will be there in Quietzco waiting for her to hold her tight, and both will wander through the flower-covered labyrinths with balconies that Joaquín knows so well. Both will walk and walk toward the sea. The train is almost silent, dragged by a growing silence that carries Delia with it, and she is dreaming ...

The train has left behind all living things, cities, fields, people, animals. It also left time in its wake and now is slowly progressing into the shadows. Delia opens her eyes and sees nothing; only dark shadows, one after the other ... one after another as if they were endless. Delia searches for the gentleman in the shadows. The train doesn't move anymore, as if dead. Have we arrived at Quietzco? Delia shouts, "Sir, Sir!" but gets no answer. Where is the gentleman? And in the darkness she stumbles. "Are we already in Quietzco?" Delia asks, out of breath.

"Where? What place? I don't know what you're talking about. Besides," a very different voice says, "I've never seen you before and I don't understand what you're talking about."

"Don't you know me? We've traveled together all the way. I'm asking about Quietzco. Surely you haven't forgotten the things you told me? I'm asking you if the train has reached Quietzco!"

"What's this nonsense about a train? There is no train here. Please, one side, let me go! I'm in a hurry. This woman must be crazy ... " mumbled the man as he walked away.

Delia doesn't know what to do. She is lost in the night, lost in the darkness. She does not know what to do, she feels alone ... with a huge, endless loneliness. She can see nothing in the dark. Large, motionless, silent, shapeless shadows.

Delia screams, "Sir! Sir!" and no one answers. She keeps on searching everywhere, further on, all around. She wanders from one place to another in the shadows. She looks for the gentleman from the train, searching high and low. She looks for her own things, but she has nothing. She carries nothing. Her hands are empty, those hands she is waving in the dark.

The night is heavy with summer. Immense, forsaken, endless night. A night that has forgotten what light is like. And the light is lost, buried on the other side of night. A deathly still night, without wind or noise, as if it were inside her, an inner darkness that has found a home in her and is remaining there forever, forever, forever ...

Translated by Delia Hufton

Breaking the Speed Record

Cristina Peri Rossi

He had begun the fourteenth lap. He was a good runner: the papers announced him as the favorite and even forecast a new record. They had been waiting for a new record for several years, one always waits for this kind of thing. And now this theory of a Brazilian physicist, a madman he thought: that the speed of light does not always remain the same. What could this mean? he asked himself. The papers had said that he was in condition to beat the record. So, had Einstein made a mistake? Or was light also trying to beat a record? In his fifteenth lap the crowds gathered around the track; already he had a good lead, a considerable lead, for he was born to run ... in the warm sunshine, and how warm it was! What did it mean to be born to run? Those lap two-thirds through the race, and still keeping up a wonderful pace" ... long distance runner ... controlled rhythm, when he set off he didn't hesitate a moment in separating himself from the rest and establish from the start who would be the winner. If they thought that he was going to hold himself back, that he would not sprint away from the team in order to save his strength and leave the final pitiless conflict to the last meters, they were mistaken. He was now running, away from the elbows of the other runners, with nobody coming in his way and with all the track empty in front of him, as fast as light, if light is still moving through space at a constant speed. Somewhere else—beyond the oval racing track around which he was running over and over again, as in a tormented dream—his trainer would be anxiously looking at his stopwatch. To think that the speed of this ray of sun shining across the track was not constant! As constant as his pace. Seventeenth lap, only seven more to victory ... this ray of sunshine racing like a breathless runner. The rest had remained behind, he had passed them several laps before; now it was the case of beating someone else, the legendary runner who had established the last record, the final record up till now, if only the speed of light would remain constant. At the twenty-first lap he began to suspect that he would accomplish what had been forecast; in spite of being tired, his rhythm was excellent, he was running along the track with a steady step, his movements were elastic and light, "as light as a gazelle," as the announcer put it, "elegant, as if running did not cause him any problem." He had a confused glimpse of the faces of the spectators; there was no need to see them more clearly, only the track turning in his mind . . . and his trainer would keep his eyes unremittingly fixed on the stopwatch; now he was passing the young runner with red hair and blue shorts whose breathless panting did not bode well, next runner number seventeen, completely outpaced by the rest, several laps behind him in one of the laps which he had run earlier on, with the brightness of the sun on the track. Everyone's eyes were clouding over, blinking through the drops of sweat; there remained only three more laps according to his calculations, three more laps before the little man with the flag designed like a chess board would let it drop at the moment he crossed the finish line, the end of the track, the ribbon which meant that the mad race was over . . . and then he heard a shout, a single shout, it was his trainer calling out assuredly that he was about to accomplish what had been forecast, that he was about establish a new record, the best in the world in the ten thousand meters on the level as flat as a pan.

It was then that he felt an enormous desire to stop. Not that he was tired; he had trained for a long time and all the experts felt that he would succeed; in fact, he was only running in order to establish a new record. But, now, this irresistible desire to stop. To lie on the side of the track and never get up again. Attention: it is forbidden to touch a runner once he has fallen. If he gets up under his own power, he can continue the race. But no one is allowed to help him stand up again. This uncontrollable desire to sit at the side of the track and look up at the sky. Surely there would be trees, he thought. Interwoven branches, quivering leaves and at the top, perhaps a nest. The smallest leaves shaking in the breeze, this same breeze which alters the speed of light, no longer constant, according to the Brazilian physicist. "I am nothing exceptional," he had said a few nights before to an elderly admirer, "I am just somebody who knows how to organize time."

His trainer waved to him excitedly: only one more lap. Only one. And his speed had not diminished. He passed a runner who was panting with his hand on his ribs. That dry pain under the ribs, the tightness that makes it so difficult to breathe. Once it begins, the race is over and you might as well get off the track—although one does not do so out of a sense of pride. That discomfort in the spleen, as he had learned during his years of training. An organ of which we are rarely conscious because it only troubles us when we have made an unusual effort, when we have run too much. And now this unknown and uncontrollable longing to stop, to rest by the side of the track, look at the trees, breathe deeply. The laps are all the same, they merge in one's memory and one no longer knows whether it is the twenty-third or the twenty-fourth, the sixteenth or the seventeenth, as it happened to that boy who thought he had finished and threw himself on the ground. Somebody—most likely his trainer or one of the judges—went near him and without touching him, informed him that he was mistaken (he had figured it wrong) and there were still three laps to run. And the poor chap with his muscles in a knot. Unable to get up. And if he did get up, it would be only to start running again, unless he fainted beforehand. But nothing like this would ever happen to him. He ran with ease, as if it were the most natural thing to do, as if he could run forever. With a rhythm which was constant, with an unvarying stride, unlike light which had deceived him and which now, it seemed, was moving at uneven speed. He was about to beat the record. But what now of the indescribable pleasure of stopping, sliding gently towards the side, the side of the track, a few meters away from the end, just a little before the finish line, slipping slowly to the ground and lifting his head up ... the tall trees, the blue sky, the slow-moving clouds, the curly, bunched-up branches ... the leaves quiver, he looks upwards and watches the rhythmic flight of the birds ... he does not hear the hubbub of the people crowding around him; undoubtedly they are reproaching him, insulting him, his trainer is furious ... to see the rest of the runners go past him, see their shorts, some are panting heavily, one is raising his hand to his chest, you will not finish, you will not reach the end; but high up the trees float in the air, in an unreal atmosphere, unseen by anyone else; now comes the blond fellow suffering from a cramp and beginning to limp ... have I seen that bird before? ... and the announcer describing the unexplainable event. His speed had been constant but suddenly, as that of light, it longed to stop. And he raised his eyes to the sky.

Translated by Psiche Bertini Hughes

Big-bellied Cow

Nélida Piñón

It was not really a burial, it was more of a simple ceremony. The family had been reluctant, but when he demanded their appearance he was imposing an authority that had been obeyed ever so many times. There ran through him now that effort that unlocks life as everything drains off in grief.

It had been difficult carrying the animal. And that place had been chosen because it was precisely there that he had come to know the nature of its species.

Although his wife resisted—you're out of your mind, what will the neighbors say—with the help of his oldest son he opened the great pit, despite the animal having grown thin in its illness. Even so, a great deal of earth was needed to cover those horns. The meanness of a space which his arms could still measure.

"Leave me now." After dismissing the temptations of the world, he looked at the soft earth piled up as a protection. How could he abandon Dapple to animals who would come to eat the remains, and that flesh would soon be divided among beaks and on its way to strange insides after having fallen outside there, and it only brought grief to his heart when he thought of it. Linked to Dapple by so many mysteries, those homey patches that did away with meaning and which only he could understand. It had to be that way, in any other way the transfer would not have taken place, and he would never murder out of love and habit a companion in life, which is the way of eternal possession; it was death by capitulation.

He had not even seen Dapple born. He had bought that foolish appearance when it was still young, for unknown reasons in a marketplace far from home. He had chosen her absent-mindedly, as one who had grown tired of evaluating living things, tying the cord about her neck; the stumps of something soon to be born were piercing her head. When he reached home, a great excitement announced the birth of his grandchild.

"It's a boy, Father," that huge man who considered himself the owner of the father who had conceived him came to announce. Even though the new fatherhood had softened his usual crudeness, the son lamented, but he calmed down with the idea of a grandson. His path was growing shorter, that much the world was making clear. The dialogue died out like an act of accommodation, and he forgot about the animal in need of care, and the grandson who was already upsetting the rhythm of the household. His wisdom excluded pleasant feelings.

There she was in the pasture. As she ate grass, her frailness was not aware of to whom she had come to belong. He smoked his pipe, thinking that things are acquired so that they may start growing. And they were like that for a long time, one close to the other, the man entering into the growth of the animal.

When he needed his neighbor's bull to breed Dapple, he became confused, not knowing how to proceed. Which was not proper. After all, such an innocent request for men of the land who had acquired the habit of yielding to anything that brings on growth. He led her along with the shame of one bringing a daughter to receive the son of some stranger, to lend that beloved flesh to the unknown lust of a procreator. Dapple was innocent, and he masked his embarrassment.

He hid those notions in front of the owner of the bull who was to make a calf in Dapple. But he examined the bull imprisoned in his pen with rage. Still covering up, he asked his neighbor for help. "Get a farmhand, I've got a cramp and I have to go take care of it." He took care of it more than was necessary, calculating the time minutely. When he came back, docilely, like one who had condoned the use, Dapple was through. On the road the man whistled, pretending to ignore the animal. The fear of perceiving something that was visibly changed. What would he have done had he perceived the wound—not what one thinks of as mutilated and requiring care, but something which is done for such a fate and which is resented for precisely that reason. He wanted to say: look, Dapple, you don't know that I'm your owner and that's why this thing bothers me; if you knew, it would be easy to explain why I let it be done, but the fact is that we're never aware that someone owns us. And he made an effort, but he never reached that clarity once and for all which would release him and let him live with the earth and its sacred fruit.

Until the calf was born, he ignored her pregnancy, her quivering belly. The whole blame was on him for having allowed the rape. He felt sorry for the animal, something justified only by friendship. The awareness that he used, in its measure and clearness, to judge people of the house, he began to use on Dapple, and more intensely. She had become the release of his secrets. In spite of his affliction, many were the times that he confessed before the animal.

When the cow's body had grown large, bulging out on both sides, he finally responded to the vitality of that growth and came to accept things in their proper places. He became adjusted to the pain that Dapple would suffer. For there was in things a spot of light proportionate to their acceptance. He watched over the brevity of that opulence, and she was silent as she slowly browsed, her eyes so sad, an acute melancholy drawing off whatever blame there was. Like any animal that is relieved, the prosperous belly was being fed.

Interrupting his peace, the oldest grandson asked: "Cows are nice, aren't they, grandfather?"

"Nice, yes."

"So nice that you'd like to eat them."

"Eat what, boy?" Annoyed, he looked at his grandson's face, at that avidity which was corrupting his old age.

"Just any old piece. But I feel sorry, that's why I wouldn't. Grandfather, Dapple is a big-bellied cow, isn't she?"

"A what?"

"A big-bellied cow. A cow that's grown so much that all of a sudden she's going to change into something else."

"thing else."

"Something like that. Big-bellied cow, big-bellied woman, big-bellied dog, isn't it all the same thing? They get so big you think they're never going to stop, but I like it. Everything that grows should be respected."

"Who taught you that?"

"I learned it all by myself. I only said it so nice because it came out together."

"Came out together?"

"What I was thinking and what I imagined."

"Oh, I see."

"Like, what would you think if Dapple had baby chicks?"

"Baby chicks?"

"If everything that came out of her came out chicks, how many chicks would Dapple have?"

"That's foolish. Where did you hear of a cow having chicks?"

"Did you ask Dapple if she'd rather have chicks?"

"No."

"Then try to find out before you get mad at me."

The boy's appearance grew calmer as he went away. The man did not lose heart, he tried to forget his grandson with the same harshness of a person who forgets other things which still mattered.

When it was time for the birth of the calf, the patient work was taking place in Dapple. The drivel was flooding out of her mouth just as the blood would flow when the heavy weight had finished deforming her. His wife and son helped him until the gelatinous thing appeared, filthy, raising itself on indecisive legs now in a leap of life, as if inside the big-bellied cow—that grandson could make expressions useless in the same way that he deformed the appearance of branches with his jack-knife—it had been standing for a long time, strolling over the pastures of the world.

With time, Dapple grew used to those uncomfortable maternal duties, the small creature beside her emptying her udder, the exact abundance of that white liquid which would even produce butter, a splendid nature that aimed at fullness and avoided any loss. The strength of the animal had been passed on to the calf, but even so it could benefit man.

One afternoon, in that same pasture, he went over to Dapple. He looked her over with complete audacity, as a person who is shortly going to be lost and stops to find out up to what point he has been saved, how much more he understood something that let itself be possessed. More and more tired, he became aware of a briefness in life, so brief that the time of a man was measured according to the action of that same man. Demanding the dignity of analysis in order to understand the world, his life, which rested on a daily sharing of life with an animal. Forced into that mutual contemplation, they would perceive in the end which of them would let himself be more easily exploited.

"Here, Dapple."

The cow approached, her balance softening the nerves that might have cropped out as she walked. And the man and the cow looked at each other. In spite of the meanness of things, any effort at all would clarify what not even the vitality of a friendship had managed to alter. The man owed himself a painful exhaustion in order to understand a friend. A pause invigorated them. He examined that animal who had brought him prosperity, never in revolt against her species, and who belonged to him without such a possession appearing as sores on her body. He did not know whether the animal had given in or whether he had bowed before that animal's necessary habits. "Now, Dapple, we're going to find out what this feeling is like."

The purchase of an animal was a kind of slavery, once its benefit was found, there should be a peaceful clarification of what there is between a cow and a man. But as he accepted the small animal and it grew, the man softened too, as a person stretches out on his bed with fatigue, free of the aberrations that certain kinds of work always instill, free of the life that distinguishes him without the least selection. Could the complete alliance between the man and that cow have been mutual contemplation and time passed? He was feeling more and more isolated under the eyes of the cow, in search of gentle solutions. His mouth wide-open and the tight pregnancy of the animal. She was ugly, a cow was, and he tacitly recognized it. The deformation of her loins, the sharp horns that did not even make use of the ferocity of their natural form. The man said: "Is a cow a coward too?" The animal next to her owner, given over to the analysis that was being made of her.

"So cowardly that she accepts my animosity, was that how I understood her?" Then the shortness of the day, and the man was content with what forgiveness had eliminated.

The man spoke, what joins us together is your age. And tranquilly he wanted rest. But even that was not enough for someone who wanted so much. More than age, the living together assured the security of the animal, who accepted all and any land to feed upon. The gentleness that he was analyzing was precisely what had become settled in his flesh, in his time as a man. The resemblance between the man and that cow was the misshapen companionship of those who are equal in the difficult struggle. He patted the animal's head, which she lowered softly in obedience.

"I never want your obedience again."

As one who settles into her comfort, the animal did not move at all. The same sad look lost behind the mountains. Irritated, he rejected that head. Rebelling not against the animal who was enjoying the satisfaction of suffering in her body, but against the life that linked him to things, to that cow, affording him the skill of hesitation. Under the aggrieved eyes of the cow, he had the bitter joy of discovering himself being the only thing looked at. The cow's complete look, along with its intensity, did not leave him, he was the universal cause of an animal. A sob tightened his world, and he knew that he was joined to the sad beast whose solitude embodied his. Having come together in time, identical old age made them obstinate. The cow's wrinkled hide, the forewarning of an illness that would bring her down, and the man's easily irritated skin, not that any wound could be seen, for that was the destruction shown by the cow, but rather a texture without moral uplift, a perplexity in the face of such full powers. The grandchildren were spread over the land, the cow had also spread so many things, even her manure had been a splendid performance, her duty to man.

It bothered him to know that he was the owner of one who, not sensing possession, let herself be dominated by a look, the only virtue of the surrender. Later, things grew calm. The abandonment of old people who can barely resist. Everything in him was tumbling down, his sex too, he would never make another child. She too, the cow, could not give shelter to new flesh.

With time they ceased their examination. They were invaded by the desire of one who does not move. It was understanding. And the cow had to fall ill. The man recognized that servitude and he played the game with death. He pretended not to see the illness that was invading that carcass, the protruding bones were the illness that was establishing itself inside. Severe, the man struggled so that she would die in peace, so that the cow's freedom would not extinguish his.

When his son suggested that the animal be put to death, he sternly hid his face. At dinner, despite his hunger, his eating was different. He abandoned the noise of chunks being chewed and ate elegantly, not letting greed interfere with the operation. His wife looked at their sons, daughters-in-law, grandchildren. A look that communicated the arrogance she had seen in the father. But he did not notice, he had been able to forget the aggressiveness and strength of the meat of the usual meal. After that he returned to the barn, where the cow had discreetly begun to die.

Until she died. Then, energetically, the father notified the family: "Everybody will come to Dapple's burial." Ignoring the reaction provoked, he contented himself with the furtive look of that obedience.

Quite early in the morning they began the work of removal. She was so thin that her bones were showing, but it was not for that reason that Dapple was ugly, ugly, yes, because her appearance was fatal, but the kind of beauty that goes with suffering was there, expressed so well by her horns as they pointed up and cleaned the sky. They dragged the body along the ground over to the wooden cart drawn by other powerful cows who were indifferent to him. The dust cloud filled his heart, and he was made contrite by that scar on the earth, that last piece of skillful work done by Dapple, the cow, his friend. Then she was borne to the pasture, where lost in their reflections, they could recognize things in that legitimate obscurantism that comes with lighting a candle in the darkness: in the beginning the darkness and the shadows are the limiting outline of what is revealed and learned.

Sliding into the pit, the animal remained there. The man went about covering her, and since everything was made of earth, there was not even any need to choose. Veiling forever the softness of those horns that had been reserved for peace.

The family left him as he had requested. He was going to stay there until he was drained dry. From that instant on he would go with other animals, his task would stay the same, except for his heart, for his tranquility of a man who can also die.

Translated by Gregory Rabassa

To Seize the Earth

Josefina Pla

The adobe house stands beside the river. It was among the first to enjoy such luxury, and Don Blas had been obliged to work hard on it, for in this new land he, like everyone else, had had to draw strength from weakness and turn his gentle-born hand to many an unexpected task. The thick walls and thatched roof keep the house agreeably cool even on the hottest days. Ursula, the old Indian woman, has sprinkled the earthen floor with water and scattered paraíso leaves on it. Outside, the sun is burnishing the topmost leaves of coconut palms and banana trees. When Blas turns his head on the pillow he can see, through breaks in the fence, the glitter of distant yellow waves: the river, running high. From time to time, a castaway island of water hyacinth floats past, carrying with it the mystery of the jungle depths, knotted occasionally in the scaly coils of a viper.

How often, in those forty years, has Blas de Lemos thought to follow the path traced by the water hyacinths! ... But he could never bring himself to tear his feet from this warm, red earth, blinding in its splendor, seductive in its docility, so different from the stark, dry land where he was born—how long ago? ... seventy years, seventy-five? ... He has lost count, for the stars here are not the same, and a different calendar of harvests and disillusionment exists. His own land never smiled, but the soil was fertile and reliable. The earth here seems soft and generous, yet utterly lacks discipline ... Helpless on his bed, Blas watches the somber mountains and gray plateaus glide past his inner eye, the interminable wheatfields, the vineyards laden with globes of sugar blackening under the sun. The memory of the sea opens then in his breast, a wide, salty, bluegreen chasm. Never again will he see it: of that he is sure now. Never again. It has been over forty years since he first trod these banks, two years since he has been nailed into this coffin of a bed, lying parallel to the river, and with each clump of water hyacinth that passes, he sends a saudade floating to the distant sea; though he is unsure of late whether it is the somnolent blue Mediterranean for which he thirsts, or the furious green Atlantic, mad with solitude, from which he barely escaped on his way here so many years ago. How remote all of that is now. How conceited he had been. And how adroitly God uses men when they think they are exercising their own free will ...

Since yesterday he has been failing. That is why he had Ursula notify the Franciscan, Fray Pérez.

Ursula squats on her heels at the foot of the bed, chewing tobacco, her movements small and precise. She is quieter than the breeze in the grass outside. Through the slits at the sides of the typoi she wears, he catches sight of her coppery breasts, large and pendulous, like certain native fruits. How old is Ursula? ... Fifty? Perhaps younger. She was barely twelve when he, half lecherous, half amused, chose her as a pledge of alliance and unity from the nubile flock offered by a chieftain in full regalia. This old Ursula (whose age is counted not by her own years but by his, by the years of Don Blas) has hair as black and smooth as the wings of a crow, whereas he, Don Blas, is balding at the temples, and his remaining hair clings in whitish tufts to his small, wrinkled head. Years ago, so many years, his young wife Isabel, barely more than a child, used to stroke it:

"Pure gold, my lord."

Ursula, too, calls him che caraí.

She moves about the room, silent and slow, birdwing black hair. On the surface of her face that is like cracked, oiled wood, Blas perceives with subtle melancholy the lees of the years-long male squeezings overlying the imperturbable course of that dark blood. His other Indian woman, María, had died young, giving birth to his only daughter—Cecilia, the daughter of his old age. Ursula, on the other hand, had given him six sons. Six vigorous youths. Youths? They are already men, some of them graying, scattered now among the border towns and forts, even the last, Diego, the youngest. He, Blas, had never been able to get along very well with his sons. They had always been closer to their mother. Even when, without speaking, they merely allowed her to serve them. From time to time they would converse with her in their own language, a language whose secrets he, Blas, was never entirely able to plumb. Almost as soon as they were able to walk, recent arrivals to life on this earth, they knew an infinity of things about it that he, Blas de Lemos, would forever find a mystery. He always felt when he was near them, even holding them on his lap, that the world of those creatures through whose veins his blood irremediably coursed was a world apart: a world in which he, Blas de Lemos, was called only to contribute semen, declining, diminished in the daily offering, while the woman silently took it up, growing with it until she could nurse, at her long, dark breasts, sons of a color like that of the earth, always strange somehow, their full lips silent, their dark eyes glowing with exclusive knowledge, so that when they said "oré ... " they traced around themselves a circle with no room in it even for him, their father, their progenitor; a space wrought from the jungle, where mysterious cries spiralled upward in the half-light of a copper planet. A world in which he had never been entirely at ease. He thought of Diego, his last-born son, the only one who had inherited his blue eyes. Blas loved him above all the others for that reason, although he never told him so; that color seemed to cast a little light on the dark path between their souls ... Diego, far away like all the rest ...

"Did you send word to Fray Pérez, Ursula?"

"I sent word, che caraí."

A voice near the house shoos away an insect. Cecilia. Cecilia, with her fair skin, her black braids, her eyes that would seem Andalusian were they not set so high. Blas thinks of her with tenderness. She is betrothed. Young Velazco, the youngest son of his old friend Pedro Velazco, who has just died, is to be her husband. She moves through the doorway as though borne on the abundant light: Cecilia with her clean typoi, the flower in her braid, the diligence of her bare feet.

"How do you feel, father? ... "

The Spanish trills softly on her lips. You might think she came from some unknown province of Spain. The girl squats near the head of her father's bed and takes up her embroidery hoop. A delicate wheel of convergent rays is beginning to appear on the fabric stretched over it. Her needle flashes in and out. From time to time a small brown hand reaches up to rest on her father's forehead. The shadows slowly draw in toward the bottom of the fence. The yellow of the river dissolves in a flood of sunlight. A tall shadow looms in the doorway. Cecilia hurries to welcome the lean, dark-skinned Franciscan, kisses his hand. Then she and Ursula withdraw to the back of the house. Only God may witness this conversation between Blas de Lemos and his confessor.

Father Pérez has left, promising to return with the Holy Oils. He has opened a painful furrow of light in the conscience of Blas de Lemos. Under his stern interrogation, shades long since at rest have risen up to drift like somnambulists into the hard, slanting shaft: Doña Isabel, her image polished like the chiaroscuro of an ancient relief. Abandoned so very young in the Castilian manor. The promise he had often repeated to himself, that he would send for her, was an empty one. She was pregnant when he left. Years later he heard she had given birth to a son; that she had named him Blas, after her forgetful husband. Young Blas—but no, he would no longer have been a youth; a man by then, with a yellow beard, perhaps, and blue eyes—his son had died in that battle . . . where was it now? . . . ah, yes, Lepanto, where the Spanish forces are said to have gained such high honor . . . He tries in vain to imagine the son he never saw . . . And Isabel? It has been years since he has had news of her. Perhaps she has died. She might be living still, a recluse in her manor or withdrawn into a convent, like so many other abandoned wives and sweethearts. He tries to imagine Isabel as she must be now, if she is still alive, old and ailing: impossible. He sees her stubbornly girlish, fair and slim as a stalk of wheat. Forty-one years . . . Who would think time could pass so quickly? Who would think such memories could endure in the far reaches of the soul? When all was said and done, the dream had not been sad; but he would like to awaken . . .

"Have you laid out the fur-lined jerkin for me today, Doña Isabel? . . . I am going hunting."

"I have, my lord. And Gonzalvico has greased the new baldric."

How far away all of that is now! And how fast the long road passed under his feet as he battled by day and kept watch by night, arquebus in hand, whenever he was not sowing his white seed in that dark current that received it impassively, turning a shade lighter, only never in the gaze!

"Not many people will hasten to come here. Poor land, Blas."

"Yes, Pedro. We are going to be very lonely."

"We will have to produce people. By the sheer force of our loins! . . . " (Laughter).

The first years were hectic, fraught with trials. Years rich in danger and poor in rewards. Blas was called to go with Ayolas to El Chaco. His childhood friend Jerónimo Ortiz, he of the perpetual smile, the ready guitar, went instead. He did not come back. He, Blas, could have been a commander: he preferred to be among those bearing arms. Up one trail with Irala, down another with Cabeza de Vaca, from one settlement to the next. And when his left arm was crippled beyond use, he took up the pen. He had written a great deal. Bulletins and messages, pages that had travelled, folded and sealed, along elfin roads cleared today, devoured by the jungle on the morrow; or had dreamt through months of wind and salt in the cabin of a brigantine lost between sky and sea, homeward bound ... And he had written his memoirs. He wrote down what he did, and also a little of what he was unable to do in these meek, tenacious lands. He kept the bundle of papers under his pillow. Part of his conversation with Fray Pérez had been about the papers.

"I have not decided yet, Father, what I want to do with them. If, when you come to give me Extreme Unction, my right hand points to the pillow ... take them, Father, take them and burn them, because that will be what I have resolved, the better to lay my soul to rest ... "

"It will be done as you say, my son."

There they are, under his pillow, and still he does not know what he is going to do with them. The title, "Anthology of Adventures and Crucible of Disillusionments of a Spanish Gentleman in the Indies," is somewhat pretentious. He has not reread them for some time, yet he can recall whole paragraphs:

" ... These are green lands, lands of a green so rich that you would swear they had taken for themselves all the green that is wanting in Castile. And there are strange flowers and beasts, such as our father Adam must have seen when he awoke, full grown and without remorse, on that first morning. But these swift, gaudy sunsets know nothing of the measured, lordly cadences of our skies; and these extravagant trees helmeted with pieces of the dawn are naught but show, mere flowers; they bear no fruit capable of nourishing and satisfying a man ... "

" ... And you embrace them, they never reject you, and they have none of the coyness of pampered ladies; yet you emerge from their arms like one stricken with dropsy, who cannot quench his thirst for all the water he may drink. And your ear will wither before it hears the words you dream of, and your tongue will long in vain to surrender its sweetness, for there will be no vessel to receive it ... "

(Isabel, Isabel! ...)

" ... And they carry your sons in their arms until their backs break, and give them the breast until their beauty is ruined. And you could kill those sons and they would say nothing, but you feel that although you could sacrifice them like Abraham, they are not your sons at all, for when you look at them there is in their eyes a secret passageway, through which they slip away from you and go to find their mother in corners known only to them, where you can never reach them ... "

" ... And you give them orders and they obey you with lowered eyes; you wish to surprise them in rebellion, to no avail; their lips close over thoughts you can never make your own and their feet spin paths you can never unravel. And their obedience cheats you of their love, and their silence is peopled with strange songs ... "

" ... And you taught them to play your clear-toned guitar, so different from those strange instruments of theirs that sound like stifled moans, and they learned quickly; but when they began to play alone, their music was no longer the music you knew, and it was like a dream in which someone has changed your face and your mirror no longer recognizes you ... "

" ... And they listen attentively to the men of God who bring His Word, and gladly receive the waters of baptism; but you know that when they have welcomed it forever it will not be the same, because they will have discovered that He can also have a face like theirs, and they will change the face He has ... "

Heresy as well. What can a white man, twice lost in the dark entrails of this land, write to save himself from oblivion? ... Heresy. A man has sons to recover himself in them; Blas de Lemos has not been able to find himself in one of his many sons. Only Diego's eyes shine from time to time in his memory, like lamps that seek to reveal something to him. Under the pillow, the bundle of papers rustles softly when Blas de Lemos ever more sorrowfully turns his head ...

The sun has moved to the other side of the roof and strikes the wall over the bed. Warm shadows begin to lengthen toward the river. From time to time the cry of a sailor is heard. Blas asks, or thinks he asks:

"Whose voices are those? ... Are there ships from Spain coming in? ... "

"They are ships, father, that are preparing to settle Buenos Aires. Don Juan de Garay himself is sending them."

Buenos Aires. He was there. He tasted the hunger, knew the terror. It no longer makes him uneasy. His tired eyes open to distinguish with difficulty the faces that bend over him in the dusk, laden with dreams that are beginning to retreat from him along with the memories: Ursula, Cecilia, young Velazco. Cecilia's betrothed. He is a good-looking young man, light-skinned, his smooth, dark hair softened with tawny lights, black eyes set deep above the broad cheekbones. Despite his twenty-five years, he has no beard. The youths of this land tend to be beardless ... Blas gives his blessing to the young couple kneeling beside the bed. Into his soul, where loneliness begins to swell, a strange tremor seeps, faint as a wisp of smoke: where will she go, this child of his whose union he has just blessed, with that mystery and secret wisdom of hers, forever interdict for him? ... The bundle of papers rustles again under his pillow ...

The yellow river, has it turned to blood? ... Blas floats in a world half shadow, half light. Someone bends over him, solemn and slow. It is the Franciscan, Fray Pérez, accompanied by an acolyte. He has brought the Holy Oils. The time has come for Blas de Lemos, and though he may have lived the life of a sinner he will die a Christian death. The ceremony unfolds among the murmured Latin phrases and soft weeping: Cecilia. It is finally over. Ursula rearranges the bedclothes over the body, now consecrated for the earth, of Blas de Lemos, and returns to her vigil at the foot of the bed. Blas drifts slowly back toward his castaway light. At times everything appears to gleam with the brilliance of copper: then all is mist and someone invisible is carrying him gently on a litter along unfamiliar roads, toward something also unfamiliar, but which for him can be called peace. Now and then voices buzz softly in the shadows. The clouded glass clears: Someone is kneeling at the head of his bed.

"Your blessing, father."

It is Diego, his youngest son. All his sons were far away, but Diego has come.

At the foot of the bed, Ursula automatically wipes her hands on her skirt, stammers in surprise. Diego was very far away ... now he is here ...

"I am going to Buenos Aires with Juan de Garay. Your blessing, father."

Blas's hand falters upward like an old bird, coming to rest uncertainly on the forehead of young Diego. He looks at him: sees the blue eyes, strange in the earthen color of the face. As with the running brooks of his childhood, Blas de Lemos can see into their farthest depths. In this dark face, rough-hewn but noble, in these blue eyes, Blas de Lemos recovers, for a dazzling instant, his own long-vanished youth. Here, in these eyes, he discovers the crazed and dreaming blood destined to spill without repose or truce over the four corners of the earth.

"God bless you and lead you by the hand. May your blood prosper and your descendants be many ... "

Perhaps he also meant to say: joyful. But he is unable to say it, he does not know why.

He is happy nonetheless, with a joy that is almost painful, almost like coming to life again. The blue eyes seem to multiply into infinity, peopling a boundless space with their glint of hope.

Infinitely tired, Blas de Lemos moves his hand toward the head of the bed.

It would seem that he is trying to touch his temple. But the Franciscan, motionless in his corner, understands. He approaches the deathbed, slides his hand under the pillow. The bundle of papers passes quickly into his sleeve. One last look at the bed where the reddish light of the candle plays; at Ursula, her arms hanging at her sides; at Cecilia, wiping away her tears with a corner of her white shawl. He leaves the house. Blas has seen nothing, heard nothing. He has returned to his world of alternating light and shadow, the light fading as the shadows deepen.

At dawn, something like a cloud or an enormous wing veils the irresolute sky outside the door. Ursula and Cecilia have run to the river bank. If Blas were awake, he would know it was the ships setting sail with the colonists of Santa María del Buen Ayre aboard. But Blas de Lemos is lying motionless on the bed. His right hand is reaching down, as if to seize the earth.

Translated by Catherine Rodríguez-Nieto

Park Cinema

Elena Poniatowska

Señorita:

As of today, you will have to strike my name from the list of your admirers. Perhaps I ought not to inform you of this decision, but to do so would be to betray a personal integrity that has never shied away from the exigencies of the Truth. By thus divorcing myself from you, I am acting in accordance with a profound change in spirit, which leads me to the decision never again to number myself among the viewers of your films.

This afternoon—or rather, this evening—you have destroyed me. I do not know whether this matters to you, but I am a man shattered to pieces. Do you understand what I am saying? A devotee who has followed your image on the screens of first-run houses and neighborhood theaters, a loving critic who would justify the very worst of your moral behavior, I now swear on my knees to renounce you forever, though a mere poster from *Forbidden Fruit* is enough to shake my resolve. As you may see, I am yet a man seduced by appearances.

Comfortably ensconced in my seat I was one in a multitude, a creature lost in an anonymous darkness, who suddenly felt himself caught up in a personal sadness, bitter and inescapable. It was then that I was truly myself, the loner who suffers and now addresses you. For no brotherly hand reached to touch mine. While you were calmly destroying my heart on the screen, all those around me stayed passionately true. Yes, there was even one scoundrel who laughed shamelessly while I watched you swoon in the arms of that abominable suitor who dragged you to the final extremes of human degradation.

And let me ask you this, señorita: Is he worthless whose every ideal is suddenly lost?

You will say I am a dreamer, an eccentric, one of those meteorites that fall to earth against all calculated odds. You may dispense with your hypotheses: it is I who is judging you, and do me the favour of taking greater responsibility for your actions, and before you sign a contract or accept a co-star, do consider that a man such as I might be among your future audience and might receive a fatal blow. It is not jealousy that makes me speak this way, but, believe me: in *Slaves of Desire*, you were kissed, caressed and assaulted to excess.

I do not know whether my memory makes me exaggerate, but in the cabaret scene there was no reason for you to half-open your lips in that way, to let your hair down over your shoulders, and to tolerate the impudent manners of that sailor who yawns as he leaves you, who abandons you like a sinking ship after he has drowned your honor on the bed.

I know that actors owe a debt to their audience; that they, in a sense, relinquish their free will and give themselves up to the capricious desires of a perverse director; moreover, I know that they are obliged to follow point by point all the deficiencies and inconsistencies of the script they must bring to life, but let me state that everyone, even in the worst of contingencies, retains a minimum of initiative, a fragment of freedom— and you could not or chose not to exercise it.

If you were to take the trouble, you might say in your defense that the very things I am accusing you of today you have done ever since your screen debut. True, and I am ashamed to admit that I cannot justify my feelings. I undertook to love you just as you are. Pardon—as I imagined you to be. Like anyone who has ever been disillusioned, I curse the day that linked my life with your cinematographic destiny. And I want to make clear that I accepted you when you were an obscure newcomer, when no one had ever heard of you, when they gave you the part of that streetwalker with crooked stockings and worn-down heels, a part no decent woman could have accepted. Nonetheless I forgave you, and in that dirty and indifferent theater I hailed the birth of a star. It was I who discovered you, I was the only one who could perceive your soul, immaculate as it was despite your torn handbag and your sheepish manner. By what is dearest to you in the world? Forgive the bluntness of my outburst.

Your mask has slipped, señorita. I have come to see the vileness of your deceit. You are not that creature of delights, that tender, fragile dove I had grown used to, that swallow innocent in flight, your face in my dreams hidden by a lacy veil—no, you are a tramp through and through, the dregs of the earth, a passing fancy in the worst sense of the word. From this moment on, my dear señorita, you must go your way and I mine. Go on, go, keep walking the streets, I have already drowned in your sewer like a rat. But I must stress that I continue to address you as "señorita" solely because, in spite of the blows you have dealt me, I am still a gentleman. My saintly old mother had instilled in my innermost being the importance of always keeping up appearances. Images linger, my life as well. Hence ... señorita. Take it, if you will, as a sort of desperate irony.

I have seen you lavish kisses and receive caresses in hundreds of films, but never before did you receive your fortunate partner into your spirit. You kissed with simplicity like any good actress: as one would kiss a cardboard cutout. For—and I wish to make this clear once and for all—the only worthwhile sensuality is that which involves the soul, for the soul surrounds our body as the skin of the grape its pulp, as the peel contains the juice within. Before now, your love scenes did not upset me, for you always preserved a shred of dignity albeit profaned; I was always aware of an intimate rejection, a last-minute withdrawal that redeemed my anguish and consoled my lament. But in *Rapture in the Body*, your eyes moist with love, you showed me your true face, the one I never wish to see again. Go on, confess it: you really are in love with the scoundrel, that second-rate flash-in-the-pan comedian, aren't you? What avails an impudent denial? At least every word of mine, every promise I made, was true: and every one of your movements was the expression of a spirit that had surrendered itself. Why did you toy with me the way they all do? Why did you deceive me like all women deceive, wearing one different mask after another? Why would you not reveal all at once, in the beginning, the detestable face that now torments me?

This drama of mine is practically metaphysical, and I can find no possible solution. I am alone in the nighttime of my delirium. Well, all right, my wife does understand me completely, and at times she even shares in my distress. We were still revelling in the sweet delights appropriate to newlyweds when, our defenses down, we saw the first of your films. Do you still remember it? The one about the dumb athletic diver who ended up at the bottom of the sea because of you, wetsuit and all. I left the theater completely deranged and it would have been futile effort to try to keep it from my wife. But at least she was completely on my side, and had to admit that your deshabilles were truly splendid. Nor did she find it inconvenient to accompany me to the cinema six more times, believing in good faith that the enchantment would

be broken by routine. But, alas, things grew worse with every new film
of yours that opened. Our family budget underwent serious modifica-
tions in order to permit cinema attendance on the order of three times
a week. And it goes without saying that after each cinematographic
session we spent the rest of the night arguing. All the same, my mate
did not get ruffled. For after all, you were but a defenseless shadow, a
two-dimensional silhouette, subject to the deficiencies of light. And my
wife good-naturedly accepted as her rival a phantom whose appearance
could be controlled at will, although she wasted no opportunity to have
a good laugh at our expense. I remember her pleasure on the fatal night
when, due to a technical difficulties, you spoke for a good ten minutes
with an inhuman voice, almost that of a robot, going from a falsetto to
deepest bass. And while we're on the subject of your voice, I would have
you know that I set myself to studying French because I could not resign
myself to the abridged subtitles in Spanish, colourless and misleading. I
learned to decipher the melodious sound of your voice, and with that accomplishment came the intolerable scourge of hearing atrocious words
directed at your person or issuing from your very lips. I longed for the
time when these words had reached me by way of a priggish translation;
now, they were slaps in the face.

The most serious aspect to this whole thing is that my wife is showing
disquieting signs of ill-humor. Allusions to you and to your on-screen
conduct are more and more frequent and ferocious. Lately she has concentrated on your intimate apparel and tells me that I am talking in vain
to a woman of no substance. And sincerely now, just between ourselves,
why this profusion of infamous transparency, this wasteful display of intimate bits of filmy acetate? When the only thing I want to find in you is
that little sparkle, sad and bitter, that you once had in your eyes ... But
let's get back to my wife. She makes faces and mimics you. She makes
fun of me too. Mockingly, she echoes some of my most heart-rending
sighs. "Those kisses that pained me in *Unforgettable You* still burn me
like fire." Wherever we may be, she is wont to speak of you; she says we
must confront this problem from a purely rational angle, from a scien-
tific point of view, and she comes up with absurd but potent arguments.
She does no less than claim you are not real and that she herself is an
actual woman. And by dint of proving it to me, she is demolishing my
illusions one by one. I do not know what will happen to me if what is
so far only a rumor should turn out to be the truth: that you will come
here to make a film, that you will honor our country with a visit. For the
love of God, by the holiest of holies—stay where you are, señorita!

No, I do not want to go see you again, for every time the music dies away and the action fades from the screen, I am overwhelmed. I'm speaking of that fatal barrier represented by the three cruel letters that put an end to the modest measure of happiness of my nights of love, at two pesos apiece. Bit by bit I have relinquished the desire to stay and live with you on film, and I no longer die of pain as I am towed away from the cinema by my wife, who has the bad habit of getting up as soon as the last frame has passed. Señorita, I leave you here. I do not even ask you for an autograph, for should you ever send me one I would be capable of forgetting your unpardonable treason. Please accept this letter as the final act of homage of a devastated soul, and forgive me for including you in my dreams. Yes, more than one night I dreamt about you, and there is nothing that I have to envy those fly-by-night lovers who collect a salary to hold you in their arms and ply you with borrowed eloquence.

Your humble servant

P.S.

I had neglected to tell you that I am writing from behind bars. This letter would never have reached your hands, had I not feared that the world would give you an erroneous account of me. For the newspapers (which always twist things around) are taking advantage of this ridiculous event: "Last night, an unknown man, either drunk or mentally deranged, interrupted a showing of *Slaves of Desire* at its most stirring point, when he ripped the screen of the Park Cinema by plunging a knife in the breast of Françoise Arnoul. In spite of the darkness, three members of the audience saw the maniac rush towards the actress brandishing a knife, and they got out of their seats to get a better look at him so they could identify him at the time of arraignment. This was easily done, as the individual collapsed once the crime had been committed."

I know that it's impossible, but I would give anything for you to remember always that sharp stab in your breast.

Translated by Teres Mendeth-Faith and Elisabeth Heinicke

The Story of a Cat

Teresa Porzencanski

(Burials are generally all similar; the same anonymous cross on the perennially black car sways back and forth according to the bumps on the pavement. No procession is more orderly and better arranged than the one made up of the relatives who in two shining automobiles exude pain just behind the hearse. The whole thing seems like a sinister fantasy, showing off artificial flowers and memorable signatures in an album and statements that flatter the personality of one who, according to everyone, was here.

One who was here: the image of God on earth, the reason for Creation, the sixth day of labor.)

It would have been different if, during the fraction of a second before death, Mary had looked in a different direction; now she was looking at the warm motionless hind legs covered with long grey fur which was inevitably washed every week. It would have been different for a cat to die in the jungle, in a circus cage, or in a park, rather than on the printed rug with roses where Mary slid on her knees so many times a day. Dying just like that, puffed up and tense and moving inside, with her first litter, dying just like that, on the shiny tile, next to the television set that had a big twenty-three inch screen that lit up the darkness of the living room every night, sending out into the useless silence of their faces the perfect images of the perfect advertisements. Dying like that, according to Mary, made no sense. The cat's six years of life, the same six years as Mary's life, had been spent in that frightful world, on that corner of the printed rug with roses in order for death like that to happen, without any green grass fertilized by the conscientious urine of the afternoons, without any ants going around the openings in the black earth spurred on by the old rake, without the happy lice that survive on so many other dying cats. It would have been different if death had come from the pain of giving birth, on a straw mat suddenly writhing because of the life that was just now rocking again, rocking just now again, forgetting the long aimless walks, the curious sniffing of the trash bins where the expensive filth of the summer houses was smashed together, rocking again after so many instances of wildly forgetting the rites: "Wetting on the carpet is forbidden." "No mating with an ownerless cat." "No giving birth because kittens are a nuisance, and they get everything dirty, and you have to drown them or give them away, but nobody wants them," Mary. "Lock up that cat so she does not give us a damn litter of kittens," "that cat is turning into a slut, Tuesday I will get her fixed so she will never have kittens, no matter how much it costs, fixed and ornamental at least an angora, ornamental."

But death, which arrived, was before the rug got soaked, hot, under Mary's eyes: a long, calm rattle, and the definitive quiet, almost obscene, of death, on the dry terrible rug, dry and sterile, dry and delicately woven by anonymous hands, delicate and washed by other helpful and dark hands, that, nevertheless, did not stamp any wetness into it. Night fell in the land of dying cats and Mary watched the world changing. The maid dressed in white was a magic fairy flying with a feather duster, over the dining room. Between the half-closed venetian blinds of the living room, every brilliant and overpowering star opened a seductive eye on the piece of furniture that once was deformed, mutilated, powerless trees. On the other side of the enormous mirror Mary walked on a long path which had all the little graves, all graves of cats ready to give birth: Mary's, 1808, Moni's, 1515, the pig's, 1611, the magpie's, 1901, along with little grey gravestones lit up by fireflies.

And the family dinner was the distorted inferno of the zoo. The faces were reflected in the iridescent crystal of the goblets: mama-magpie, daddy-pig, grandmother-owl, sister-hen, aunt-hyena, and uncle-rhinoceros, served graciously by Juana, farily-slave in a starched uniform. And Mary-queen contemplating the tablecloth crocheted during the months in which the magpie in labor had not died before giving birth on a printed rug, rather she had begotten her, Mary-queen, so Mary could eat that viscous liquid called vegetable, under the observation of the courteous animals and wear beautiful velvet and learn to play the beautiful piano, a beautiful melody, audible, only on the beautiful days when guests came, when the happy magpie shouted at the pig to be quiet so Mary-queen could practice there, happily smiling the melodic repressions that her parrot-teacher transmitted to her every Monday,

Wednesday, and Friday, from five to six, by man's calendar.

And, at last, dessert, swimming in the viscous ocean of melted sugar, chewed by the great jaws of the pig and the hyena, which by then seemed to have satisfied to some extent their big appetites. Graciously the dishes were served and taken away: "Juana, take away the food, clear the table, arrange the couch, wash the dishes, sweep the rug, be careful not to break the crystal, go to your room, sleep." Juana, sleep; sleep, Juana; Juana, sleep; sleep, Juana, put Mary-queen to bed.

"Moni."

"Mary! Are you still awake?"

"What happened to the cat?"

"There is a place at the bottom of the world, behind the mirror, where all the dead rest."

"Even cats that are going to give birth?"

"Of course."

"Moni."

"What?"

"Why in the world did she die? Yesterday she was fine. Juana was going to take care of her while she gave birth."

"Juana knows why she died."

"Yes, who killed her?"

"Shhhh! They are going to wake up."

Shhh, mandatory silence brings on sleep, brings it on, in the swaying on the wall paper with drawings for children, the silence to bring on the ingenious and deaf sleep over the interruptions. Shhhh, and suddenly the shouting, jumping out like crazy notes from a piano out of tune up to the tense and frozen pause, and later, the tranquilizing complicity of snoring.

(The evening silence is like this in these summer houses: spurious and dark hideouts, in which the years accumulate a variety of pills and forgotten things.)

The grey morning surprises the kitchen: the open cupboards airing out their things, the tiles soaped by the recent scrubbing, the marble, blinding white. And Juana, on her knees, like a stout angel, soaping up the floors on which there are no tracks.

"Am I bothering you?"

"No, child, what's the matter?"

"Nothing, nothing, nothing."

(Nothing, slave of the vultures, nary a fairy, Mary, nary a fairy.) Nothing.

"Juana, what happened to the cat?"

"She died, that's all."

"But why? Wasn't she all right?"

"Oh dear, my child. Your mother gave me rat poison to put in her milk yesterday. She said that the kittens would be bothersome and that they were not angora."

("Aha, magpie-witch, witch, witch. It is all clear now.")

(On the printed rug, dry and sterile and dry, the gruesome idea had been gradually developing, or perhaps, in the orderly coming and going of lunch, or perhaps, in the useless and quiet face in front of the television set or in the tense moments or nighttime silence. And the murder had taken place, taken place, the filth. And right now, the stench of garbage and the ants would be on the grass, and urine would be fertilizing the earth, but far away, like in a phantasmagoric vision. And the witch would continue to discuss free will and contraceptives, in the morning mass in which other witches also were talking about the sacred principles of the church with reference to maternity.)

The summer is flooded with the lights on the garden, and the siesta. Reddish, the gravel shines, while the faucet like an elbow by the gate leaks rhythmically. May sways back and forth on the swing in the front: the pine trees, the asphalt and the lawn, the house and the roof; the roof, and the roof ... Mary contemplates the sky: on the swirl of green foliage the golden rays reflect; the path extends in the distance and the shadows cut it off abruptly. All at once a figure faintly appears, coming closer, vague, stylized, colorless, within the radiant gleaming of things. And Mary makes a dash for it: the porch, the kitchen, Juana the slave-fairy listening to the radio soap-opera of fifteen to three, the remains of the roast, bewildered by the flies, the overwhelming silence of the siesta.

"I saw her! I want to die, to die. I saw her. She found me."

"Who, my child? What's the matter?"

"The Virgin, Juana, the Virgin, all transparent, and with the child in her arms."

(The pews are lined up before the altar in devout and obedient rows. Along the isle the long candles burn down indolently. One of the faithful stretches out a vacillating hand with a plate in which the offering rings, inert. And the morning sermon extends out over the repressed whispers, over the furious feathers of exclusive hats, and the knees, perfect for not having to scrub the floors of summer homes with poorly-paid female servants and heretics of the morning. And the dome, a warm womb that feeds and warms inside, closes inexorably exactly at noon, when a portion of consumed morality spills across the marble entrance, and across the punctual excrement of their consciences.)

"The Virgin! But, really?"
"She had a child in her arms, but it was dead, and its face, it was the face of a cat!"

Translated by Roland Hamilton

Death and Transfiguration of a Teacher

María Teresa Solari

The teacher was dead; she had been cut up by the girls who, after killing her, cannibalistically disposed of her remains. The teacher was a poet endowed with great sensitivity and a romantic temperament, having started writing at twenty, although her career was now over at thirty-five. They were going over the scene of the crime. All the students were presumed guilty. They were interrogating the top student in the class:

"Now please tell us everything from the start ... "

The girl, a young thing with a blank expression on her face, grabbed one foot and sardonically exclaimed:

"Here."

"What's that supposed to mean? What are you doing with your foot? Get to the point!"

"I mean, I started on her foot. I took off her sock and bit into the heel."

"You can't be serious!"

The principal was nonplussed. Actually, all that was left were the gnawed-on bones. They left a little sign on the macabre residue: "Anatomy Lesson," it said.

One of the murdered teacher's poems went:

Oh, bittersweet youth,
object of my abject toil ...

And nothing else. She had published only one book, entitled *Destiny*. She was timid in conversation and at times could not seem to express herself. When she got frustrated during the torture of her classes,

she turned red and her mouth trembled. But she was incapable of raising her voice. And the classroom noise of the students' uninterrupted
chattering seemed to envelop, disorient and paralyze her. She often
talked about poetry. She tried to explain the magical power of poetic ut-
terance. Something like the supreme effort of the poet to rise above the
maddening crowd and to create. Somewhere in the back of the classroom a girl started going meeeeeooow, smothering the poetry of the
impassioned rhapsodist. The laughter sharpened in tone. The class became a single giant cat, glaring at the teacher with piercing, bloodshot
eyes. Four girls in the front row were singing some pop tune that went:

> *When I love you*
> *from the bottom of my heart*
> *my brains go*
> *suddenly into knots ...*

The teacher left the room, crestfallen. Looking out at the empty
schoolyard, she thought about her Calvary, about poets no longer having any place in this world. Why make teachers cover poets and poetry?
It was laughable, and cruel to boot. A little bird swooped down and
daintily snatched up a crumb from the gutt er. The school's dog wagged
his tail as she passed by, and without realizing it she glanced at him tenderly. At least he was sincere. The principal had called her to the office.
When she went in, she couldn't help staring at a row of stuffed animals
neatly lined up in an open cabinet. She remembered how the day before
the principal had ordered them taken out into the sun to keep down the
moths. The glass-eyed rabbit and the hawk with one wing stretched out
got to sun themselves all morning. She felt the school was lifeless, and
the principal just another stuffed animal.

"You don't seem to appreciate how serious the situation is. Your
class is a madhouse, I've noticed it when I go by. The students don't
respect you; you don't know how to make them respect you. You don't
understand the principle of authority. You've just got to face them down
and use a firm tone of voice—and make them afraid of you. You can
manage them only if they fear you. But what do you do? You talk about
poetry, sweetness and light, subtleties that they'll never understand and
they don't care about! Stick to the program, right to the end! Hammer
on those dates, yes, dates! For example: this poet was born in 1506 and
died of tuberculosis in 1526! Therefore, he lived twenty years, wrote
twenty books and a dictionary of poetry. Never made a red cent, nobody gave a damn about his books! The first was Illusion, the last, Des-

peration. Women wanted nothing to do with him, but now he's a great poet. That's all, enough for them to learn and then get on with the next writer!"

She left the office and her spirit seemed to mope along behind her, but at least it wasn't stuffed.

The day of the crime started normally enough. As she entered the classroom a student gave her a bouquet of red roses. Totally unheard of. Some others arranged them in a vase and placed them on the lectern. One girl got up and recited one of Bécquer's poems from beginning to end, the one that starts with "The dark swallows will return." And then, you could have heard a pin drop. One of them—the one that had recited the poem—suddenly came forward and plunged the knife into her before she knew what was happening. She died with a beatific smile on her face and then they simply ate her up. Laughter was everywhere and spring was in the air, as befit the month of October. Later they went home and no one was hungry, although some complained about upset stomachs. A few threw up, but they were mostly calm. Sensitive to the deceased's poetic inclinations, they buried the bones next to a rose-bush, but the dog—who was always hungry—dug them up. And when the principal was notified, she did not know what to make of them, since they did not match any of the bones in her collection. When the teacher did not show up the following day—she had never missed a class—the principal began to suspect something was wrong. Her suspicions were confirmed after questioning the class. There was no accounting for it; this had never happened before at her school. She tried to blame it on the noxious influence of television, but the psychologist she brought in felt that there was more to it: perhaps some of the girls in the class had a congenital predisposition to crime. She called an emergency meeting of the P.T.A. to discuss what should be done, whether to go public or adopt an attitude of prudent silence. More than one father during that long session embarked on a rambling disquisition on how damaging it would be to interrupt or perhaps even end his daughter's studies. Other, more draconian parents noted that the girls' sense of right and wrong would suffer if it were not made clear what they had done stepped out of line. Around midnight the sterner ones prevailed; they voted and it was decided to call in the authorities. But who would go to the police with the news? This duty fell to the gardener because, after all, he was the one who found the bones (and the dog chewing on them). So off he went. The police seemed more upset than anyone else. The whole thing was blown up in the press and newspapers sold like hotcakes, although after a while things quieted down and it was all conveniently forgotten. Some of the fathers had a lot of pull and reached an understanding with the court. Money changed hands, classes resumed and the girls did very well in their finals, and 99% of the class passed. The jury admitted that they were very bright. The principal decided to screen all prospective teachers for poetic tendencies, so as to avoid a repetition of this disagreeable and most inconvenient event. She found a taxidermist with literary inclinations to fill the recently-vacated position and keep her supplied with a steady stream of new specimens as well. She even felt a twinge of regret, reflecting on the lost opportunity to stuff the slain Lit teacher and label her "Poet," for an example to all the students: a dangerous breed, a egregious flaw in the Lord's creation. Later on, she and the new teacher started a Taxidermy Club which, to her surprise, proved very popular with the student body, including many of those involved in the incident of the previous year. Not only with the girl with the knife— very bright and a lot of personality, by the way—but also with the best student in the class, who—she knew—had nothing to do with it except for the cannibalism part.

Translated by John Benson

The Tale of the Velvet Pillows

Marta Traba

No one knew Nimia Sánchez until the moment she came forward, climbed the creaking wooden steps with great caution and, once on the platform, offered the mayor the velvet pillow which lay in her outstretched hands.

For a moment, however, she appeared to have changed her mind. She made a half turn, looked at the neighborhood people wearing their Sunday best, crammed together in front of the platform, and she raised the pillow so that all could see. She displayed the pillow as if it were the sacred host, and this action produced in the people, as it did in church, a moment of confusion and silence.

Perhaps there was someone, incapable of resisting the solemnity of the spectacle, who went so far as to lower his head and eyes. Then at once the pillow returned to its original position in the two outstretched palms. Nimia Sánchez executed a gracious circus-like movement, made another half turn, and at last handed the gift to its recipient. The neighborhood people were able to admire the center of the black velvet pillow on which the Colombian coat of arms was meticulously embroidered with crossed flags and gold stars that managed to shine even when the thick layer of clouds held back the sun. Nimia Sánchez was ageless and nondescript. She possessed the rare gift of complete invisibility while the rest of the neighborhood women were invisible only up to a point, always noticed and greeted by someone. (Only a few, like Feliza for instance, were perceptible at a distance; but in this moment, which corresponded to the birth of the neighborhood, Feliza had barely entered adolescence and had not yet begun to cast her famous electrifying looks which caused so many disasters).

What is certain is that after the inauguration ceremony the people only remembered Nimia Sánchez' embroidered pillow; she, the actual author of the marvel, was immediately erased from memory. By the same measure, two days later no one was able to remember how old Nimia Sánchez was, what she looked like, or how she was dressed, but the prestige of her pillow continued to grow surprisingly. On street corners women sighed about it, and in these sighs envy and desire gradually crept in. Soon, one of the greatest aspirations of the neighborhood inhabitants, not only of the women but also some of the men, was to have in their homes one of the pillows embroidered by Nimia Sánchez. One man who was more daring than the rest was able to find out where she lived and actually went to her house to place an order for a pillow. When he talked about it, it turned out that he was unable to explain anything about Nimia Sánchez, or who she lived with. Perhaps she didn't live with anyone, because he didn't encounter anyone at all in the dining room or hear sounds emanating from the kitchen, or the bathroom, or from the floor above. This fact would have caused alarm, since the houses of the neighborhood were only allotted to families with children, but as she was the creator of the embroidered pillow, the normal rules did not apply. The person who ventured to order the pillow was not even able to describe anything exceptional with respect to the furniture in Nimia Sánchez' house. It seemed as though she had the same table, chairs, and worn-out cupboards as everyone else, and that the only exception was a multitude of rag dolls and animals strewn about the floor, which the man had glimpsed from behind a door that was half-opened onto the second room of the bottom floor.

After six days, beset by growing anxiety, Nimia Sánchez presented her client with the new pillow of embroidered black velvet. She invited him to the house, had him pass through the dining room and began to repeat the identical gestures she used on the day of the inauguration. She approached with the pillow delicately laying across her extended palms and raised it by two corners, exhibiting it so that the embroidery could be seen, and then immediately handed it over. She received the stipulated payment with disdain and great dignity and promptly showed her client to the door.

Nimia Sánchez's work enjoyed a sudden increase in popularity when the rest of the neighborhood saw the pillow. The embroidery showed a giraffe in the middle of a jungle full of details right down to the stems, trunks and leaves. The extraordinary thing was precisely the leaves which were embroidered in the most strident colors without green appearing anywhere; between the lilac, blue, yellow, red and orange foliage, the giraffe had chosen to feed on some dark violet leaves which contrasted sharply with the orange. The happy owner of the embroidered pillow was obligated to patiently tolerate the parade of neighbors that wanted to see it, and in three days time Nimia Sánchez received more than fourteen new orders.

The first batch of pillows, which came with a surprising velocity from Nimia Sánchez' house, always pertained to giraffes. In order to not repeat herself, the embroiderer placed the giraffes in the most implausible settings. After situating it in a jungle, she placed it on plateaus with a large and golden sun, then between multiple suns, later between moons, and when she felt she had quite exhausted the possibilities of the African landscape, she placed it in the middle of rivers and waterfalls, and finally set it down in her own neighborhood. This last pillow visibly disconcerted its owner and the spectators. The giraffe, always in profile, was imprisoned by superimposed houses which obviously recalled the outlines of the neighborhood buildings. Nimia Sánchez put curtains with violet flowers in the windows, the likes of which didn't exist in the area, but she was not able to disguise it completely. The client felt cheated, since the magic of the pillows consisted in their ability to transport the owner to another reality, to imaginary African landscapes, forests, or plains. With a certain apprehension, the client returned the pillow with the giraffe between the houses. The following day she returned to explain herself to the embroiderer, but the door remained obstinately closed, although it was clear that Nimia Sánchez was inside. Neither did she open the door to other clients that insisted on knocking, but greeted them instead with unconcealed hostility.

During the years that followed no one heard anything more of Nimia Sánchez and people forgot about her. The happy owners of the pillows showed them as if they were precious objects, and they were indeed the only things that saved their owners from the deterioration that implacably consumed the neighborhood. While chair legs broke, painted walls filled with scratches and stains, and formica tops peeled off tables, the pillows remained resplendent, the thick gold and silver threads continuing to radiate luminously in the darkness. Meanwhile Nimia Sánchez came and went like any other inhabitant of the neighborhood but, thanks to her condition of invisibility, no one recognized her. It was during the time of the child-care center scandal and of the dark and equivocal dominion of Feliza that her name resounded once again in kitchen gossip.

A small boy, climbing in the window, had entered the daycare center to take a peek. Since it was daytime, he was able to explore at his leisure the ex-daycare center and current brothel. He went upstairs and downstairs, he traveled bewildered with his mouth open and drooling a bit through the second floor rooms crammed with cots, and on arriving at this point, he stopped in amazement. The four cots represented a commonplace spectacle for him, since in all of the homes he knew, the same thing happened, and yet being such a small boy, he was incapable of understanding. The extraordinary thing, however, was that on top of the cots covered with sheets or worn-out blankets, piles of profusely embroidered black velvet pillows glowed like something not of this world.

At first, in his anxiety the boy didn't see more than gold and silver outlines and patterns. Then he approached and recognized figures, the meaning of which escaped him. It attracted his attention that the bodies were nude and that against all logic, they were blue or green. Clumsily and with faltering words he tried later to explain to his mother in the kitchen. He described the perfectly yellow hands holding between them ... and here he got confused and was not able to continue on, in spite of his mother's pinches.

From his confused and gasping story, the neighbors were able to make out that, one, given the enormous quantity of pillows, Nimia Sánchez had taken up her work again in a feverish manner, and two, that something dark and loathsome now moved through the embroidery. The landscapes no longer dealt with giraffes, forests, and rivers, but with something else which they intuited, but were unable to state explicitly. One of the women, more pious than the rest, affirmed in a harsh voice that it was necessary to report the situation, and she went to see the priest. Once she started to explain the reason for her visit, there was no turning back; the priest, furious and cursing incoherently, stalked off towards the sacristy.

He must have guessed it, however, because the next day, almost at dawn, the people of that block saw the sacristan knocking at Nimia Sánchez' door. He entered and was there for a short while. It was futile to ask him anything afterward, since he belonged so little to this world. After the incident, the neighbors once again entertained themselves, keeping watch over Nimia Sánchez' house. They noted that for three days she did not even show her face in the street, and on the fourth she left carrying, in her unique manner, a large package wrapped in newspaper which, without a doubt, contained a pillow. The only surprising and unusual thing was that she carried it wrapped. A neighbor woman who was one of her clients stopped to ask her in a humble voice if she would show the pillow to her, but Nimia Sánchez just glared at her and continued directly to the church.

She went in and came out of the dark cave where the priest was located in no more that a matter of minutes.

It was Sunday.

At the usual hour the people met for mass; the women, many small children interspersed among them, and a few old people, sat near the entrance. A long time passed and the priest did not appear. Noon arrived and the women, a little afraid, looked at each other and shrugged their shoulders. At last two got up, crossed the black corridor which led to the sacristy and the priest's quarters, and knocked. They knocked a long time without answer. Finally the door opened slightly and the sacristan appeared wide-eyed and slavering, murmuring incomprehensibly. It wasn't possible to understand him until he shut the door and they heard the lock turn. The people outside withdrew in the midst of frightened comments.

Nothing was seen of the priest for fifteen days. When he climbed up to the pulpit two Sundays later, he looked like he had one foot in the grave. A sudden decrepitude had overtaken him, dispelling the vainly apocalyptic air which had held the people in terror of hell. He died shortly thereafter and although no one understood clearly what had transpired, they all assumed it had to do with Nimia Sánchez' black velvet pillow—which no one ever got to see.

Translated by Jean *Vaughn*

Up Among the Eagles

Luisa Valenzuela

You're going to find it hard to believe what I tell you because these days who knows anything about life in the country? And up there, life on the mountain, up among the eagles? But you get used to it. Oh, yes. I can say that, I who never knew anything but the city, see how I am now, the color of earth, carrying my pails of water from the public fountain. Water for myself and water for others. I do it to eke out a living; I've done it ever since the day I made the foolish mistake of climbing the path that borders the cliff. I climbed up, and when I looked down and saw the green dot of the valley far below, I decided to stay here forever. It wasn't that I was afraid, I was just being prudent, as they say: threatening cliffs, beyond imagination; impossible even to consider returning. I traded everything I had for food; my shoes, my wrist watch, my key chain with all my keys (I wouldn't be needing them now), a fountain pen that was almost out of ink.

The only thing of any value I have left is my polaroid camera; no one wanted it. Up here they don't believe in preserving images; just the opposite: every day they strive to create new images, they invent new images only for the moment. Often they get together to tell one another about the incorporeal images they've been entertaining. They sit in a circle on the dirt floor in the darkness of their communal building—a kind of hut—and concentrate on making the vision appear. One day, out of nothing, they materialized a tapestry of non-existent colors and ineffable design, but they decided that it was but a pale reflection of the mental image, and they broke the circle in order to return the tapestry to the nothingness from which it had come.

They are strange creatures; normally they speak a language whose meaning they themselves have forgotten. They communicate by interpreting pauses, intonations, facial expressions, and sighs. I tried to learn

190

this language of silences, but it seems that my tongue is not meant for such subtleties. At any rate, they speak our language when they refer to trivial matters, the daily needs that have nothing to do with their images. Even so, some words are missing from their vocabulary. For example, they have no word for yesterday or tomorrow, before and after, or one of these days. Here everything is now, and always. An unsatisfactory imitation of eternity, like the tapestry I've already mentioned. Have mentioned? Oh, yes, I'm the only one that uses that verb tense; I may also be the only one who has any notion of conjugations. A vice left over from the world down there, knowledge I can't trade anyone, because no one wants it.

"Will you trade me a few beans for a notion of time?" I went around asking the women in the marketplace, but they shook their heads emphatically. (A notion of time? They were incredulous; a way of being, of moving on a different plane? That has nothing to do with the kind of knowledge we're after.)

Who dares speak of the passage of time to the inhabitants of this high place where everything endures? Even their bodies endure. Death neither decays nor obliterates them; it merely stops them in their path. Then the others, with exquisite delicacy—a delicacy I've seen only in connection with newly dropped kids or certain mushrooms—carry the body beyond the rushing stream and with precise symmetry arrange it in the exact place it had in life. With infinite patience they have succeeded in creating, on the other side, a second population, one that obliterates time, an unmoving reflection of themselves that is secure because it is mummified, unmodifiable.

The only change they permit themselves is with their images. They grow, yes, they grow, and reach adulthood with a suspicion of implicit old age, and they stay that way until they die. In contrast, I note with horror that I have a sprinkling of gray hairs, and wrinkles are lining my face, premature, of course, but who could keep her youth in this dry air, beneath skies like these? What will become of me when they discover that time passes in my life, and is leaving its mark?

They are absorbed in other concerns, in trying to retain visions seemingly of jewelled palaces and splendors unknown on this earth. They glide through their astounding worlds while it is all I can do—very infrequently and with extreme stealth—to take a photograph of myself. I crawl along at ground level, in spite of the fact that I am in an elevated land floating in clouds. They say that the altitude deranges those of us who come here from sea level. But it is my belief, my fear, that they are

the ones who are deranged, that it's something ancestral, inexplicable—
especially when I see them sitting on their haunches, as they almost always are, looking inward in contemplation. I'm always looking outward,
I search every path, almost nonchalantly nourishing my fear, something
silent and my own. They watch me go by carrying water, with the pole
across my shoulders and the two pails dangling from the pole, and I
would like to think they do not suspect my fear. This is twinned, it has
two faces, not at all like the fear that kept me from returning after I had
climbed the mountain. No, this is not simple fear; it reflects others, and
becomes voracious.

On the one hand, I am here, now. A now that grows and changes
and expands with time and, if I am lucky, will continue to evolve. I do
not want them to be aware of this evolving, as I have already said, and
even less do I want to be like them, exempt from time. For what would
become of me if I kept this face forever, as if surprised between two
ages? I think about the mummies in the mirror city, oh yes, absolutely,
only mummies are unchanged by time. Time does not pass for the dead,
I told myself one day, and on a different day (because I, if not they, am
very careful to relate question to calendar) I added: nor does it pass for
those who have no concept of death. Death is a milestone.

The inhabitants here, with their language of silence, could teach me
the secrets of immobility that so closely resemble immortality, but I am
not eager to learn. Life is a movement toward death; to be static is
already to be dead.

"Stay here, little lady, nice and quiet here with us," is one of the few
things they consent to say to me in my own language, and I shake my
head energetically (one more way of insuring movement), and as soon
as I am out of their vision, I begin to run like a madwoman along the
neglected paths. More often than not I run up, not down, but either
way, I don't want to get too far from the town, I don't want to stumble
into the still city and find myself face to face with the mummies.

The secret city. I don't know its exact location, but I know everything about it—or maybe I only suspect. I know it has to be identical
to this humble little clump of huts where we live, a faithful replica with
the exact same number of bodies, for when one of them dies the oldest
mummy is thrown into the void. It's noisy in the secret city. The noise
announces its proximity, but it also serves a basic purpose: scraps of tin,
of every size and shape, hang from the rafters of the huts to scare away
the buzzards. They are all that moves in the secret city, those scraps
of tin to scare away the vultures, the only thing that moves or makes a

sound, and on certain limpid nights the wind carries the sound to where we the living dwell, and on those nights they gather in the plaza, and dance.

They dance, but oh so slowly, almost without moving their feet, more as if they were undulating, submerged in the dense water of sound. This happens only rarely, and when it does I feel an almost uncontrolable urge to join in the dance—the need to dance soaks into my bones, sways me—but I resist with all my power to resist. I am afraid that nothing could be more paralyzing than to yield to this music that comes from death. So that I won't be paralyzed, I don't dance. I don't dance and I don't share their visions.

I have not witnessed a birth since I have been here. I know they couple, but they don't reproduce. They do nothing to avoid it, simply the stillness of the air, the immobility, prevents it. As for me, at this point, I don't even go near men. It must be admitted that men don't come near me either, and there must be a reason, considering how often and how closely they approach almost everything else. Something in my expression must drive them away, but I've no way of knowing what it is. There are no mirrors here. No reflections. Water is either glaucous or torrential white. I despair. And ever so often in the privacy of my cave, sparingly and with extreme caution, I take a new photograph.

I do this when I can't stand things any longer, when I have an over-whelming need to know about myself, and then no fear, no caution, can hold me back. One problem is that I am running out of film. In addition, I know perfectly well that if they find my photographs, if they place them in chronological order, two things can happen: they will either abom-inate or adore me. And neither possibility is to be desired, both are too much like being stone. There are no alternatives. If they put the photographs in order and draw the conclusions. If they see that when I arrived, my face was smoother, my hair brighter, my bearing more alert. If they discover the marks of time, they will know that I have not controlled time even for a moment. And so if they find I am growing older, they will not want me to continue to live among them, and they will stone me from the town and I will have to face the terrifying cliffs.

I don't even want to think about the other possibility. That they will adore me because I have so efficiently and so concretely materialized these images of myself. I would then be like stone to them, like a statue forever captive and contained.

Either of these two quite lapidary prospects should be sufficient rea-son to restrain my suicidal impulse to take yet another photograph, but it isn't. Each time, I succumb, hoping against hope that they will not be alerted by the glare of the flash. Sometimes I choose stormy nights; perhaps I conjure the lightning with my pale simulacrum of its rays. Other times I seek the protection of the radiance of dawn, which at this altitude can be incendiary.

Elaborate preparations for each of my secret snapshots, preparations charged with hope and danger. That is, with life. The resulting picture does not always please me but the emotion of seeing myself—no matter how horrible or haggard I appear—is immeasurable. This is I, changing, in a static world that imitates death. And I feel safe. Then I am able to stop and speak of simple things with the women in the market and even understand their silences, and answer them. I can live a little longer without love, without anyone's touch.

Until another relapse, a new photo. And this will be the last. On a day with the sound of death, when the minimal activity of the town has come to a halt and they have all congregated to dance in the market plaza. That deliberate dancing that is like praying with their feet, a quiet prayer. They will never admit it, but I suspect that they count to themselves, that their dance is an intricate web of steps like stitches, one up, two stitches backward, one to the right. All to the tinkling of the faroff tin scraps: the wind in the house of the dead. A day like any other; a very special day for them because of the sound that they would call music, if they were interested in making such distinctions. But all that interests them is the dance, or believing they are dancing, or thinking of the dance, which is the same thing. To the pulse of the sound that floods over us, whose origins I cannot locate, though I know it comes from the city of the dead. A sound that threatens to engulf me.

They do not call to me, they don't even see me. It's as if I didn't exist. Maybe they're right, maybe I don't exist. Maybe I am my own invention, or a peculiar materialization of an image they have evoked. That sound is joyful, and yet the most mournful ever heard. I seem to be alive, and yet ...

I hid in my cave trying not to think about these things, trying not to hear the tinkling; I don't know from where it comes, but I fear toward what it may lead me. With the hope of setting these fears to rest, I begin my preparations for the last photo. A desperate attempt to recover my being, to return to myself, which is all I have.

Anxiously, I await the perfect instant, while outside, darkness is weaving its blackest threads. Suddenly, an unexpected radiance causes me to trip the shutter before I am ready. No photograph emerges, only a dark rectangle which gradually reveals a blurred image of a wall of stone. And that's all. I have no more film so I may as well throw away the camera. A cause for weeping were it not for the fact the radiance is not fading. A cause for uneasiness, then, because when I peer out I see that the blazing light is originating from the very place I wanted not to know about, from the very heart of the sound, from a peak just below our feet, and that now the radiance comes from millions of glittering scraps of tin in the moonlight. The city of the dead.

Spontaneously, I set forth with all my stupid photos, responding to an unfathomable impulse that may be a response to a summons from the sonorous radiance. They are calling me from down there, over to the left, and I answer, and at first I run along the treacherous path and when the path ends I continue on. I stumble, I climb and descend, I trip and hurt myself; to avoid hurtling into the ravine I try to imitate the goats, leaping across the rocks; I lose my footing, I slip and slide, I try to check my fall, thorns rake my skin but at the same time save me. Rashly, I rush ahead, because I must, I will reach the city of the mummies, I will give my faces to them, I will place my successive faces on the mummies and then at last I will be free to take the path to the valley without fearing stone, because I will take the last photograph with me and I am myself in that photograph and I am stone.

Translated by Margaret Sayers Peden

Penelope's Silver Wedding Anniversary

Rima de Vallbona

The preparations for the party have created an atmosphere of anxiety, you'd think we were going to be entertaining royalty. Maybe something exciting is finally going to happen in this sleepy place. Even I'm restless. I try to fit the nervous hours into my daily work, but it's no use. Everything breaks away from the habitual routines, the well-defined limits and rolls on towards the unexpected. Damn it! Will it happen? What?

A party's a party, fool. Relax those nerves. They're rightening like violin strings. Don't jump every time the china clinks as Julia, the old housekeeper, washes it.

"To think that I once held her in my arms when she was just a tiny little thing. Look at her now! I never would've believed that I could hang on for so many years. It's just incredible!" Julia goes on whistling her litany through the black gaps in between her few remaining teeth. She washes and washes, conducting a kitchen symphony of porcelain, crystal, silverware and running water. That unbearable garlic and fried-food smell pervades the air and turns my stomach. Though I really can't tell if it's the smell or what may happen tonight.

The noise, the smell of cooking mixed with the piercing aroma of jasmine, roses and gardenias all nauseate me and open chasms between me and the things I normally handle with ease, almost with disdain. It's as if I were desecrating a sacred object. When I picked up a teaspoon, I dropped it superstitiously. Damn nausea! The cigarette I was about to light seemed alive in my mouth, so I let it fall and then lacked the energy to pick it up.

In the next room Charito and Laura sing while they make their beds. Magical, impossible sailboats form in the air as they flap the fresh, clean sheets whose whiteness dazzles in the sunlight. As I lie unraveled on

196

the couch, their young arms invite me to enter their intimate circle of laughter and song, to taste their kissing. "They're your cousins, David, orphaned cousins, and you must love and respect them always. You're bad, David! You'll pay in hell for what you've done. You have to go to confession and never sin with them again!" How soft and tender was their skin in the river waters! Never again have I experienced such complete and total paradise: the multicolored vegetation cascading into the water in a transcendental suicide of branches thickened with parasites and bulrushes. And the silence pierced by a thousand noises, bursting into a locust's soft whir, or into the plop of a ripe peach striking the earth, or into the river's rush, or the rush of the blood laden with new, healthy pleasure. "You'll be damned to hell! That's a mortal sin!" Ah, but it was paradise, Mom, the paradise which opened its doors to me at fourteen. The taste of moist virginal flesh inviting me to joyously sample it like a fresh, crisp apple! Swollen with pleasure, their young bodies would sway in the river waters. I closed my eyes and let myself go ... let myself go ... let myself go ... They allowed me to penetrate the boundaries of their sensuous arms and legs that wrapped around my body like a fleshy net. There I surrendered myself to the magic of release after long nights calming the hard, shameful pain in my groin. Surrender was paradise. Hell was each night in my bed as I suffered the sinful swelling. That was hell.

But Mom—such a good woman, poor thing—was unable to understand then as she is now, that games, bicycles, marbles, desks, books and multiplication tables aren't everything. There she sits knitting on the sofa next to the window—waiting for something? Knitting, always knitting. She's waiting for something. I know she is waiting for something. Every quick, nervous movement of her needle says that she is waiting. She's been waiting for so long! What has she knitted all that time? She must have collected a roomful of bedspreads, pillows, sweaters, booties, hats, scarves. Where does she find room for them all? Now, amid the bustle and getting ready for the party—damn it—Mom's knitting is making me strangely uneasy. Where on earth could she put all those things if she has never worn them or given them away? Is there a secret stash somewhere in the house? Where? White wool, always pure white. Ever since I was a child, I would watch her knit by the window, humming some sad old waltz, and then she should kiss me as she shook with anguish. "Why do you knit so much, Mom?" She would just keep knitting, and teardrop trickled down her cheek whenever I asked her. "Where's that white sweater you knitted last week?" Then she would silently rise from the sofa and go to check on Julia's dinner preparations. I always asked her about it but Mom's knitting never bothered me as it does today. The very first words I can remember her saying to me were "Sinful boy! You'll go to hell! You're a bad boy!" Then she would trail off muttering "Sausage, potatoes, beans, laundry, roses, knitting. I must knit, I must finish these booties." As she intones "I must," it's as if everything alive in her drains off into the grave and she goes on making soup or kneading dough.

When she hears a love song or the canary's warble, something suddenly seems to stir within her ... but then she starts up again talking about the same old things as if life were routine and just a household chore. Dad just tolerates the chatter; it isn't coherent, not at all. Strings of words, apparently meaningful, but not really. The funny thing is that each word sounds as if she carried the thing named right there in her mouth.

"Leave her alone, David, she's happy there in her own world, a simple woman's world. Married twenty-five years and not a single complaint, not one. She's happy just to knit, cook, arrange flowers and move the furniture around. If the real world were like that, everything would be a bed of roses. Look, look here at this gray hair—that's what you get chained to a desk all day."

Mom doesn't have a single gray hair but her eyes suggest gravestones and the life entombed inside. In the mornings when she awakes her complexion is moist, as if the dew had watered the slight wrinkles that are starting to appear around her eyes. Not a single gray hair. Shining hair, always clean, done up in an elegant bun. As long as she doesn't open her mouth—*bring the potato salad, Julia*—you'd think she had popped out of a museum painting of some royal family. But once she starts talking about everyday things in her unpretentious way and with that peculiar accent from her home town, she seems crude and common. It makes you want to muzzle her, hide her in a corner, plug your ears and block out the awful sound that clashes with her beauty and elegance. Why can't she leave the bananas, cabbage and vegetables alone? Mom, Mom! How many times has she embarrassed me with that *Oh, these tomatoes are overripe!* and *Mmm, what tender green beans!* They look at me and shrug their shoulders, unable to understand her simple world, and then resume their conversation ...

Today's party. What for? What is it that's bothering me? Just another party. I feel like gagging. Is there any more room at all in Mom's knitting room? Is she going to stay by the window? White wool, white wool, white wool ... "Oh, those nights at the Opera House, the Music Hall ... to take in the splendor of the chandeliers! To dance every night until your shoes wore out, a new pair every night, just to wear them out." When did she say all that? No, she never did. I just dreamed it in one of those childhood daydreams that so easily pass for reality. "And the girls were always jealous of my dance card. All the boys wanted to dance with me." A vague remembrance of hearing it from her lips. Maybe it wasn't her. Someone else. Probably one of those vain old bags that always talk your ear off when they visit. White wool, kitchen—nausea, nausea—its the same little world she'll never escape. Poor thing. Just like grandmother and all the others, no wings to fly away towards the endless horizon, no dreams of conquest ... Oh hell, what a bunch of tripe. It's all so dumb, the knitting room, the fragile little woman, a shadow, empty inside ... What silly thoughts!

Charito is warm, vibrant as she trembles against me for a moment and then slips away like a fish. She is so tender pressed against me, alive with unquenchable ardor in her beautiful, perverted virginity. "You'll suffer in hell! You're bad!" Mom said that because she just doesn't understand how Charito feels when she rubs up against me and we go for it. Mom doesn't know anything about that. I wonder if she has ever felt it with Dad—or anyone? No way. She's different, all she cares about it white wool and kitchen. Strange, when the teacher would talk about the Tinoco dictatorship I would think about Mom, vivacious and laughing, with curly hair and a low-cut dress—*Pelico Tonico made a pass at me too, but I* ... It's absurd, she's not that old and besides she's my mother, who can say ...

The party finally starts, guests arrive. Little by little the pretense, lies and gossip penetrates and solidifies in the interstices between them. Laughter, greetings, all bullshit. Nausea haunts me, will Mom start stuffing herself with bananas, tomatoes, stew and pies? She looks so beautiful in that black dress that sets off the reddishness in her hair, just regal. If she would just keep quiet, stay away from the commonplace. What? What are they saying? She's going to make an announcement? Everyone's eyes are on her. Dad is dumbfounded. This can't be happening! She has never spoken to a crowd before. With all those vultures waiting around for someone to slip up, how could she dare to speak up?

"Mom, for crying out loud ... why did you have to have that damn drink, you know what it does to you. Come on, let's go ... "

"No, I have an important announcement for my friends. Let me go, David, and tell your father I haven't had a drop to drink."

"Mom, please shut up for the love of God!"

She climbed up on a platform and majestically silenced everyone. She had the most marvelous, regal air about her. If she could just stay that way and be quiet ...

"I would like to be candid with all our dear friends, you who have known us all our twenty-five years of marriage. How could I celebrate our silver wedding anniversary without sharing *my* happiness with you?" (Why did she emphasize *my*? What about Dad? She's drunk, she just can't handle champagne.)

"Can you imagine what it is like to be married to a cruel, selfish, stubborn, lecherous man for twenty-five years,—*God damn it, she's gone crazy!*—the sleepless night and exhausting days working, living by his side?—*Christ, this is unreal! Nightmare! This can't be happening, she's no good at expressing herself, she's drunk, get her out of here!*—I won't bore you with the details, all the tears I've shed during the past twenty-five years ... What's that murmuring? I just want to share with you why I'm so happy. Well, here it is: David is now a man and no longer needs me. As for my husband ... Today I celebrate my freedom. Have you ever seen a prisoner who has just paid his debt to society? Well, you're looking at one now.—*I can't take any more, everything is coming down around my ears*—Today I am throwing off the yoke of marriage. I am now free to dispose of my time as I please. No more crummy trips to Galveston or Freeport while he takes his mistress to Acapulco, Capri and Biarritz! I'm going around the world.—*She's crazy, crazy, crazy!*—And the best thing about today is the end of the silence that practically destroyed me. Drink up; drink, my friends, to freedom, to this joyous day for both me and my husband!—*Dad, poor Dad, how humiliating!*—Right dear, isn't that a relief? I'm the one that made the stink so you can play the suffering husband, just as always. Let's just drink to it, no bad feelings, good friends like we've always been."

The feeling of unreality that had pursued me since morning hit me with such force that I thought the martinis had finally done me in. I had the strangest sensation that the distance between other objects and myself were somehow sacred. Material objects which I once touched without noticing now disappeared from sight. They shunned contact, slipping away into nothingness, vanishing in the nightmare.

Mom was still on the platform when I noticed the black dress had a very provocative neckline. Her neck—I'd never seen it that way before—was firm, young, like Charito's, disquieting. No, for Christsake, what's happening to me? She's my mother. There she is, laughing ... laughing... laughing with that good-looking gray-haired fellow. They gaze at each other raptly, lustfully, whispering thing I can't even imagine. The martinis ... I'm plastered. Mom, Dad, twenty-five years, the anniversary, that man: Dr. Manzione, yes, it was Dr. Manzione the one that pulled her through that long illness. He saved her life ... now he's saving her from ... hell ... slut ... She's bad just like all the rest ... They're just looking at each other ... And Dad? It's the martinis, I can't even remember my name.

She can't. She can't leave the salads, tortillas, soups ... Dammit! Let her keep knitting by the window! I'll buy her all the white wool she wants so she'll fix that sinful neckline and stop staring at Dr. Manzione that way. She was born to knit.

"I still have the rest of my live to enjoy, just for me. Why not now while there's still time? Slavery is illegal now, isn't it? (She's no good, she's looking at Dr. Manzione like Charito looks at me when we're together. She's gone to hell. My clean, pure mother, tireless knitter of useless things. This is pure hell, I thought that ...)

Things got even stranger when she produced her knitting (white wool, white, white everywhere!) and started passing it out among the guests: they all got into it and started putting things on until they were completely covered in whiteness, white, white wool ... finally fusing into a white mass of arms, legs, a shrieking, frenzied confusion of freedom and lust.

Translated by Mary G. *Parham*

Cloud Cover Caribbean

Ana Lydia Vega

September, agent provocateur of hurricanes, signals for war, filling the seas with urchins and rays. Suspicious breezes swell the guayabera, makeshift sail for a makeshift vessel. The sky is a conga drum stretched tight for a *bembé* of the gods.

An ugly thing, this meaty arm of sea separating Antenor from the pursuit of happiness. The sharks don't amount to a pimple on a mosquito's ass beside the real dangers lurking. But he must muscle through. This is his second day amidst monotonous waves that seem to roll off of the clouds. Since leaving Haiti he has not sighted so much as a fishing boat. It is like playing discoverer while secretly wondering if the world is legitimately round. Any minute now he might confront the edge and drop into the fabled abyss.

The putrid mangos, emblems of diarreah and famine, the war cries of the macoutes, the fear, the drought—it's all behind him now. Nausea and the threat of thirst once the meager water supply runs out—this is the here and now. For all its menace, this miserable adventure at sea is like a pleasure cruise compared to his memories of the island.

Antenor settled in beneath the broiling cauldron of sky. Between the boat's rocking merengue and his own weary body he could have sunk into slumber like an island village, and would have, had it not been for the Dominican shouting for help. You didn't have to know Spanish to understand that the man was shipwrecked and wanted a lift. Antenor helped him aboard as best he could. In that instant there came upon the little skiff a mocking, derisive spirit of the sort that inhabit the Caribbean tradewinds. So violent was its arrival that it nearly capsized the boat. At last they managed to quell it.

"Thanks, brother," said the man from the Dominican Republic, with a sight of relief that moved the sail to pity.

The Haitian passed him the canteen, then almost had to tear it from his hands to keep him from drinking it all down. After some long exchanges of looks, mutually impermeable words and exhausting gestures, they reached the cheerful conclusion that Miami couldn't be far away. And each told the other, without either understanding, what he was leaving behind—which was very little—and what he was seeking. Then and there was spoken the royal pain of being black, Caribbean and poor; deaths by the score were retold: clergy, military and civilians were roundly cursed; an international brotherhood of hunger and solidarity of dreams was established. And as Antenor and the Dominican— his name was Diogenes, a neoclassical baptismal flourish—reached the very thick of their bilingual ceremony, new calls were heard to reverberate under the forbidding vault of the heavens.

The two of them raised their eyes to the waves and described the kinky hair of a Cuban bobbing along, hanging on to the proverbial plank of the shipwrecked sailor.

"A house full of screaming kids and grandma just had a baby," said Diogenes, frowning. The Haitian understood almost as if he had grown up on the Dominican side of the island. Another passenger, another soul, another stomach, to be exact.

But the Cuban howled so mightily, and with such undeniably Santiagan overtones, that at last they yielded and pulled him aboard with a quintessentially Caribbean "what the fuck," as the boat began to rhumba.

Despite the urgency of the situation, the Cuban had the good sense to ask, "You people going to Miami?" before taking hold of the Dominican's indecisive hand.

Again the quarreling picked up steam. Diogenes and Carmelo, which was the restless Cuban's Christian name, raised an unearthly ruckus. Antenor intervened from time to time with a meek "Mais oui" or a "C'est ça," when the fury of the moment called for it. But he did not for a minute enjoy the Spanish language monopoly on a vessel which, whether destined for exile or not, was sailing after all under Haitian colors.

With Diogenes carrying counterpoint, and with a discreet touch of Haitian maracas for backup, Carmelo related the misadventures which had driven him from the shores of the Greater Antilles.

"I'm telling you, my friend, it was work, work, work day and night, no matter where you turned your head ... "

"Hey, in Santo Domingo there wasn't any work to be had ... "

"It was cut that cane, boy, day in, day out."

"Hey, man, where I'm from they bring in all the madamos from Haiti to do the cutting. The rest of us can lie there and rot for all they care."

The Haitian twitched. The Dominican had mentioned his half of the island, albeit at supersonic speed. He said nothing. Better not rock the boat any further; it was already giddy with the slap-happy rocking of the waves.

"I'll tell you, boy, there is always a stirfry of trouble somewhere," said the Cuban, initiating with this unhappy choice of words a search for food.

In a shoebox inherited from a trashbasket in a rich neighborhood, Antenor had put some cassava bread, two or three ears of corn, a pack of tobacco and a bottle of rum, staples which he had gathered for the voyage with the greatest of difficulty. Lest one charitable act overshadow another, he had taken the precaution of sitting on the box. But a major in black marketeering had given the Cuban a keenly developed sense of smell.

"Nigger, come up off that box," he said, eschewing formality and eyeballing the shoebox as if it were the very Ark of the Covenant.

Antenor pretended not to hear, though Carmelo's intentions were plainly polyglot.

"Get out of there, madamo, 'cuz it stinks of rum and tobacco," Diogenes translated, quickly forgetting the vows of mutual aid spoken with his fellow islander prior to the Cuban's arrival.

Still Antenor played dumb. Our undisputed world record illiteracy rate might pay off here, he thought, assuming the most vacant attitude possible in the face of his brother's demands.

Their impatience growing and their indignation rising at Antenor's passive resistance, they at length administered him one tremendous shove, which nearly sent him overboard on an underwater voyage. And they fell upon the box as if here, indeed, were the celebrated Horn of Plenty.

After eating the cassava bread and the corn, the two rogues renewed their comparative socio-economic analysis of the Caribbean nations. Carmelo chewed while Diogenes cocked an elbow, relishing the rum as though ogling the Statue of Liberty's charms under her threadbare tunic.

"I plan to go into business in Miami," said Carmelo. "I have a cousin who started out as a lowly pimp and now has his own, well, dating service."

"The land of opportunity," the Dominican concurred, his rum-fogged breath hot in the Haitian's face.

Antenor had not let out a peep since they had put him in quarantine. But his eyes were two black dolls pierced through by enormous needles.

"In Cuba," Carmelo went on, "dating services are banned, you know. Now, tell me, how is a person supposed to live with all that restriction?"

"Hey, in the Dominican Republic there's so many whores that we have to export them," rejoined Diogenes with a guffaw of such explosive resonance that it scared a shark that was trailing fuse-like behind the boat.

"Tout Dominiken se pit," grumbled Antenor from his little Fort Allen, which remark Diogenes, fortunately, did not hear, immersed as he was in more ponderous concerns.

"The problem," Carmelo said, digging deeper, "is that in Cuba the women think they are equal to the men and, you know, they don't want to get out and work the streets."

"That may be true now, but the Cuban women used to put out with the best of them," said his friend, recalling the internationally renowned rear ends of Cuban women.

The nostalgic allusion to the Batista era was none to the liking of Carmelo, and the Dominican's line of conversation was getting under his skin. Thus out of nowhere he parried, "Anyway, how is Santo Domingo looking since the hurricane? People who know the city say you can't tell the difference." He capped his dubious joke with a laugh that could be heard back in Guantanamo.

The Dominican went pale—no small accomplishment—but chose to contain his wrath in deference to the Cuban passenger's formidable biceps, the fruit, no doubt, of the accursed cane cutting.

Masking his change of mind, he searched for the canteen. The sea was in open revolt and the boat was rocking like a mambo's hips in Dambala worship. The canteen rolled to Antenor's inconvenient feet. The Dominican challenged. Antenor grappled with him. The Cuban smiled, following the struggle with the benign condescendence of an adult watching children quarrel.

Just then it began to drizzle. The wind, the waves and the great Antillean brawl conspired in that ill-fated boat to rekindle the hopes of the shark. They might as well have been going to China.

The Haitian threw the canteen into the water. Better to die than to quench the thirst of a Dominican cur. Diogenes bolted up, aghast. That's to remind you that we invaded you three times, Antenor thought as he bared his teeth to his countrymen.

"Trujillo was right," the Dominican lowed, charging the Haitian's belly like a raging bull.

The boat looked like a patron saint's day float on the loose. Carmelo at last emerged from his indifference and gave notice, "Easy does it, gentlemen, c'mon goddamnit, we're going to capsize the boat."

And capsize it they did, quite as the future Miami businessman had prophesied. Capzised and rained on, with wind and thunder for background music and the wholesome enthusiasm of the sharks.

But in the precise instant in which our heroic emigrees might have succumbed to the perils of the Bermuda Triangle, there came the deep raw droning sound of a horn, like the chant of a priest at a politician's requiem.

"A boat!" cried Carmelo, waving his arm wildly about like a sadist with a cattle prodder.

The three unfortunates united their voices in a long, shrill, hopeful cry for help.

Some time later—and don't ask me how the hell they kept the sharks at bay; clearly it was a joint miracle involving the Virgin of Altagracia, the Caridad del Cobre and the Seven African Powers—they lay rescued, tired but content, on the deck of the boat. On the deck, that is, of the American boat.

The captain, an Aryan and Appolinean sea dog of ruddy complexion, golden hair and very blue eyes, drew near for a quick verification of the disaster and said, "Get those niggers down there and let the spikes take care of 'em." Words which our untutored heroes did not understand as well as our more literate readers will. Whereupon the Antilleans were taken, sans tender loving care, into the ship's hold, in which, amidst wooden crates and moldy trunks, they exchanged their first post-wreck glances: a blend of relief and fright, sauteed in some lightly browned hopes.

Moments later the Dominican and the Cuban had the pleasure of hearing their mother tongue spoken. A little fractured, but unmistakable. Even the Haitian welcomed the sound. He seemed to recall it from his tenderest childhood memories and was beginning to suspect he would hear it for the rest of his life. The parched lips of each man in the trio were bending northward into a smile when a Puerto Rican voice grumbled through the semi-darkness.

"If you want to feed your belly here, you're going to have to work and I mean work hard. A gringo don't give anything away. Not to his

own mother."
   And he handed them dry clothes on the end of his black arm.

Translated by Mark McCaffrey

The IWM 1000

Alicia Yáñez Cossío

A man is only what he knows

—F. Bacon

Once upon a time, all the professors disappeared, swallowed and digested by a new system. All the centers of learning closed because they were outmoded, and their sites were converted into living quarters swarming with wise, well-organized people who were incapable of creating anything new.

Knowledge was an item that could be bought and sold. A device called the IWM 1000 had been invented. It was the ultimate invention: it brought an entire era to an end. The IWM 1000 was a very small machine, the size of an old scholarly briefcase. It was very easy to use—lightweight and affordable to any person interested in knowing anything. The IWM 1000 contained all human knowledge and all the facts of all the libraries of the ancient and modern world.

Nobody had to take the trouble of learning anything because the machine, which could be hand-carried or put on any piece of household furniture, provided any information to anybody. Its mechanism was so perfect, and the data it gave so precise, that nobody had dared to prove it otherwise. Its operation was so simple that children spent time playing with it. It was an extension of the human brain. Many people would not be separated from it even during the most personal, intimate acts. The more they depended on the machine, the wiser they became.

A great majority, knowing that the facts were so ready at hand, had never touched an IWM 1000, not even out of curiosity. They did not know how to read or write. They were ignorant of the most elementary

208

things, and it did not matter to them. They felt happy at having one less worry, and they enjoyed the other technological advances more. With the IWM 1000, you could write any type of literature, compose music, and even paint pictures. Creative works were disappearing because anybody, with time and sufficient patience, could make any work similar to and even superior to one made by artists of the past without having to exert the brain or feel anything strange or abnormal.

Some people spent time getting information from the IWM 1000 just for the pleasure of knowing something. Some did it to get out of some predicament, and others asked it things of no importance whatsoever, simply for the pleasure of having someone say something to them, even though it might just be something from their trivial, boring world.

"What is *etatex*?"

"What does *hybrid* mean?"

"How do you make a chocolate cake?"

"What does Beethoven's *Pastorale* mean?"

"How many inhabitants are there actually in the world?"

"Who was Viriato?"

"What is the distance from the Earth to Jupiter?"

"How can you get rid of freckles?"

"How many asteroids have been discovered this year?"

"What is the function of the pancreas?"

"When was the last world war?"

"How old is my neighbor?"

"What does *reciprocal* mean?"

Modulations of the voice fell on some supersensitive electronic membrane, connected with the brain of the machine, and computed immediately the requested information, which was not always the same because, according to the tone of voice, the machine computed the data concisely or with necessary references.

Sometimes two intellectuals would start to talk, and, when one of them had a difference of opinion, he would consult his machine. He would present the problem from his own perspective, and the machines would talk and talk. Objections were made, and many times these did not come from the intellectuals but from the machines, who tried to convince each other. The men who had begun the discussion would listen, and when they tired of listening, they would be thinking which of two machines was going to get the last word because of the power of the respective generators.

Lovers would make the machines conjugate all the tenses of the verb *to love*, and they would listen to romantic songs. In offices and administrative buildings tape-recorded orders were given, and the IWM 1000 would complete the details of the work. Many people got in the habit of talking only to their own machines; therefore, nobody contradicted them because they knew how the machine was going to respond, or because they believed that rivalry could not exist between a machine and a human being. A machine could not accuse anyone of ignorance: they could ask anything.

Many fights and domestic arguments were conducted through the IWM 1000. The contestants would ask the machine to say to their opponent the dirtiest words and the vilest insults at the highest volume. And, when they wanted to make peace, they could make it at once because it was the IWM 1000 and not they who said those words.

People began to feel really bad. They consulted their IWM 1000's, and the machines told them that their organisms could not tolerate one more dose of pep pills because they had reached the limit of their tolerance. In addition, they computed that the possibilities of suicide were on the increase, and that a change in lifestyle had become necessary.

The people wanted to return to the past, but it was too late. Some tried to put aside their IWM 1000, but they felt defenseless. Then they consulted the machines to see if there was some place in the world where there was nothing like the IWM 1000; and the machines gave information and details about a remote place called Takandia. Some people began to dream about Takandia. They gave the IWM 1000 to those who had only and IWM 100. They began to go through a series of strange actions. They went to museums; they spent time in the sections which contained books looking at something that intrigued them a great deal—something that they wanted to have in their hands—little, shabby syllabaries in which the children of past civilizations learned slowly to read poring over symbols, for which they used to attend a designated site called a school. The symbols were called letters; the letters were divided into syllables; and the syllables were made up of vowels and consonants. When the syllables were joined together, they made words, and the words were oral and written ... When these ideas became common knowledge, some people were very content again because these were the first facts acquired for themselves and not through the IWM 1000.

Many left the museums to go out to the few antique shops that remained, and they did not stop until they found syllabaries, which went from hand to hand in spite of their high prices. When the people had the syllabaries, they started to decipher them: *a-e-i-o-u, ma me mi mo mu, pa pe pi po pu*. It turned out to be easy and fun. When they knew how to read, they obtained all the books they could. They were few, but they were books: *The Effect of Chlorophyll on Plants*, *Les Miserables* by Victor Hugo, *One Hundred Recipes from the Kitchen*, *The History of the Crusades* ... They began to read, and, when they could obtain facts for themselves, they began to feel better. They stopped taking pep pills. They tried to communicate their new sensations to their peers. Some looked at them with suspicion and distrust and labelled them lunatics. Then these few people hastened to buy tickets to Takandia.

After a jet, they took a slow boat, then a canoe. They walked many kilometers and arrived at Takandia. There they found themselves surrounded by horrible beings, who did not even wear modest loincloths. They lived in the tops of trees; they ate raw meat because they were not familiar with fire; and they painted their bodies with vegetable dyes.

The people who had arrived in Takandia realized that, for the first time in their lives, they were among true human beings, and they began to feel happy. They looked for friends; they yelled as the others did; and they began to strip off their clothes and throw them away among the bushes. The natives of Takandia forgot about the visitors for a few minutes to fight over the discarded clothing ...

Translated by Susana Castillo *and* Elsie Adams

Biographies

Dr. Zapata holds a Ph.D. in Hispanic Literature from the University of California at Irvine. Born in Mendoza, Argentina, she is now a tenured professor of Hispanic Literature at San Jose State University, where she has taught since 1969.

She has published several books and numerous articles on contemporary Latin American literature. Among her works are *Detrás de la reja* (the first critical anthology of Latin American women writers), *Ensayos hispanoamericanos* (criticism), *Tiempo ajeno*, *Cantos* and *Cruz del sur* (poetry). Her poetry has been recorded for the Library of Congress in Washington, D.C.

Dr. Zapata directed Conference of Inter-American Women Writers held in April 1976 at San Jose State University. This was the first conference held in California on Latin American women writers, and the second in the country. Her work has pioneered a new field and her leadership in this relatively new area of study has been internationally recognized.

Isabel Allende (Chile, 1942 –)

Isabel Allende is a Chilean born in Lima, Peru, in 1942 where her parents were on diplomatic duty. She began working at the United Nation's Food and Agriculture Organization in Santiago, Chile, and was drawn towards the field of journalism. She currently resides in the San Francisco Bay Area. With the publication of *La casa de los espíritus* (1982), Isabel Allende became one of the best-known Latin American novelists. The book was translated into more than twenty languages and was followed by *De amor y de sombra* and *Eva Luna* (1984 and 1987 respectively). Her short story collection *Los cuentos de Eva Luna* is in press.

Dora Alonso (Cuba, 1910 –)

Dora Alonso has worked as a journalist in print and in radio as well as a writer of novels, short stories, poetry, theater and children's literature. In 1936 the magazine *Bohemia* awarded her recognition for her short stories, and she received a poetry prize in 1942. Her book *The Year 1961* chronicles her experiences as a war correspondent at Playa Girón. Since then, she has twice received the Casa de las Américas prize: first for the novel *Tierra inerme* (1961) and later for the children's book *El valle de la pájara pinta* (1979).

_____ **Helena Araujo (Colombia, 1933 –)** _____

Helena Araujo was born in Bogota, Colombia where she lived until 1970, contributing in cultural events, journalism and literary magazines. Since 1971 she has lived in Lausanne, Switzerland and teaches at the Université Populaire andalso collaborates in courses at the Université de Lausanne. She has published *La M de las Moscas* and *La Carta Abierta* (short story collections), *Fiesta en Tesauquillo* (novel) and a collection of essays on Latin American women writers, *La Scherezada criolla* (1989).

_____ **María Luisa Bombal (Chile, 1910 –)** _____

María Luisa Bombal was born in Viña del Mar where she was educated by Franciscan nuns. After the death of her father, she went with her family to Paris at age thirteen. She studied drama and received a degree in philosophy and letters from the Sorbonne. In 1931 she returned to Chile and worked in theater. Two years later she moved to Buenos Aires where she published short stories in the magazine *Sur*: "Las islas nuevas" (1938), "El árbol" (1939) and "María Griselda" (1946). Her most successful novels are *La última niebla* (1935), *La amortajada* (1938) and *La historia de María Griselda* (1977).

_____ **Rosario Castellanos (Mexico, 1925 – 1974)** _____

Born in Mexico City, Rosario Castellanos studied philosophy both in her country and abroad. Her work is characterized by an extremely lucid and cerebral examination of her identity as a woman and a Mexican; she also shares José Vasconcelos' and David Alfaro Siquieros' fascination for Indian subjects. Having worked in journalism and taught in both Mexican and foreign universities, she became Mexico's ambassador to Israel, where she died in a freak accident in 1974. Her principal novels are *Balun-Canan* (1951) and *Oficio de tinieblas*, which was awarded the Sor Juana Inés de la Cruz prize in 1962. Her short stories have been published in two collections: *Ciudad Real* (1960) and *Los convidados de agosto*.

_____ **María Amparo Dávila (Mexico, 1928 –)** _____

Amparo Dávila was born in 1928 in Pinos, Zacatecas and lived in San Luis Potosí for a number of years. She currently lives in Mexico City. In addition to contributing to Mexico's leading magazines for over thirty years, she has published three volumes of poetry: *Salmos bajo la luna* (1950), *Perfil de soledades* (1954) and *Meditaciones a la orilla del sueño* (1954). She has also published three short story collections: *Tiempo destrozado* (1959), *Música concreta* (1964) and *Arboles petrificados* (1957). She has received numerous literary prizes including the Premio Xavier

Villaurrutia.

_____ **Guadalupe Dueñas (Mexico, 1920 –)** _____

Guadalupe Dueñas was born in Guadalajara in 1920. Her short story collection *Tiene la noche un árbol* was published in 1958 by Fondo de Cultura Económica and won for her the José María Vigil Prize in 1959. She wrote *Máscara para un ídolo* in 1959 with the aid of a grant from the Centro Mexicano de Escritores. Her short stories have been widely anthologized in Spanish, English and German.

_____ **María Virginia Estenssoro (Bolivia, 1902 – 1970)** _____

María Virginia Estenssoro's story was originally published in *El cuento boliviano* edited by Armando Soriano Badani (Buenos Aires: Eudeba). Her most representative works are the short story collection, *El occiso* (1937) and the posthumously published collection of poems, *Ego inútil* (1976).

_____ **Rosario Ferré (Puerto Rico, 1942 –)** _____

Rosario Ferré was born in Puerto Rico in 1942. She received a Ph.D. in Comparative Literature from the University of Maryland. A magazine publisher, poet, short story writer, essayist and literary critic, she has also written children's stories and recently published her first novel, *Maldito amor* (1986). In 1976 she published *Papeles de Pandora*, a collection of short stories and poems and in 1980 the poetry collection *Fábulas de la garza desangrada*. Her three volumes of children's stories are *El medio pollito* (1978), *La mona que le pisaron la cola* (1981) and *Los cuentos de Juan Bobo* (1982). Her collection of feminist essays, *Sitio a Eros*, appeared in 1980.

_____ **Elena Garro (Mexico, 1920 –)** _____

Elena Garro studied at the Universidad Autónoma de Mexico where she worked as a choreographer. She practiced journalism in both Mexico and the United States and was married for a time to the poet and essayist Octavio Paz. In 1954 she began writing for film and in 1958 published *Un hogar sólido*, a collection of three one-act plays. Other plays include *La mudanza* (1959), *El rey mago* (1960), *La señora en un balcón* (1963), *El árbol* (1963) and *La dama boba* (1964). She was given the Xavier Villaurrutia Prize for her first novel, *Los recuerdos del porvenir* (1963). Her collection of short stories *La semana de colores* appeared in 1964.

_____ **Nora Glickmann (Argentina, 1944 –)** _____

Nora Glickmann is an Associate Professor in the Department of Romance Language at Queens College, C.U.N.Y. She published *Uno de sus Juanes* in 1983 and *Leib Malaj y la trata de blancas* in 1984. She specializes in Latin American literature and several of her short stories have appeared in English and Portuguese translation.

Lucía Guerra (Chile, 1942 –)

Lucía Guerra was born in Chile in 1942. She traveled to the United States on a Fulbright Scholarship for postgraduate study in Linguistics and Literature. She is currently a Professor of Latin American Literature at the University of California, Irvine. She published the essay *La narrativa de María Luisa Bombal: una visión de la existencia femenina* in 1980 and edited a volume of essays on women entitled *Mujer y sociedad en América Latina* (1980). *Más allá de las máscaras* (1984), her first novel, met with critical acclaim in the United States and abroad. Together with Richard Cunningham, she has translated various works of María Luisa Bombal into widely-read English translations. She is currently working on her second novel, *Muñeca brava*.

Liliana Heker (Argentina, 1943 –)

While still a teenager, Liliana Heker published her first collection of short stories, *Los que vivieron la zarza*. She edited the literary *El Ornitorrinco* (formerly *El Escarabajo de Oro*) during the seventies, a difficult decade for all forms of expression in Argentina. Her last novel *Zona de Clivaje* was published in 1987.

Vlady Kociancich (Argentina, 1941 –)

Coraje (1970) was the first short story collection published by Vlady Kociancich, a student of Jorge Luis Borges. Her novel *La octava maravilla* (1982) was well received in Spain and Argentina. It was followed by two more novels, *Abisinia* (1985) and *Los últimos días de William Shakespeare* (1984). Her new short story collection *Un hombre de familias* is in press.

Luisa Mercedes Levinson (Argentina, 1910 – 1987)

Luisa Mercedes Levinson was born in Buenos Aires. She published her first novel in 1951—*La casa de los Felipes*—which was rewritten in 1969. Four novels followed which include *Concierto en mi* in 1956. She won the Buenos Aires Municipal Prize for 1954, 1955 and 1956. Some of her other works are *A la sombra del buho* (1972) and the short story collections *Las tejedoras sin hombre* (1967) and *El estigma del tiempo* (1977). Her daughter (also represented in this anthology) is the well-known writer Luisa Valenzuela.

Clarice Lispector (Brazil, 1925 – 1977)

In 1925, while her family was en route to Brazil from the Ukraine, Clarice Lispector was born. She was not only a successful author of novels, short stories and children's literature, but also a teacher, reporter and noted translator. Her first novel *Perto do coracao selvagem* (1944) won the Gra'a Aranha Prize. Several other works followed. Her other novels include *O lustre* (1946), *A cidade sitiada* (1949), *A maci no escuro* (1961) and *A paixio segundo G.H.* (1964). She died of cancer shortly after the release of *A hora da estrela* (1977). Several of her works have been published posthumously.

_____ **María Elena Llano (Cuba, 1936 –)** _____

María Elena Llano was born in Cuba in 1936. She is a journalist working with the cultural section of La Habana's new agency "Latin Press." Her works written for radio and television have been recognized by various awards. In addition to writing theater, short stories and poetry, she also produced humoristic journalism and is an art critic. *La reja*, a volume of short stories, was introduced in 1966. She has since published a collection of poems and a second volume of short stories. Her short stories have been translated into several languages and are included in a number of anthologies.

_____ **Carmen Naranjo (Costa Rica, 1931 –)** _____

Carmen Naranjo has published short stories, novels and poetry. She published the novel *Los perros no ladraron* in 1966 and in 1982 won the short story prize for the collection *Ondina* in the 1982 Certamen Latinoamericano competition. Her other publications include *Diario de una multitud*, *Mi guerrilla* and the short story collection *Otro rumbo para la rumba* (1989).

_____ **Olga Orozco (Argentina, 1920 –)** _____

Olga Orozco lives and writes in Buenos Aires. Her first book was *Desde lejos* (1946), followed by *Las muertes* (1951) and *Los juegos peligrosos* (1962). She also published *Museo salvaje* in 1974 and *Los cantos de Berenice* in 1977.

_____ **Antonia Palacios (Venezuela, 1910 –)** _____

Antonia Palacios published *Ana Isabel, una niña decente* in 1949. She received the Premio Nacional de la Literatura in 1976 for the short story collection *El largo día ya seguro*. Other collections include *Viaje al Frailejón* (1959), *Crónica de las horas* (1964) and *Textos de desalojo* (1974).

_____ **Cristina Peri Rossi (Uruguay, 1941 –)** _____

A translator and journalist, Cristina Peri Rossi holds a degree in the humanities and lives in Barcelona. She published the novels *El libro de mis primos* and *La nave de los locos* in 1969 and 1984 respectively. Among her short story collections are *Los museos abandonados* (1968), *Indicios pánicos* (1970) and *El museo de los esfuerzos inútiles* (1983). She has also published collections of poetry.

_____ **Nélida Piñón (Brazil, 1937 –)** _____

Nélida Piñón lives and works in Rio de Janeiro. A journalist, she works with various mewspapers and literary journals. She is Brazilian correspondent for the Latin American magazine *Mundo Nuevo* and is assistant editor of *Cadernos Brasileiros*. She published her first novel, *Guia-Mapa de Gabriel Arcanjo*, in 1961. Among her collection of fiction are two prize-winning novels, *A Casa de Paixio* (1972) and *Tebas do Meu Coracio* (1974). Her short story collections include *Sala de Armas* (1973) and *O Calor das Coisas* (1980). In 1972 she received the Mario Andrade Prize from the Sao Paulo Society of Art Critics.

_____ **Josefina Pla (Paraguay, 1909 –)** _____

Josefina Pla was born in Spain's Canary Islands, but has spent most of her life in Paraguay where she has worked in radio, newspapers, education, art, history and fiction. She is known first as a poet and secondly as a writer of fiction. In 1963 she published the short story collection *La mano en la tierra*, followed by *El espejo y el canasto*. Among her more recent novels are *La nave del olvido* (1985) and *Alguien muere en San Onofre Cuarumí* (1985). Recent volumes of poetry include *Tiempo y tinieblas* (1983) and *Cambiar sueños por sombras* (1985).

_____ **Elena Poniatowska (Mexico, 1933 –)** _____

Born in Paris, she came to Mexico at the age of ten. She has written for the magazines *Excelsior* and *Novedades* and her works include *Lilus Kikus* (short stories, 1954), *Melés y Teléo* (theater, 1956), *Palabras cruzadas* (interviews, 1961), *Todo empezó el domingo* (commentary, 1963) and the novel *Hasta no verte, Jesús mío* (1969), *La noche de Tlatelolco* (journalism, 1971), *Querido Diego te abraza Quiela* (novel, 1978), *De noche viernes* (short stories, 1979), *Fuerte es el silencio* (short stories, 1980) and *La flor de lis* (novel, 1988).

_____ **Teresa Porzencanski (Uruguay, 1945 –)** _____

Teresa Porzencanski is a professor of social work and anthropology. As well as appearing in numerous anthologies, she has published *Historias para mi abuela* (1970), *El acertijo y otros cuentos* (1972), *Esta manzana roja* (1972), *Intacto el corazón* (1976), *Construcciones* (1979), *La invención de los soles* (1981) and *Una novela erótica* (1986).

_____ **María Teresa Solari (Peru,)** _____

María Teresa Solari's story appeared originally in *Antología del cuento fantástico peruano* (Universidad Mayor de San Marcos, 1977).

######### Marta Traba (Argentina/Colombia, 1930 – 1984) #########
Marta Traba graduated from the National University of Buenos Aires as a professor of literature in 1950. She was instrumental in founding Bogota's Museum of Modern Art. She published some of her short stories in *Pasó así* (1967), and received the Casa de las Américas prize in 1966 for *Las ceremonias del verano* (1966). The novels *Los laberintos insolados* and *La jugada del sexto día* both followed in 1970, and *Conversación al sur* in 1981. The novel *En cualquier lugar* (1984) and the short story collection *De la mañana a la noche* (1986) were published posthumously.

######### Luisa Valenzuela (Argentina, 1938 –) #########
A precocious writer, she started publishing and worked with Jorge Luis Borges in the National Library while still a teenager. She published her first novel, *Hay que sonreír*, in 1966. She received a Fulbright Scholarship and has taught at Columbia University. Other works include *El gato eficaz* (1972), *Como en guerra* (1977) and short story collections: *Los heréticos* (1967), *Aquí pasan cosas raras* (1975) and *Cambio de armas* (1982). *Cola de lagartija* appeared in Gregory Rabassa's English translation, *The Lizard's Tail*.

######### Rima de Vallbona (Costa Rica, 1931 –) #########
Rima de Vallbona was born in San Jose, Costa Rica. She holds the Cullen Chair in Spanish at the University of St. Thomas (Houston, Texas) where she has been teaching since 1964. She has a Masters degree from the University of Costa Rica and a Doctorate in Modern Languages from Middlebury, Vermont. Dr. Vallbona has also received diplomas from the Sorbonne, France, and the University of Salamanca, Spain. She has published the following books: *Noche en vela* (novel), 1968; *Yolanda Oreamuno* (literary study), 1971; *Polvo del camino* (short stories), 1973; *La salamandra rosada* (short stories), 1979; *La obra en prosa de Unice Odio* (literary study), 1981; *Mujeres y agonías* (short stories), 1982; *Las sombras que perseguimos* (novel), 1983; *Baraja de soledades* (short stories), 1983, and *Cosecha de pecadores* (short stories), 1988.

######### Ana Lydia Vega (Puerto Rico, 1946 –) #########
Ana Lydia Vega is a professor at the University of Puerto Rico and teaches Caribbean Literature and French. She was first published in the anthology *Vírgenes y mártires* (1981) which contained six of her short stories. Her collection of short stories *Encancaranublado* (1983) won the Casa de las Américas award. She also earned the Premio Internacional Juan Rulfo for the story *Pasión de historia* (1984).

_____ **Alicia Yáñez Cossío (Ecuador, 1929 –)** _____

A journalist, poet and professor of literature, Alicia Yáñez Cossío published *Bruna, Soroche y los Tíos*, winning the Premio Nacional in 1971. Her other two novels are *Yo vendo unos ojos negros* (1979) and *La Cofradía del mullo del vestido de la virgen Pipona* (1985). She has published two short story collections, *Más allá de las islas* (1980) and *El beso y otras fricciones* (1975) in which her story "The IWM 1000" first appeared.

Translators

Elsie Adams has as her areas of specialization British literature and women's studies. She is the author of *Bernard Shaw and the Aesthetes* as well as other scholarly works, including a co-authored feminist anthology. She holds a Ph.D. in English and is currently Professor of English and Comparative Literature at San Diego State University.

John Benson is a freelance translator. He has read papers at regional and international conferences on the relationship between Severo Sarduy's and Marshall MacLuhan's philosophies and also on the outlook for Latin American literature in translation.

Cedric Bussette is Professor of Hispanic Literature at Santa Clara University and translator of the works of Carmen Naranjo.

E.D. Carter, Jr. is professor of Spanish and Chair of the Department of Foreign Languages and Literatures, California State University, Los Angeles. His publications include *Julio Cortázar: Life, Work and Criticism* (1986); *Otro round: Ensayos sobre la obra de Julio Cortázar* is in press. Professor Carter has translated stories by Silvina Ocampo and the novel, *Victoria*, by Anderson Imbert.

Susana Castillo, originally from Ecuador, is the author of *El "Desarraigo" en el teatro venezolano* and of numerous articles on Latin American theater. Her areas of specialization are the contemporary Latin American theater and women's studies. She holds a Ph.D. in Romance Languages and is currently Professor of Spanish at San Diego State University.

Ina Cumpiano is a Ph.D. candidate in Comparative Literature at the University of Iowa. In addition to writing two books of poetry, she has contributed translations to *Poetry World* and *Nosotras: Latina Literature Today*.

Richard Cunningham is author of the novels *The Place Where the World Ends* (1974) and *A Ceremony in the Lincoln Tunnel* (1978). Together with his wife, Lucía Guerra, he has translated María Luisa Bombal ("The Tree" and *La última niebla*) as well as Guerra's story "The Virgin's Passion."

Leland Guyer is Chair of the Department of Spanish and Portuguese at Macalester College in St. Paul, Minnesota. His publications include a book, *Imagística do Espaço Fechado na Poesia de Fernando Pessoa*, a translation of Ferreira Gullar's masterpiece *Peoma Sujo* and a number of articles on Portuguese, Brazilian and Spanish poetry and fiction.

Roland Hamilton is professor of Spanish at San Jose State University and author of *Americanismos en las obras del padre Bernabé Cobo*. He has translated two books on the Incas, *History of the Inca Empire*, and *Inca Religion and Customs*, in press.

Elisabeth Heinicke, presently teaching at Boston University, collaborated with Teresa Méndez-Faith on the translation of Elena Poniatowska's story.

Delia Hufton, born in Uruguay, holds a Ph.D. in Linguistics from Stanford University and and is a professor of Linguistics and Translation at San Jose State University. She publishes translations and articles on *lunfardo*, an argot spoken in and around Buenos Aires.

Psiche Bertini Hughes, Ph.D. (London) lectures in Latin American Literature at the University of London Extra-Mural Department. Her recent publications include an essay on "Latin American Women Writers" and an interview with Cristina Peri Rossi in *Unheard Words*.

Sylvia Erhlich Lipp lives in Canada and won a University of Miami "Letras de Oro" First Prize in the area of twentieth-century novel translation for *A la sombra del búho* by Luisa Mercedes Levenson.

Alberto Manguel was born in Buenos Aires and has worked for the BBC. His published collections of translations include: *Black Water: The Book of Fantastic Literature* and *Other Fires: Short Fiction by Latin American Women* (1986). He has translated major contemporary Latin American writers and currently resides in Canada.

Mark McCaffrey is a Hispanist and translator who lives in Williston, Vermont. His work has appeared in numerous anthologies, including the recent *Tales from an Urban Landscape: Contemporary Puerto Rican Fiction*, Waterfront Press, 1989.

Teresa Méndez-Faith is a professor of Spanish at St. Anselm College and is an assayist, textbook author and literary critic. Among her recent publications are *Con-Textos literarios hispanoamericanos* and articles on the literature of Paraguay and the Southern Cone.

Julian Palley is professor of Spanish Literature at the University of California, Irvine. His bilingual anthology of the Spanish poet Jorge Guillén, *Affirmation*, appeared in 1970. He has published two anthologies of the poetry of Rosario Castellanos: *Meditación en el umbral* (Mexico: Fondo de Cultura Económica, 1985) and the bilingual version, *Meditation on the Threshold* (Tempe, Arizona: Bilingual Press, 1988). He has authored two volumes of poetry: *Spinoza's Stone and Other Poems* (1976) and *Bestiary* (1987).

Mary Parham received a Ph.D. in Romance Languages from UCLA

after receiving an M.A. from New York University. A recent Fulbright Scholar to Belize, she is currently working on an anthology of Belizean literature. She has published widely on topics in Latin American and Portuguese literature and is a published poet. She teaches Spanish at the University of Houston-Downtown.

Gregory Rabassa, Ph.D., Litt.D., is a professor of Romance Languages and Comparative Literature at Queen's College and the Graduate School at CUNY. He has translated Gabriel García Márquez's *Cien años de soledad (One Hundred Years of Solitude)* and most of the contemporary Latin American writers, including Luisa Valenzuela's *Cola de lagartija (The Lizard's Tail)*. He is considered a leader in the field of Latin American literature in English translation.

Catherine Rodríguez-Nieto is a free-lance translator living in the San Francisco Bay Area. She has translated contemporary Latin American writers such as Elsie Alvarado de Ricord, Lucha Corpi, Amparo Dávila, Marta Traba and Elena Garro. Her work has appeared, among other places, in Dories Meyer's anthology of Spanish-American women writers.

Margaret Sayers Peden is a Professor of Spanish at the University of Missouri, Columbia. Among her translations are *Woman of Genius, the Intellectual Autobiography of Sor Juana Inés de la Cruz* (1982), Carlos Fuentes' *Old Gringo* (1985) and Octavio Paz's *Sor Juana Inés de la Cruz, Or the Pitfalls of Faith*. She also translated Isabel Allende's latest novels *Of Love and Shadows* and *Eva Luna*.

Gustavo V. Segade is a professor of Hispanic Literature and directs the English/Spanish Translation Certificate Program at San Diego State University. His publications include *Critical Issues in Contemporary Latin American Poetic Theory* (Berkeley: Quinto Sol Publications, 1978) and the translation of Sergio Elizondo's *Perros y antiperros*. As a poet, his long poem, "State of the Art," received the First Prize in Poetry at the Chicano Literary Contest, University of California, Irvine, 1986.

Beatriz Teleki is a professor of Hispanic Linguistics at Trinity College and has published articles on Sor Juana Inés de la Cruz, Virginia Woolf, José Gorostiza and Xavier Villaurrutia, among others. She has also authored a book on the works of the Argentine poet Evaristo Carriego.

Jean Vaughn received her Master's degree in Spanish from San Jose State University. She is currently working on a Ph.D. in Comparative Literature at the University of California, Santa Cruz. She is coauthor of *Politics of the Heart*, Pollack and Vaughn (Ithaca: Firebrand Books,

1987).

Diana Vélez teaches translation and creative writing at the University of Iowa. She collaborated with Rosario Ferré on the translation of "A Poisoned Tale."